Democratisation in the Maghreb

DEMOCRATISATION IN THE MAGHREB

J. N. C. Hill

EDINBURGH
University Press

Edinburgh University Press is one of the leading university presses in the UK. We publish academic books and journals in our selected subject areas across the humanities and social sciences, combining cutting-edge scholarship with high editorial and production values to produce academic works of lasting importance. For more information visit our website: edinburghuniversitypress.com

© J. N. C. Hill, 2016, 2018

Edinburgh University Press Ltd
The Tun – Holyrood Road
12 (2f) Jackson's Entry
Edinburgh EH8 8PJ

First printed in hardback by Edinburgh University Press 2016

Typeset in 11/13 JaghbUni Regular by
Servis Filmsetting Ltd, Stockport, Cheshire
and printed and bound in Great Britain by
CPI Group (UK) Ltd, Croydon CR0 4YY

A CIP record for this book is available from the British Library

ISBN 978 1 4744 0897 4 (hardback)
ISBN 978 1 4744 3215 3 (paperback)
ISBN 978 1 4744 0898 1 (webready PDF)
ISBN 978 1 4744 0899 8 (epub)

Contents

Acknowledgements

The scale of my debt is almost unfathomable; broad and deep and wide. For it is the direct inverse of the seemingly limitless assistance friends, colleagues and well-wishers have provided over the past months and years. Their help has been active and passive, sustained, vital, and willingly, generously, provided. Daunted, and doomed never to give full and proper acknowledgement to all whom I should, I would like sincerely to thank Wyn Bowen, Bob Folely and Kate Utting for giving me essential time and space in which to research and write; Nicola Ramsey, Ellie Bush and their colleagues at Edinburgh University Press for their professionalism, efficiency and patience; Neil Curtis for his attentive copy-editing; Sebastian Elischer and Matthijs Bogaards for helping me better to understand Levitsky and Way; the reviewers, anonymous and not, for their useful feedback on the proposal and earlier drafts; Andrew Stewart, Ashley Jackson and Ken Payne for their sustained encouragement and interest when they had far more pressing calls on their time; and my family for their questions, enquiries, stoicism and reassurance. Finally, I should like to give special thanks to Sophie Hague. Yet again, she has improved the typescript beyond measure, put up with more, and done so always and unhesitatingly. It is to her that this book is dedicated, with love and gratitude.

Abbreviations

AA	Association Agreement
AAV	Green Alliance of Algeria (Alliance de l'Algérie)
AC	Association Council
ADFM	Democratic Association of Moroccan Women (Association Démocratique des Femmes du Maroc)
AIS	Islamic Salvation Army (Armée Islamique du Salut)
AMDH	Moroccan Human Rights Association (Association Marocaine de Driots Humains)
ANEP	National Agency for Advertising and Publicity (Agence Nationale d'Edition et de la Publicité)
AP	Action Plan
APP	Popular Alliance for Progress (Alliance Populaire Progressiste)
AQIM	Al Qaeda in the Islamic Maghreb
ATI	Tunisian Internet Agency (Agence Tunisienne d'Internet)
AWI	Justice and Benevolence association (Justice et Bienfaisance/Al-Adl Wal-Ihsan)
BMENA	Broader Middle East and North Africa
CC	Constitutional Court (Cour Constitutionelle)
CCo	Constitutional Council (Conseil Constitutionnel)
CDR	Committee to Defend the Revolution (Conseil de Défense de la Révolution)
CENI	Independent National Electoral Commission (Commission Electorale Nationale Indépendante)
CESE	Economic and Social Environment Council (Conseil Economique, Social et Environnemental)
CFSP	Common Foreign and Security Policy
CIS	High Islamic Council (Conseil Islamique Supérieur)
CM	Council of Ministers (Conseil des Ministres)
CMJD	Military Council for Justice and Democracy (Le Conseil Militaire pour la Justice et la Démocratie)
CNCD	National Coordination for Change and Democracy

	(Coordination Nationale pour le Changement et la Démocratie)
CNP	National Press Council (Conseil National de la Presse)
COD	Coordination of Democratic Opposition (Coordination de l'Opposition Démocratique
CP	Press Code (Code de la Presse)
CPM	Coalition of the Majority (Coalition des Partis de la Majorité)
CPRN	Charter for Peace and National Reconciliation (Charte pour la Paix et la Réconciliation Nationale)
CR	Congress for the Republic (Congrès pour la République)
CSF	Civil Society Facility
CSFAR	Supreme Head of the Royal Armed Forces (Chef Suprême des Forces Armées Royales)
CSO	Superior Council of the Ulema (Conseil Supérieur des Oulémas)
CSPJ	Superior Council of the Judiciary (Conseil Supérieur du Pouvoir Judiciaire)
CSS	Superior Council of Security (Conseil Supérieur de Sécurité)
DRS	Department of Intelligence and Security (Département du Renseignement et de la Sécurité)
EBRD	European Bank for Reconstruction and Development
EDF	European Development Fund
EEAS	European External Action Service
EIB	European Investment Bank
EMDH	Euro-Mediterranean Human Rights Network (Réseau Euro-Méditerranéen des Droits de l'Homme)
EMP	Euro-Mediterranean Partnership
ENA	North African Star (Étoile Nord Africaine)
ENP	European Neighbourhood Policy
ENPI	European Neighbourhood and Partnership Instrument
ERT	Tunisian Radio Establishment (Établissement de la Radio Tunisienne)
ETT	Tunisian Television Establishment (Établissement de la Télévision Tunisienne)
EUSR	European Union Special Representative
FAO	Food and Agriculture Organization
FASP	Foreign Affairs and Security Policy
FDI	Foreign Direct Investment

FDTL	Democratic Forum for Work and Freedoms (Forum Démocratique pour le Travail et Les Libertés)
FFD	Democratic Forces Front (Front de Forces Démocratiques)
FFS	Socialist Forces Front (Front des Forces Socialistes)
FIS	Islamic Salvation Front (Front Islamique du Salut)
FLN	National Liberation Front (Front de Libération Nationale)
FMF	Foreign Military Financing
FNDD	National Front for the Defence of Democracy (Front National Pour la Defense de la Democratie)
FTA	Free Trade Agreement
GIA	Armed Islamic Group (Groupe Islamique Armé)
GSPC	Salafist Group for Preaching and Combat (Groupe Salafist pour la Prédication et la Combat)
GUNT	Transitional Government of National Unity (Gouvernement d'Union Nationale de Transition)
HACA	High Authority for Audio-Visual Communication (Haute Autorité de la Communication Audiovisuelle)
HAPA	High Authority for the Press and Broadcasting (Haute Autorité de la Presses et de l'Audiovisuel)
HCE	High State Council (Haut Comité d'État); High Council of State (Haut Conseil d'État)
HIRORRPTD	Higher Commission for the Achievement of the Objective of the Revolution, Political Reform and the Transition to Democracy (Haute Instance pour la Réalisation des Objectifs de la Révolution, de la Réforme Politique et de la Transition Démocratique)
IDB	Islamic Development Bank
IER	Equity and Reconciliation Committee (Instance Equité et Réconciliation)
IfS	Instrument for Stability
IISS	International Institute of Strategic Studies
IRMA	Resurgence of the Abolitionist Movement (Initiative pour la Resurgence du Mouvement Abolitioniste)
IS	Islamic State
ISIE	Higher Authority for Independent Elections (Instance Supérieure Independante pour les Élections)
LADDH	Algerian League for the Defence of Human Rights (Ligue Algérienne pour la Défense des Driots de l'Homme)

LDF	Leaders for Democracy Fellowship
LNG	Liquefied Natural Gas
MCC	Millennium Challenge Corporation
MDA	Movement for Democracy in Algeria (Mouvement pour la Démocratie en Algérie)
MDS	Socialist Democrats Movement (Mouvement des Démocrates Socialistes)
MEDA	Accompanying Measures (Mesures d'Accompagnment)
MEFTA	Middle East Free Trade Area
MEI	Movement for the Islamic State (Mouvement pour l'État Islamique)
MENAFATF	Middle East and North Africa Financial Action Task Force
MEPI	Middle East Partnership Initiative
MIA	Armed Islamic Movement (Mouvement Islamique Armé)
MNP	National Popular Movement (Mouvement National Populaire)
MOU	Memorandum of Understanding
MP	Popular Movement (Mouvement Populaire)
MRI	Islamic Revival Movement (Mouvement de la Renaissance Islamique)
MRN	National Reform Movement (Mouvement pour la Réforme Nationale)
MSP	Society of Peace (Mouvement de la Société pour la Paix)
MTI	Islamic Tendency Movement (Mouvement de la Tendence Islamique)
MUP	United Popular Movement (Mouvement d'Unité Populaire)
MVCF	February 25th Movement (Mouvement du 25 Février)
MVF	February 20th Movement (Mouvement du 20 Février)
OADP	Organisation of Democratic and Popular Action (Organisation de l'Action Démocratique et Populaire)
OAS	Organisation of American States
OMDH	Moroccan Human Rights Organisation (Organisation Marocaine des Droits Humains)
ONEM	National Organisation of the Children of Mujahidin (Organisation Nationale des Enfants de Moudjahidine)
OSCE	Organisation for Security Co-operation in Europe
PAM	Modernity Party (Parti Authenticité et Modernité)
PASC	Programme of Support to Civil Society
PCT	Tunisian Communist Party (Parti Communiste Tunisien)

PDP	Progressive Democratic Party (Parti Démocrate Progressiste)
PfDSP	Partnership for Democracy and Shared Prosperity
PJD	Justice and Development Party (Parti de la Justice et du Développement)
PND	National Democratic Party (Parti National Démocrate)
POLISARIO	Popular Front for the Liberation of Saguia el-Hamra and Río de Oro (Frente Popular para la Liberación de Saguia el-Hamra y Río de Oro)
PPS	Party of Progress and Socialism (Parti du Progès et du Socialisme)
PRD	Reform and Development Party (Parti de la Reforme et du Développement)
PRDR	Republican Party for Democracy and Renewal (Parti Républicain Démocratique et Renouvellement)
PRDS	Democratic and Social Republican Party (Parti Républicaine Démocratique et Social)
PSD	Socialist Destourian Party (Parti Socialiste Destourien)
PSL	Social Liberal Party (Parti Social Libéral)
PT	Workers' Party (Parti des Travailleurs)
PUP	Popular Unity Party (Parti de l'Unité Populaire)
PVP	Greens (Parti des Verts pour le Progrès)
RCD	Democratic Constitutional Rally (Rassemblement Constitutionel Démocratique)
RDU	Rally for Democracy and Unity (Rassemblement pour la Démocratie et l'Unité)
RFD	Rally of Democratic Forces (Regroupement des Forces Démocratiques)
RND	National Rally for Democracy (Rassemblement National Démocratique)
RNI	National Rally of Independents (Rassemblement National des Indépendants)
RNRD	National Rally for Reform and Development (Tawassoul/Rassemblement National pour la Réforme et le Développement)
RpCD	Rally for Culture and Democracy (Rassemblement pour le Changement et la Démocratie)
RTT	Tunisian Television Broadcaster (Radiodiffusion–Télévision Tunisienne)
SCMET	Special Coordinator for Middle East Transitions
SEP	Strategic Energy Partnership

SJM	Mauritanian Journalists' Union (Syndicat des Journalistes Mauritaniens)
SLP	Student Leaders Programme
SNIM	National Industrial and Mining Company (Société Nationale Industrielle et Minière)
SNJT	National Union of Tunisian Journalists (Syndicat National des Journalists Tunisiens)
SOMELEC	Mauritian Electricity Company (Société Mauritanienne d'Électricité)
Sonatrach	National Company for Research, Production, Transportation, Processing, and Commercialization of Hydrocarbons (Société Nationale pour la Recherche, la Production, le Transport, la Transformation, et la Commercialisation des Hydrocarbures)
SPRING	Support for Partnership, Reforms and Inclusive Growth
SSDS	Strategy for Security and Development in the Sahel
TIFA	Trade and Investment Framework Agreement
TSCTP	Trans-Sahara Counter-Terrorism Partnership
UC	Constitutional Union (Union Constitutionelle)
UDP	Union for Democracy and Progress (Union pour la Démocratie et le Progrès)
UDU	Unionist Democratic Union (Union Démocratique Unioniste)
UFD	Union of Democratic Forces (Union des Forces Démocratiques)
UfM	Union for the Mediterranean
UGTE	General Union of Tunisian Students (Union Générale Tunisienne des Étudiants)
UMD	Moroccan Union for Democracy (Union Marocaine pour la Démocratie
UR	Union for the Republic (Union pour la République)
USFP	Socialist Union of Popular Forces (Union Socialiste de Forces Populaires)
WTO	World Trade Organization
YES	Youth Exchange and Study

Introduction

The Maghreb's political development continues to confound expectations. Few specialists anticipated the start of the Arab Spring. Fewer still thought it would begin in Tunisia, long regarded as one of the region's most stable and prosperous countries.[1] Then, when the demonstrations did break out, most assumed Ben Ali would easily deal with them. Not only had he overcome similar challenges in the past, but he had the support of a large, well-funded and experienced security apparatus. Their shock at his downfall less than a month later was compounded by the simultaneous outbreak of copycat protests elsewhere and Libya's descent into civil war. Many now issued millennial predictions about what would happen next. Unrest would sweep the region. None of its leaders would be spared. Algeria was especially vulnerable.

Yet many of these forecasts have proved to be just as inaccurate as the conservative assumptions that preceded them. While the Arab Spring has undoubtedly wrought many significant changes to the Maghreb, its impact has not been as great as was predicted. In large parts of the region, political life has continued very much as before. Morocco's monarchy has not surrendered any of its core powers let alone become fully constitutional. Mauritania is still governed by the general and *coup d'état* leader, Mohamed Ould Abdel Aziz. And Algeria's 2014 presidential election was won comfortably by the long-serving, aging and seriously ill incumbent, Abdelaziz Bouteflika.[2]

A critical mistake made by many commentators was to overemphasise Tunisia's similarity to its near neighbours. They deduced that, if comparable circumstances to those which had led to Ben Ali's fall could be found throughout the rest of the region, then its other leaders were likely to suffer the same fate. Their suppositions and hypotheses were given additional weight and credibility by the outbreak of equally decisive protests in other parts of the Middle East. Hosni Mubarak's demise was widely seen as both a sign and a prelude, as evidence of the region's hunger and readiness for change, and the continued power of this transnational impulse and movement to enact it. Soon, the whole region would succumb to its transformational energy.

These assumptions were not without foundation. The countries of the Maghreb do share a great deal in common. And their likenesses are accentuated by the region's exceptionalism. Indeed, the Maghreb is defined by separation and similarity. It is distinct and distinguished from the regions that surround it, from the Middle East, from Europe and from sub-Saharan Africa. Yet its ties to them each are as numerous as they are varied, ancient as they are self-renewing, strong as they are subtle. Moreover, it is these connections that make it different. For the Maghreb is the sum of its parts. It is hybrid, it is distinct from each because of the influence of all. Similarity has created singularity.

Yet there are also differences within, between the Maghreb's assorted parts, peoples and cultures. Indeed, it is these variations that hold the key to explaining the region's competing political trajectories, why Morocco has not gone the way of Tunisia, why Abdelaziz Bouteflika remains in office, why the Mauritanian regime endures. The aim of this book is better to capture and contextualise these disparities while paying all due and necessary attention to the similarities. It does so by charting, examining and comparing the political development of four of the region's countries – Tunisia, Algeria, Morocco and Mauritania – over the past ten years. And, to structure and guide its analysis, it draws on Steven Levitsky and Lucan Way's concept of competitive authoritarianism and associated model for explaining regime transition.[3]

The purpose of this model is to explain the uneven spread of democracy among competitive authoritarian regimes. Levitsky and Way argue that such regimes are a product of the end of the Cold War. The conflict's conclusion not only triggered a sharp decline in international tolerance of authoritarian practices and the governments that employed them but also sparked the rapid diffusion of the 'formal architecture of democracy' and 'particularly multiparty elections' around the world.[4] These developments led to the emergence of 'civilian regimes in which formal democratic institutions exist and are widely viewed as the primary means of gaining power, but in which incumbents' abuse of the state places them at a significant advantage vis-à-vis their opponents'.[5] The model seeks to explain, therefore, why some of these regimes 'democratized during the post-Cold War period, while others remained stable and authoritarian and still others experienced turnover without democratization'.[6]

To do so, the model focuses on both international and domestic factors, regimes' 'ties to the West and the strength of [their] governing-party and state organizations'.[7] These factors are covered by the core dimensions of linkage, leverage and organisational power which, in turn, consist of various subdimensions. Levitsky and Way define linkage as 'the density of ties' between a regime and European and North American countries.[8] These bonds can take a range of forms but the most significant are economic, intergovernmental, technocratic, social, information and civil-society.[9]

In contrast, leverage is defined less by the amount of pressure European and North American countries can bring to bear on a regime, and more by the regime's ability to withstand outside influence.[10] Levitsky and Way argue that the amount of leverage the West has over a regime is determined by the size and strength of the regime's economy and state structures; the consistency with which European and North American governments pursue their foreign policies and co-ordinate them with one another; and whether a regime has a powerful patron or Black Knight who is willing and able to defend it against Western governments and offset some of the pressure placed on it by them.[11]

Finally, organisational power concerns a regime's ability to sustain itself. Levitsky and Way observe that 'modern authoritarianism is a complex and costly endeavour'.[12] To survive, a regime has to dissuade 'diverse social and political actors from challenging' it 'as well as maintain the loyalty and cooperation of powerful' individuals and groups within it.[13] Crucial to its ability to perform these functions, are its state and party structures. For, as Levitsky and Way argue, 'effective state and party organizations enhance incumbents' capacity to prevent elite defection, co-opt or oppress opponents, defuse or crack down on protest, and win (or steal) elections'.[14] A regime's organisational power is determined, therefore, by the cohesion, reach and mobilisation capacity of the ruling party and the size, effectiveness and experience of the security forces (the military, police, gendarmerie, and intelligence and security services).

Levitsky and Way's model provides an ideal framework for this enquiry for three main reasons. First, it is specifically designed systematically to capture and explain similarities and differences in experience. Second, the symmetry of circumstance encourages its renewed use. That is, the model was initially devised to explain the experiences of a range of regimes during the last, great wave of democratisation that was triggered by the collapse of the Soviet Union and the end of the Cold War. It is only fitting, therefore, that the model be applied to at least some of the countries affected during this most recent wave of democratisation. And third, the model has never been applied to this particular region which, owing to its geocultural singularity, is only imperfectly covered by Levitsky and Way's original study.[15]

The book's choice of case studies (Tunisia, Algeria, Morocco and Mauritania) is informed by two key considerations. First, by selecting these countries, the book seeks to uncover and chart region-wide issues and themes. Doing so not only allows it to determine the ways and extent to which each country was affected by what was taking place in its nearest neighbours but also to compile a carefully structured overview of the region's development over this critical period (before, during and after the Arab Spring). Second, Libya (the last remaining Maghreb country) is excluded as a case study because it is currently in the grip of civil war.[16]

The book argues that Tunisia, Algeria, Morocco and Mauritania were all competitive authoritarian a decade ago, that only Tunisia is now democratic and that, while Algeria, Morocco and Mauritania have remained competitive authoritarian, they have done so for different reasons. More specifically, the book argues that Morocco and Algeria have remained competitive authoritarian because of their high organisational powers, and Europe's and North America's inconsistent and half-hearted application of pressure on them to democratise; that Mauritania has remained competitive authoritarian, despite the regime's medium organisational power, because Europe and North America lack both the means and the will consistently to pressurise Nouakchott to democratise; and that Tunisia has democratised because the Ben Ali regime was unable to sustain itself owing to a catastrophic breakdown in its organisational power.

Inevitably, the Arab Spring casts a long shadow across the pages of this book. The passions, protests, calculations and countermeasures which comprised and defined it, have left an indelible mark on the Maghreb. And some countries have been especially affected. Tunisia is now much altered as a result. Not only did the protests start there but, such was their impact, they have entered into national folklore, become an important and powerful political memory, and added an extra facet to Tunisians' collective sense of self. Yet this book is not about the Arab Spring. The volume's purpose and goal are neither to trace the local and transnational origins of these demonstrations, nor offer any great new insight into why they began and unfolded as they did. Rather, the book is interested in the political development of four Maghreb countries over a period during which the Arab Spring took place.

This examination and this analysis lead the book to make three valuable and original contributions. To begin with, it is the first to use Levitsky and Way's model to structure its interrogation of Morocco's, Tunisia's and Mauritania's recent experiences, and organise its comparison of their and Algeria's development over the past decade.[17] By adopting this unprecedented approach, the book is able systematically to chart and compare the development of these four regimes over this vital period. It is able to contextualise the start, progression and end of the Arab Spring in the Maghreb, highlight and consider the roles played by key global actors, and examine the interplay between international and domestic factors. The book makes no claims about the originality of the information on these countries it includes, only about the ways in which this material is organised and presented. This approach is entirely consistent with that taken by Levitsky and Way in their 2010 book as they also relied on existing analyses and works for each of their cases studies.

Second, the book is the first to focus on these four countries alone. A number of existing studies of the Arab Spring examine events in some of them (usually Tunisia and Libya). Yet they invariably do so alongside other places in the Middle East.[18] By restricting its focus to Tunisia, Algeria, Morocco and Mauritania, the book privileges the Maghreb's experiences. Moreover, it is better able to address the shortfall in attention paid to some of the region's countries. Little has been written about Algeria, and even less about Mauritania.

And third, the book extends the application and broadens the applicability of Levitsky and Way's model. As the first study to apply it to the Maghreb, the book extends their model to a group of countries that resist easy categorisation as either African, Middle Eastern or European and which are, as a result, only partially covered by both their introductions to their case studies from these regions and the studies themselves. And the book also confirms that their model can be applied to these countries. That is, it demonstrates that at least some of the limits Levitsky and Way imposed on their choice of case studies are needlessly stringent.

In explaining their selection, Levitsky and Way confirmed that they excluded 'other types of hybrid (or "partly free") regime[s], including a variety of regimes in which political competition exists but nonelected officials retain considerable power, such as (1) those in which the most important executive office is not elected (e.g., . . . Morocco); (2) regimes in which top executive positions are filled via elections but the authority of elected governments is seriously constrained by the military or other nonelected bodies . . . ; and (3) competitive regimes under foreign occupation'.[19] Their justification of these parameters was that 'in all of these regimes, the power of actors outside of the electoral process generates a distinct set of dynamics and challenges not found under competitive authoritarianism'.[20]

The book challenges these restrictions on the grounds that they are unhelpful and unnecessary. First, Levitsky and Way's explanation of why these conditions are needed is both brief and vague. They argue that powerful monarchs and militaries do not fit within competitive authoritarian regimes but do not explain why this is so. Second, by insisting on these limits, they expose themselves to accusations of cherry-picking, of setting the criteria for consideration in ways that favour their model. And third, by excluding certain types of regime, they compromise their model's claim to universality. For there are numerous countries in Africa, Asia and Latin America that have politically influential kings or, more often, armed forces. If such regimes are to be ignored, then large parts of the world are placed beyond the model's explanatory reach. The book, then, uses Algeria, Morocco and Mauritania to substantiate these challenges and demonstrate the fallaciousness of the restrictions Levitsky and Way impose.

To sustain this analysis and comparison, the book is divided into five chapters. The first outlines and explains Levitsky and Way's model. It examines each of the core dimensions (linkage, leverage and organisational power) and their subdimensions. It explains how Levitsky and Way use these dimensions to assess a regime's strength. It explains how they measure strength. And it examines the interplay between dimensions, how particular scores in one (high, medium or low) shape and affect the significance of what is happening in the other two (for example, high linkage makes democratisation more likely even if leverage is low, while low linkage means that organisational power is key).[21]

The following four chapters each then applies this model to Tunisia, Algeria, Morocco and Mauritania respectively. To ensure better the consistency of their analysis and facilitate each country's comparison with its neighbours, these chapters are all structured in the same way as each other and along the same lines as Levitsky and Way's original case studies. Each chapter begins, therefore, by assessing the strength of Tunisia's, Algeria's, Morocco's and Mauritania's links to Europe and North America. The chapters systematically proceed through the various subdimensions, identifying and evaluating the significance of any ties that fall within these categories. The chapters then move on to gauge the amount of leverage Western governments have over their Maghreb counterparts. Again, the chapters do so by progressing through each of the subdimensions before determining whether the country in question has the backing of a Black Knight patron. The chapters then examine the organisational strength of each regime, looking at the robustness of their party and state structures. Finally, and again in keeping with Levitsky and Way's original case studies, the chapters trace the origins and development of the regime in question.

This analysis leads the book to arrive at a series of intriguing and noteworthy conclusions: that domestic factors have often proved to be more decisive than international ones; that the organisational strengths of the Moroccan and Algerian regimes have exceeded the determination and ability of European and North American governments to make them change; that Western states have struggled to formulate and prosecute consistent, pro-democracy foreign policies and co-ordinate their efforts with one another; that these states have continued to struggle to promote democratisation in the region and better synchronise their policies despite promising to do so; that the Algerian, Moroccan and Mauritanian regimes look set to remain competitive authoritarian for the foreseeable future; that Levitsky and Way's model can be applied to these regimes; and that their model has broader applicability than they claim.

Notes

1. Mounah Abdel-Samad (2014), 'Why Reform not Revolution: A Political Opportunity Analysis of Morocco 2011 Protests Movement', *The Journal of North African Studies*, 19: 5, 792–809, p. 792.
2. Bouteflika won with 81.5 per cent of the vote while Ali Benflis, who came second, received just 12.18 per cent. Patrick Markey and Lamine Chikhi (2014), 'Algeria's Bouteflika Wins Re-Election with 81.5 Percent: Official Results', *Reuters*, 18 April, <http://www.reuters.com/article/2014/04/18/us-algeria-election-idUSBREA3H0D620140418> (last accessed 29 April 2015), p. 1.
3. Steven Levitsky and Lucan Way (2010), *Competitive Authoritarianism: Hybrid Regimes after the Cold War*, Cambridge: Cambridge University Press.
4. Ibid. p. 5.
5. Ibid. p. 5.
6. Ibid. p. 5.
7. Ibid. p. 5.
8. Ibid. p. 43.
9. Ibid. pp. 43–4.
10. Ibid. p. 41.
11. Ibid. p. 41.
12. Ibid. p. 56.
13. Ibid. p. 56.
14. Ibid. p. 56.
15. Arslan Humbaraci (1966), *Algeria: A Revolution that Failed*, London: Pall Mall Books, p. 10; Michael J. Willis (2012), *Politics and Power in the Maghreb: Algeria, Tunisia and Morocco from Independence to the Arab Spring*, London: Hurst and Company, p. 9.
16. Libya's exclusion is consistent with Levitsky and Way's own guidelines for case study selection which include rejecting any country 'in which comparative authoritarianism collapses before the completion of a single presidential

term' or in which it is 'difficult to identify *any* kind of organized political regime'. Levitsky and Way, *Competitive Authoritarianism*, p. 32.

17. J. N. C. Hill (2015), 'Linkage, Leverage and Organisational Power: Algeria and the Maghreb Spring', *Zeitschrift für Vergleichende Politikwissenschaft / Comparative Governance and Politics*, 9: 4, 1–19

18. For example, see: John R. Bradley (2012), *After the Arab Spring: How Islamists Hijacked the Middle East Revolts*, Basingstoke and New York: Palgrave Macmillan; Lin Noueihed and Alex Warren (2010), *The Battle for the Arab Spring: Revolution, Counter-Revolution and the Making of a New Era*, New Haven and London: Yale; and Tariq Ramadan (2012), *The Arab Awakening: Islam and the New Middle East*, London: Allen Lane.

19. Levitsky and Way, *Competitive Authoritarianism*, p. 32.

20. Ibid. p. 32.

21. Ibid. pp. 70–1.

1

Levitsky and Way and Competitive Authoritarianism: Leverage, Linkage and Organisational Power

Levitsky and Way developed their model in response to the momentous events of the late 1980s and early 1990s. Glasnost and perestroika, the withdrawal of Soviet hegemony over Eastern Europe, the fall of the Berlin Wall and the collapse of the USSR itself set in train the powerful forces which not only led to the crucial changes in international attitude which so interest Levitsky and Way but also helped create several of the states they have since examined.[1] In the space of just a few years, authoritarian practices were dismissed as inappropriate and the regimes which employed them worthy of censure. Liberal democracy was confirmed as the preferred and only truly legitimate political system.[2] The amount of material support provided to dictatorships was either reduced or ended entirely, while that offered to governments which were willing and trying to democratise was increased. Indeed, just as colonialism had been quickly ruled unacceptable following World War II, so authoritarianism was deemed undesirable in the wake of the Cold War.[3]

Yet the triumph of democratic ideals these changes heralded was by no means total. While the number of democracies in the world certainly increased, especially in Eastern Europe, authoritarianism lingered on.[4] As well as surviving in some of the places where it had long been practised, it was adopted by many of the governments of the new states that emerged out of the Soviet Union.[5] Moreover, some of the regimes which claimed to have embraced democracy – claims that they often tried to substantiate by pointing to new practices they had adopted or alterations to their political processes and systems they had made – had done so reluctantly, half-heartedly and imperfectly. Levitsky and Way describe such semi- or pseudo-democracies as competitive authoritarian.

Of course, the Third Wave of democratisation and the Arab Spring remain inextricably interlinked. First, there is the term 'Arab Spring' itself which is derived from that of the 'Prague Spring' that was applied to the Czechoslovakian government's ill-fated efforts in 1968 to challenge Soviet hegemony by extending its citizens' civil and political rights.[6] Memories of the Prague Spring later fed into the popular protests that helped launch and sustain the Third Wave and have also been invoked elsewhere in the world including North Africa. Indeed, in March, April and May 1980, Algeria's Kabyle minority launched a series of protests against the government which were quickly dubbed the Berber Spring.[7] The Arab Spring, therefore, is named after a vital moment in Eastern European history which has provided succour and inspiration to pro-democracy activists everywhere for over fifty years.

Then there are the activities themselves. Very broadly, both the Third Wave and Arab Spring were phases of democratisation of international scale and import. Numerous countries in multiple regions were affected by them. Their transnational dimensions helped give them much of their early energy as populations followed and understood the significance of what was happening elsewhere, and drew courage and inspiration for what they, in turn, might achieve. In both instances, the world (or substantial parts of it, at least) appeared to be in flux with profound and, for the most part, popular changes being demanded and made. New political vistas seemed to be opening up while the momentum of events placed them tantalisingly within reach. And, more specifically, the Arab Spring was made possible and necessary only by the Third Wave's failure to bring fundamental and lasting change to the region. Certainly the countries of the Maghreb were affected by the powerful forces it unleashed and encapsulated. In March 1992, Mauritania held its first ever multiparty parliamentary election.[8] Then, in October 1999, Tunisia staged its first competitive presidential election.[9] And, between June 1990 and December 1991, Algeria organised its first multiparty local, regional and national assembly elections.[10] Indeed, of all the region's countries, Algeria experienced the most far-reaching changes, coming close to undergoing democratic transfers of power at three of its four levels of government.[11]

And, after they had each begun, the Third Wave and Arab Spring followed similar trajectories. Both caught the international community by surprise and opened with an outpouring of energy, dynamism and optimism. Some governments fell quickly. Others sought to save themselves with platitudes and reforms, to bargain their ways out of their crises. Others still were more robust and turned to their militaries, police forces, intelligence and security services to save them. Some of these efforts were in vain as more regimes collapsed and others stood on the brink. Yet, in the end, by the time all the early energy, dynamism and optimism had dissipated, the full extent of democracy's gains were not quite as great as had initially been hoped for or seemed possible.

Indeed, just as the Third Wave did not trigger the lasting collapse of any of North Africa's established orders, so the Arab Spring has failed fully to deliver on its early promise. Perhaps inevitably, its piecemeal and partial achievements have breathed new life into the interests and questions that originally motivated Levitsky and Way. Indeed, why has this phase of democratisation stalled? Why have not more of the region's countries liberalised? Why, despite their seeming similarities, have they experienced such different political outcomes? Why has Tunisia democratised? Why have Algeria, Morocco and Mauritania remained competitive authoritarian?

The aim of this chapter, therefore, is to chart and explain Levitsky and Way's model in preparation for its application to the book's four case studies. In pursuit of this goal, the chapter is divided into four sections. The first provides an overview of the dimensions of leverage, linkage and organisational power, focusing, in particular, on the interplay between them; how the strength of one renders the others more or less important. The following three sections are each organised along the same lines. The second section examines the dimension of leverage: the principal ways in which it is exercised and how it is quantified. This section also defines a Black Knight patron: what a state or regime must do to qualify as one. The third section examines the dimension of linkage: the main forms it takes and how its strength is measured and categorised. And the fourth section examines organisational power: the state and other structures on which it is based.

Leverage, Linkage and Organisational Power: an Overview

In 2010, Steven Levitsky and Lucan Way published their highly acclaimed book, *Competitive Authoritarianism: Hybrid Regimes after the Cold War*. In it, they set out their model for explaining regime transition: why some regimes become democratic while others remain or become authoritarian, and others, still, become partial democracies or competitive authoritarian. Their reasons for devising their model can be divided into two broad categories – to explain the broad and profound international and domestic political developments which had taken place in the world over the past two decades, and their dissatisfaction with existing attempts to do so.

The main real-world development which motivated Levitsky and Way was the end of the Cold War and resultant spread of democracy and competitive authoritarianism. As Levitsky and Way note, competitive authoritarianism was not born out of the ashes, or smashed-up fragments, of the Berlin Wall. On the contrary, it had been exhibited, on and off, by regimes the world over since the 1920s. Yet, for all that, it had remained a limited phenomenon, never widespread, restricted to just a handful of countries. From the late 1980s onwards, however, it proliferated. The end of Soviet hegemony over Eastern Europe and collapse of the USSR created propitious political, economic, social and cultural conditions for its spread.[12]

More specifically, the demise of the Soviet Union had three crucial consequences. First, it led to a sharp decline in the amount of military and economic assistance provided to those authoritarian regimes that were supported by one or other of the superpowers. Clearly, the USSR no longer existed to provide the help and support that it once had. And the countries that replaced it, including the new Russian Federation, had neither the means nor inclination to assume its responsibilities. Meanwhile, with the Soviet Union gone, the United States could afford to reconsider which regimes to back, and in what ways and to what extent. The fiscal and security challenges the ending of this support presented its various client regimes, exacerbated the economic problems that many of them were experiencing. So much so that a raft of dictators were left 'with little choice but to liberalize or abandon power'.[13]

Second, the USSR's implosion encouraged the diffusion of democracy around the world in two distinct ways. To begin with, it caused the global balance of power to shift decisively westwards. Not only was there now no 'military, economic, and ideological alternative to the liberal West',[14] but its victory greatly enhanced the appeal of its political structures and practices. To those regimes eager to achieve similar levels of wealth and prosperity as the United States, Britain and France, the lesson was clear: embrace democracy. And they were given additional incentive to do so by the concentration of much of the world's remaining development resources in Western hands. To qualify to receive further outside economic assistance, these regimes had little choice but to acquiesce to Western demands and adopt 'formal democratic institutions'.[15]

Indeed, the end of the Cold War enabled European and North American governments to refocus their foreign policies as never before. With the Soviet Union gone, they were free to promote and protect democracy around the world with far greater vigour. As well as putting military and diplomatic pressure on regimes to liberalise, they also devised a new form of leverage: political conditionality.[16] From the early 1990s onwards, the United States, Britain and France declared that all future economic assistance they provided would be tied to democratic and human rights. Regimes would be given support only if they held regular multiparty elections and respected the personal liberties of all their citizens.[17]

12

The imposition of these conditions formed part of a broader, more ambitious project to construct an international legal framework to facilitate the defence of democracy around the world.[18] The third key development, therefore, was the creation of the means by which citizenries could be better informed of their rights and their governments more closely monitored and held to account. During the 1990s, a 'transnational infrastructure', made up of 'international party foundations, election-monitoring agencies, and . . . international . . . and non-governmental organizations', was established which exploited the 'new information technologies' to draw 'international attention to human-rights abuses, lobb[y] Western governments to take action against abusive . . . [regimes], and help protect and empower domestic opposition groups'.[19] By the end of the decade, therefore, Western governments were aided and abetted in their efforts to protect democracy by a rapidly growing, and increasingly well-funded and sophisticated global apparatus.

These changes not only provided dictators with powerful incentives to democratise but also raised and made clear the costs they would incur if they failed to do so.[20] Indeed, they were presented with a zero-sum choice. Hold multiparty elections and the West would look kindly upon them. Their requests for support would receive favourable hearings. And international human rights groups would review their efforts with sympathy and offer encouragement. Refuse, however, and the opposite would happen. European and North American governments would condemn their rule and work to destabilise it. Their applications for assistance would be rejected. And human rights organisations would expose their foibles, provide damning assessments, and encourage their political rivals and publics to protest.

Yet, crucially, these changes neither marked nor brought about democracy's total victory. For the pressure to democratise exerted by the West was compromised in at least two critical ways. To begin with, it was not rigorously applied. Some regimes, including many in sub-Saharan Africa, were consistently and strictly held to account. Others, however, were not. Economically important and militarily powerful countries, such as China, were treated with reverence and caution. While close and strategic allies, such as Saudi Arabia, Kuwait and Qatar, were similarly indulged. And even when pressure was applied, Western governments were often satisfied with the sometimes superficial reforms it brought about. They became overly fixated on the holding of multiparty elections at the expense of the quality of these votes (the extent to which they were free and fair) and the amount of respect governments paid to their citizens' broader civil and human rights.[21]

13

As a result, many dictators around the world found ways to alleviate or avoid this pressure (if any was placed on them at all). And they often did so by meeting some of the international demands made of them. They quickly recognised and cynically exploited the West's preoccupation with elections to ensure that they held regular ballots which were at least partially free and fair. Indeed, while these votes were seldom hailed by election monitors as completely open and transparent, they were usually sufficiently competitive to elicit only mild rebukes and tepid warnings. Regimes learned to practise just enough democracy to avoid the levels of international criticism which might have imperilled their holds on power and existence.[22]

So, while the changes in the international environment brought about by the end of the Cold War forced many regimes to moderate their behaviour and at least be seen to pay greater respect to their citizens' civil liberties and human rights, they did not establish democracy as the minimum acceptable standard of political organisation and conduct.[23] What was instituted instead was multiparty electoralism. Certainly, democracy was confirmed as the preferred political system that most governments had to at least claim to aspire to implement if they did not practise it already. And the West did encourage and pressurise authoritarian regimes to embrace it. But often, Washington, London, Paris and Brussels were prepared to accept something less. As long as these regimes held 'passable elections' then the West was usually satisfied.[24]

It was in this twilight world of rhetoric and appearance, encouragement and pressure, negotiation and compromise that competitive authoritarianism thrived. Between 1985 and 1995, the number of such regimes grew exponentially from 'a handful . . . to nearly three dozen'.[25] Yet their rapid proliferation did not augur well for democracy. For, as Levitsky and Way argue, competitive authoritarianism is not necessarily a stepping stone towards full liberalisation or a temporary state. Regimes can remain like this for as long as they are willing and able to. Indeed, by 2010, there were more than a dozen regimes around the world that had been competitive authoritarian for at least fifteen years.[26] Moreover, not all those which ceased being so went on to become democratic. In fact, only a minority did, with the rest growing more authoritarian.[27]

The first explanatory dissatisfaction which helped drive Levitsky and Way to devise their model, therefore, was the 'assumption that . . . [competitive authoritarian] regimes are (or should be) moving in a democratic direction'.[28] Just because they look more like democracies than dictatorships do, does not automatically mean that they will become democratic. On the contrary, competitive authoritarian must be understood as a distinct regime type that will not inevitably turn into something else.

And the second main dissatisfaction which motivated Levitsky and Way was the underexamination of 'the relationship between the international environment and regime change'.[29] This neglect was somewhat anomalous given the dramatic increase in the number of studies in the post-Cold War period into the ways in which the international sphere and global developments affect democracy's spread. And it manifested itself in two noteworthy ways. To begin with, insufficient effort was made 'to either adjudicate among the various mechanisms of international influence . . . [diffusion, direct democracy promotion, multilateral conditionality, democracy assistance and transnational advocacy networks] or integrate them into a coherent theoretical framework'.[30] That is, either too little was said about the different ways in which these means worked and the relative significance of their respective contributions, or just one or two of them were examined while the rest were completely ignored.[31]

Second and related to this, too many studies pay insufficient attention to country-by-country and region-by-region variations in the effectiveness of these mechanisms and the West's democracy-promotion efforts more broadly. In particular, they fail to note or adequately chart: how diffusion was more effectual in Eastern Europe than in the former Soviet Union;[32] how Western governments were more concerned about the fate of democracy in Latin America than in either Asia (where 'power politics' took precedence) or Africa (where its pursuit was mostly 'rhetorical');[33] or how human rights organisations were better able to establish themselves in Eastern Europe and Latin America than in either the Middle East or sub-Saharan Africa.[34] Indeed, for Levitsky and Way, too many studies fail to register the unevenness of the international environment's influence on regime development (how it affected some countries more than others) or the disparate ways in which it achieved effect (whether by diffusion, as in Poland, or transnational advocacy networks, as in Nicaragua).

Levitsky and Way's reasons for developing their model, therefore, were threefold. First, they wanted to address the explanatory shortcomings they identified in existing studies into democratisation in the post-Cold War period. They sought more carefully to chart and theorise the international environment's influence on regime development. Second, they wanted better to explain the origins and spread of competitive authoritarianism. Though such regimes were not new, their rapid increase in number from 1990 onwards gave them an international significance they had never had before. And third, they wanted to chart more accurately the full range of development trajectories of these regimes in order to counter the erroneous assumption that competitive authoritarianism was a temporary prelude to democracy.

While competitive authoritarian is a distinct type of regime, it is also a hybrid because it combines both democracy and authoritarianism. Levitsky and Way define authoritarianism as the absence of any

> viable channels . . . for opposition to contest legally for executive power.[35] This category includes closed regimes in which national-level democratic institutions do not exist . . . and hegemonic regimes in which formal democratic institutions exist on paper but are . . . [a] façade [*sic*] . . . In hegemonic regimes, elections are so marred by repression, candidate restrictions, and/or fraud that there is no uncertainty about their outcome. Much of the opposition is forced underground and leading critics are often imprisoned or exiled.[36]

Competitive authoritarian regimes, in contrast, include constitutional safeguards that allow opposition groups to compete for control of the government. Elections are held regularly and are open to rival parties and candidates. And, between and during ballots, these groups are largely free to campaign, recruit and operate openly. Their leaders are not imprisoned or forced into exile and hiding.[37]

Levitsky and Way adopt a largely procedural definition of democracy built around a series of essential attributes. To be democratic, a regime must hold 'free, fair, and competitive elections'; have 'full adult suffrage'; protect 'civil liberties, including freedom of speech, press, and association'; and be free from 'nonelected "tutelary" authorities (e.g. militaries, monarchies, or religious bodies) that limit elected officials' power to govern'.[38] To these, they add a further, non-procedural attribute: the establishment and maintenance of 'a reasonably level playing field between incumbents and opposition'.[39] By reasonable, they mean that the advantages enjoyed by incumbents (*all* incumbents), such as having patronage to bestow, vote-winning money to spend, the ability to launch 'clientelist social policies' and 'privileged access to media and finance' are not so great as seriously to impair the opposition's ability to compete for power.[40] In competitive authoritarian regimes, on the other hand, 'incumbent abuse of the state violates at least one of three defining attributes . . . : (1) free elections, (2) broad protection of civil liberties, and (3) a reasonably level playing field'.[41]

Elections can be considered free when 'there is virtually no fraud or intimidation of voters'.[42] And they can be considered fair when opposition parties are able to 'campaign on [a] relatively even footing' with incumbents and are not repressed, harassed or 'systematically denied access to the media or other critical resources'.[43] In competitive authoritarian regimes, elections are held but do not meet these standards. Ballots are usually competitive, as opposition parties and candidates are permitted to participate in them and there is only a small amount of fraud, but not free and fair.[44] Voter lists are manipulated, ballot boxes are stuffed and stolen, polling-booth results are changed and fabricated, opposition supporters are threatened, election monitors are intimidated, voters are prevented from casting their ballots, and opposition parties are excluded from parts of the country.[45] By such means, incumbents ensure that they and those they back triumph. Yet, in these regimes, such abuses are never so serious, are never so great as to render the outcome of the election unbelievable and meaningless. Incumbents are willing to cheat but they want the result to stand and be (broadly) accepted. Their cheating cannot be so egregious, therefore, as to make this impossible.

Civil liberties are not only vital to the practice of democracy but their protection and exercise provide confirmation of its health. By having the freedom to speak, meet, say and read what they want, a country's citizens are engaging in democracy. Moreover, in doing so, they provide proof that theirs is a democratic country. In competitive authoritarian regimes, these freedoms are imperfectly enshrined and only partially respected. Independent newspapers, radio stations and television networks exist but they and their staff are routinely threatened, fined and silenced. Opposition parties and other civil society groups are able to operate openly but their members and supporters are frequently attacked, intimidated, arrested and imprisoned. On some occasions, such is the ferocity of this repression that it resembles that practised in full dictatorships. More often, though, it is subtle and legalistic with regimes making 'discretionary use of legal instruments – such as tax, libel, or defamation laws – to punish opponents'.[46] While such prosecutions may be technically correct, they are pursued selectively against regime opponents.[47] And, though such repression is not heavy enough to drive them into hiding or exile, it is greater than that allowed in democracies. By these means, competitive authoritarian regimes intimidate all but the most courageous parties, individuals, civil groups, and media outlets into remaining silent.[48]

In such circumstances the political playing field is tilted decisively and unfairly in favour of the incumbent. Of course, those who hold power in democracies also enjoy a number of advantages. Yet not so many, nor to such an extent, that their rivals have little chance of winning. To distinguish between what is reasonable and what is not, therefore, Levitsky and Way set three criteria for assessing a playing field's evenness. They argue that it is unfairly unbalanced if 'state institutions are widely abused for partisan ends . . . incumbents are systematically favored at the expense of the opposition, *and* . . . the opposition's ability to organize and compete in elections is seriously handicapped'. [49]

They also identify three factors which are particularly important in determining whether a playing field is level. The first is access to state resources, whether those in power abuse their positions 'to create or maintain . . . disparities that seriously hinder the opposition's ability to compete'.[50] Sometimes, such manipulation is open and even legal, with incumbents overtly channelling public funds to themselves, their parties and their clients. More often, though, it is clandestine or surreptitious, with those in power unlawfully siphoning off state monies, 'systematically deploy[ing] . . . state buildings, vehicles . . . communications infrastructure . . . and . . . employees . . . on behalf of the governing party', and 'monopoliz[ing] access to private-sector finance', using their 'discretionary control over credit, licenses, state contracts, and other resources to enrich themselves via party-owned enterprises, . . . benefit crony- or proxy-owned firms that then contribute money back to party coffers, . . . or corner the market in private-sector donations'.[51] By these means, office-holders in competitive authoritarian regimes are able to gain huge, material advantages over their competitors, far in excess of those that their counterparts in democracies are able to achieve.

The second key factor is access to the country's media. In many competitive authoritarian regimes, opposition parties and candidates are not only given less coverage but also less favourable coverage than those they are seeking to oust. State-owned television channels, radio stations and newspapers invariably do not give them as much airtime or as many column inches as the incumbents. Independent media outlets are often more favourably disposed towards them but are usually fewer in number and have more limited geographic and demographic reach. Finally, what privately owned stations and titles there are tend to be 'linked to the governing party – via proxy ownership, patronage, and other illicit means'.[52] As a result, opposition groups are rarely afforded the same media platform as those in power, while their candidates, policies, initiatives and actions are presented far less favourably.

The third critical factor is access to the law. In many competitive authoritarian regimes, the autonomy of the country's courts and other supposedly independent bodies with the power to make legally binding decisions, has been seriously impaired by those in office. Through a variety of means, such as interfering with appointment processes, packing judiciaries and electoral commissions with supporters, bribery, blackmail and coercion, incumbents have extended their influence over many of the institutions charged with holding them to account.[53] As a result, they are often able to break the law with impunity and are routinely awarded favourable rulings and judgments in the cases they bring and in those brought against them.[54] Opposition groups, candidates and activists, in contrast, invariably struggle to win positive legal outcomes, and frequently find themselves in trouble for misdemeanours for which the governing party is rarely held to account and on trumped-up charges.

In addition to establishing a vital benchmark, Levitsky and Way's definition of democracy is noteworthy for the emphasis it places on the creation and maintenance of a level playing field, and the insights it offers into how they chose their case studies and the countries they selected. Certainly, most other definitions acknowledge the playing field's importance. Yet, often, they do so but implicitly through the 'dimensions of "free and fair elections" and "civil liberties"'.[55] As a result, they tend to neglect not only what goes on between ballots, 'such as skewed access to media and finance' which can greatly affect the outcomes of elections, but also those instances of incumbent interference which are not classified as civil liberty abuses.[56] By drawing attention to the quality of the playing field directly, therefore, Levitsky and Way seek to provide fuller definitional coverage.

How they defined democracy also informed the criteria they used for choosing their case studies. One of their definition's five essential attributes specified that democracies must not be subject to 'nonelected "tutelary" authorities (e.g., militaries, monarchies, or religious bodies) that limit elected officials' power to govern'.[57] Levitsky and Way embraced this requirement as a guiding principle when deciding which countries to examine in their 2010 book. As a result, they excluded 'other types of hybrid (or "party free") regime, including . . . [those] in which political competition exists but nonelected officials retain considerable power'.[58] More specifically, they rejected all regimes '(1) . . . in which the most important executive office is not elected . . . ; (2) . . . top executive positions are filled via elections but the authority of elected governments is seriously constrained by the military or other nonelected bodies . . . ; and (3) competitive regimes under foreign occupation'.[59]

Levitsky and Way's embrace of these criteria also explains their case-study selection, including their decision to exclude all Maghreb countries. Indeed, in the course of their book, they make only one, very brief, reference to the region; to identify Morocco as an example of the first type of inappropriate regime (one 'in which the most important executive office [the monarchy] is not elected').[60] Nevertheless, and even though they are not named, Algeria and Mauritania can be considered examples of the second type of unsuitable regime (those 'in which . . . the authority of elected governments is seriously constrained by the military').[61] For, not only have they both experienced army-led *coups d'état* and periods of martial rule but their political processes and elected, civilian governments continue to be subjected to significant military interference. And Libya is ruled ineligible on the grounds that, under Gaddafi, it was too authoritarian and, since his demise, it has been too unstable.[62] Only Tunisia, in fact, satisfies Levitsky and Way's stipulations since President Ben Ali regularly held elections which, by various unfair means, he dominated.[63] Of the Maghreb's five countries, therefore, four contravene Levitsky and Way's criteria for inclusion.

Yet these requirements remain open to at least two significant challenges. The first is that they are underelaborated. For, while Levitsky and Way identify specific countries and the types of regime they will not consider, as well as briefly set out their reasons for excluding them, they do not explain why these conditions matter. What is it about the amount of power wielded by the king of Morocco, for example, that makes the country unsuitable for analysis? Second, the stringency of their restrictions not only limits their model's claim to universality but also exposes them to accusations of cherry-picking. Many militaries in Africa, the Middle East, Latin America and elsewhere have played tutelary roles. So many and for such long periods, in fact, that there are few countries in any of these regions in which their political influence is not felt. Does this mean that Levitsky and Way's model simply should not be extended to them? If so, then great swathes of the world are potentially placed off limits with all the implications this has for their model's explanatory prowess. And finally, if so many regimes and regions are excluded, then are they not deliberately setting their criteria in order to discount those places which their model might struggle to explain? Are they trying to load the elucidatory dice in their favour?

At least some of these conditions, therefore, are unnecessary and unhelpful, and place needlessly severe limits on Levitsky and Way's model. This much can be confirmed by extending their analysis to Algeria, Morocco and Mauritania. Certainly the current influence of the monarchy and military in these countries cannot be questioned or denied. But, rather than view them as either extraordinary or immutable political forces, they should be considered parts of their respective country's authoritarian furniture. Making the Moroccan monarchy genuinely constitutional is one of the hurdles that pro-democracy reformers there need to clear if they are to liberalise the country's political structures and practices. Just as their Algerian and Mauritanian counterparts need to depoliticise their militaries. Rather than view these conditions as reasons to withhold Levitsky and Way's model from these regimes, they should be factored into the analysis it enables.

Competitive authoritarian regimes have split personalities. Indeed, they are defined by their dualism, by their embrace of the democratic and the authoritarian. As a result, they are marked by tension and ambiguity. Their democratic institutions and practices give opposition parties and candidates opportunities to challenge those in office for power. As long as incumbents are able successfully to exploit these processes, to command the support of a significant portion, if not outright majority, of the population and win elections without so compromising the vote as to render its result completely unbelievable and illegitimate, then this tension is contained. For, on such occasions, election outcomes and the popular will are broadly in harmony with the incumbents' desire to remain in power. Yet should this alignment not be achieved, should those in power struggle to win the backing of a large number of their citizens or feel compelled to intervene in an electoral process to the extent that the ballot loses all credibility, then this tension becomes profound and, for the incumbents, dangerous.

Indeed, in such instances, those in power are confronted with a wicked dilemma. If they respect democracy they will be lauded for doing so but increase the risk of their being ejected from office. Alternatively, if they openly and aggressively intercede in the democratic process, they will better ensure their short-term survival but at the likely expense of their domestic standing and international reputation.[64] To date, this tension and dilemma have elicited a range of responses from those in power in competitive authoritarian regimes. Their various reactions help explain the divergent political trajectories of the countries they govern.

Despite the inescapable tension at its core, which forces those who hold power to exist in a state of almost constant imbalance, competitive authoritarianism has proved remarkably durable. Of the thirty-five case studies they investigated, Levitsky and Way found that nineteen had survived for fifteen years or more.[65] This led them to identify three different development paths taken by competitive authoritarian regimes. The first was towards democratisation. In these cases, those in power held 'free and fair elections', recognised and protected civil liberties, and established 'a level playing field'.[66] The second was towards unstable authoritarianism. In these instances, 'authoritarian incumbents were removed at least once but new governments were not democratic'. Moreover they 'inherited a skewed playing field and politicized state institutions, which they used to weaken and/or disadvantage their opponents'.[67] And the third was towards stable authoritarianism. On these occasions, 'authoritarian incumbents or their chosen successors remained in power for at least three presidential/parliamentary terms following the establishment of competitive authoritarian rule'.[68]

It was to explain competitive authoritarianism better and why individual regimes followed different development paths that Levitsky and Way devised their model. At its heart are the dimensions of linkage, leverage and organisational power which, together, cover both international (linkage and leverage) and domestic (organisational power) factors. With them, Levitsky and Way have constructed a three-part, incremental argument which begins by observing that extensive linkage to the West has made competitive authoritarian regimes far more likely to democratise.[69] For high linkage not only raises the international costs of any autocratic abuses committed, make a Western response to such misdemeanours more probable, expand the number of local groups and figures with an interest in avoiding any such sanctions, and increase the amounts of material help and acclamation heaped on opposition movements but also makes maintaining an authoritarian regime far more expensive. Indeed, high linkage provides dictators and their successors with strong incentives to relinquish power quietly and govern democratically.[70]

In contrast, low linkage reduces the effectiveness of Western pressure to democratise. Step 2 of Levitsky and Way's argument, therefore, is that, in these circumstances, 'regime outcomes were driven primarily by domestic factors, particularly the organizational power of incumbents'.[71] In those regimes where the state apparatus and ruling party were well organised and cohesive, those in power were usually able to prevent elite defections and defeat any opposition challenges. But, in those countries where the state organs and governing party were poorly co-ordinated and fragmented, incumbents often lacked the 'organizational and coercive tools to prevent elite defection, steal elections, or crack down on protest' so were 'vulnerable to even relatively weak opposition challenges'.[72]

On these occasions, and step 3 of Levitsky and Way's argument, 'states' vulnerability to Western democratizing pressure (. . . *leverage*) . . . was often decisive'.[73] Crucially, this pressure achieved the greatest effect on those regimes which were susceptible to European and North American influence but were of little strategic value to them and which were not supported by a Black Knight power. Countries which were important to the West habitually had less pressure put upon them. Moreover, that which was applied was often done so with little consistency or co-ordination as Washington, London, Paris and Brussels allowed their collective or individual interests to take precedence over democracy promotion. And those regimes which had the backing of a Black Knight (usually, but not always, Russia or China) were better equipped to resist Western efforts to make them democratise even if they had low organisational power. Finally, in those countries which had few ties to the West and only weak domestic pro-democracy movements, authoritarianism frequently endured.[74]

Taken together, therefore, leverage and linkage help to explain the variation in the types and levels of democratising pressure applied by the West.[75] Different combinations of high, medium and low leverage and linkage generate a range of external environments, some of which are more conducive of democracy than others. The democratising effects of leverage and linkage, therefore, depend not only on their individual strengths but also on those of the other. When both are high then 'external democratizing pressure is consistent and intense'.[76] In such circumstances, the West is focused on what is taking place in a regime and willing to intervene if abuses are perpetrated, and provides encouragement and support to internal opposition groups. Indeed, so great is their interest and involvement that 'democratization is likely even . . . [if] domestic conditions are unfavourable'.[77]

When linkage is high and leverage low, however, this pressure is less well directed even though it remains strong. Its effects, therefore, are more indirect as it leads regimes to engage in greater self-censorship. For, while the West might not push these governments quite as hard to democratise as it does some others, they remain subject to 'intense scrutiny from international media, transnational human-rights networks, and internationally orientated domestic constituencies' which they are anxious to appease.[78] And in their efforts to do so, and thereby avoid the reputational and material penalties they know they will incur from failing to, they enact many of the pro-democracy measures and reforms advocated by the West.[79]

Conversely, when linkage is low and leverage high, external pressure is inconsistently applied. Those regimes which fail 'to meet international electoral or human-rights standards' may be severely sanctioned but often the penalty imposed on them amounts to no more than holding a ballot which broadly satisfies Western electoral expectations.[80] Not only does this give dictators considerable room for manoeuvre but, even if they are ousted from power, there is no guarantee that democracy will follow or that the pressure being applied will be sustained thereafter. While a low-linkage–high-leverage environment may raise the cost of authoritarianism, it does not guarantee, or even greatly encourage, democratisation.[81] And finally, when linkage and leverage are both low, external pressure is infrequently and ineffectively applied. In such an environment, Western governments do not always respond to serious civil and human rights abuses let alone take any countermeasures. And, even when they do, their reprisals often have little impact. In such a lax and unconducive environment, democratisation is demanded by domestic groups and organisations alone.[82]

In using these dimensions in this way, Levitsky and Way argue that their model successfully predicted what would happen in twenty-eight of the thirty-five regime transitions they examined. Furthermore, they contend that six of the seven results they got wrong were 'near misses' as their model accurately explained 'key aspects' of the regimes' evolution and forecast outcomes for them which were close to what eventually transpired.[83] Indeed, Levitsky and Way maintain that only one case fell 'entirely outside ... [of their] theoretical framework'. In adopting this model, therefore, the book is embracing an analytical framework and thesis which have been thoroughly developed and proven to work.[84]

Leverage

Levitsky and Way's understanding of leverage 'encompasses both ... regimes' bargaining power vis-à-vis the West, or their ability to avoid Western action aimed at punishing abuse or encouraging political liberalization; and ... the potential impact (in terms of economic health or security) of Western punitive action toward target states'.[85] The exercise of leverage, therefore, has two key features that cover the determination and capabilities of both those seeking (the West) and resisting (target states) democratic change. The first refers to the amount of pressure European and North American governments can bring to bear on a given country as measured by the likely political and economic consequences of individual and successive disciplinary actions. And the second relates to the ability of that country to withstand those actions and cope with their consequences. Both features must be considered, for it is possible for Western governments to put more pressure on a regime than they do others but still have less influence over it because of its greater capacity to cope with their punitive measures.[86]

The amount of leverage European and North American governments have over a regime is mainly determined by three factors. The first of these is the size and strength of the target state's economy. Unsurprisingly, countries with 'small, aid-dependent economies are more vulnerable to external pressure' than those with large ones. Indeed, states with big economies are not only better able to cope with 'the various types of pressure employed by Western powers ... such as aid withdrawal, trade sanctions, and the threat of military force' but are also better placed to prevent any penalties from being imposed in the first place.[87]

The second factor is the consistency with which European and North American governments pursue their pro-democracy foreign policies towards a regime, and co-ordinate their efforts with one another. Any significant variation in either their individual or collective aims helps the target state evade and offset any pressure placed upon it. In such circumstances, dictators are better able to play Western governments off against one another. And they usually do so by presenting both themselves and the stability of their regimes as vital to the realisation of a particular government's goals, and greater democracy as a threat to this mutually beneficial arrangement. If another Western state attempts to discipline the regime, therefore, it soon discovers the limits of at least some of its allies' support. And without their compliance, the punitive measures it has introduced are inevitably rendered less effective.[88]

Finally, the third factor is whether a regime has the backing of a Black Knight or 'counter-hegemonic' power.[89] Black Knights are powerful states with a vested interest in ensuring a particular regime's survival. Usually the role is played by either Russia or China but is occasionally performed by France and Japan. To help safeguard the existence of their client regime, a Black Knight will provide it with 'economic, diplomatic, and other assistance'.[90] And they will do so in part to enhance its ability to withstand any democratising pressure placed upon it by (any other) European and North American countries.

One of the main ways in which high leverage encourages democratisation is by making dictatorships more expensive to establish and maintain. The sanctions imposed on many of them by European and North American governments often 'trigger fiscal crises, which – by eroding incumbents' capacity to distribute patronage and . . . pay [the] salaries of civil servants and security personnel – seriously' endanger their survival.[91] So grave can the consequences be that, sometimes, just the threat of such measures is sufficient to make autocrats change their behaviour. By this method, therefore, Western states have been able to curb authoritarianism and undermine dictatorial regimes in a variety of ways, from deterring election theft, to toppling governments, to persuading autocrats to democratise, to convincing leaders who acquired power by nefarious means to relinquish it.[92]

Nevertheless, even high Western leverage is rarely sufficient by itself to bring about democratisation. Its limitations are mainly the result of the West's preoccupation with elections and comparative neglect of other issues crucial to democracy, such as human rights. While European and North American governments often respond vigorously to serious and flagrant abuses, they tend either to miss or ignore 'less spectacular' violations even when they occur before their eyes.[93] Indeed, in many elections monitored by their observers, incumbents have been able to harass opponents, abuse state resources, exercise almost complete control over the country's media and manipulate the vote and escape censure and punishment. Moreover, Western governments tend to relax whatever pressure they have been applying once a multiparty election has been held regardless of whether it leads to greater democracy.[94]

The West's fixation on elections is itself a consequence of the difficulties inherent in monitoring other elements of democratic behaviour. Ballots are easy to observe. Moreover, the European Union, United States and other national governments and international bodies, have well-established mechanisms for monitoring them. Western countries are then able to configure their policies and actions towards target states on the basis of what their observers' witness. Ensuring that regimes respect civil liberties, and construct and preserve level electoral playing fields, however, is a much harder task to accomplish. Not least, because Western governments and international bodies are poorly equipped to undertake such assignments.[95] On its own, therefore, leverage generates 'blunt and often ineffective forms of external pressure'.[96] Even when conditions are imposed on dictators, they are still often left with extensive room for manoeuvre. Too often, European and North American governments have been concerned only with the staging of multiparty elections at the expense of the quality of the votes themselves and the introduction of other, important democratic reforms. As a result, leverage has been sufficient 'to force transitions from closed to competitive authoritarian regimes,' but insufficient 'to induce democratization'.[97]

Levitsky and Way use the same grading system (high, medium and low) to determine the strength of the West's leverage over, and links to, a country, and a regime's organisational power. According to them, Europe's and North America's leverage is low if the target state satisfies any one of three criteria, has a large economy (with a total GDP of more the $100 billion), is a major oil producer (pumping more than a million barrels of oil a day during the course of an average year), or possesses or has access to nuclear weapons.[98] If a state does not meet any of these criteria but has either a medium-size economy (with a total GDP of between $50 and $100 billion) or 'a major security-related foreign-policy issue' of importance to either the European Union or United States, or a Black Knight patron (which is either a high-income country with a per capita GDP of at least $10,000 or a major military power with an annual defence budget of more than $10 billion) providing it with extensive bilateral aid (amounting to at least 1 per cent of GDP), then Western leverage is medium.[99] Finally, if a state does not meet any of these seven criteria, then the West has high leverage over it.[100]

Linkage

Crucial to determining the effectiveness of Western pressure on a regime is Levitsky and Way's second dimension, linkage. They define linkage as 'the density of ties (the economic, political, diplomatic, social, and organizational) and cross-border flows (of capital, goods and services, people and information) among particular countries and the United States, . . . EU . . . , and Western-dominated multilateral institutions'.[101] In addition to these many different types of interaction, the concept also covers an equally wide range of actors, including politicians and bureaucrats, political activists and aid, development and charity workers, journalists and intellectuals, business owners, industrialists and merchants, internet-users, expatriates and migrants, and ordinary citizens. To help capture and organise better this plethora of links and participants, and thus render them more accessible to study and analysis, Levitsky and Way divide them into six categories of connection – economic ('flow of trade, investment, and credit'), intergovernmental ('including bilateral diplomatic and military ties as well as participation in Western-led alliances, treaties, and international organizations'), technocratic ('the share of a country's elite that is educated in the West and/or has professional ties to Western universities or Western-led multilateral institutions'), social ('the flows of people across borders, including tourism, immigration and refugees flows, and diaspora networks'), information (the 'flows of information across borders via telecommunications, Internet connections, and Western media penetration'), and civil-society ('local ties to Western-based NGOs, international religious and party organizations, and other transnational networks').[102]

The forms and extent of a regime's links to the West are largely determined by history, economics and geography. Colonial pasts often sustain lingering attachments between former metropoles and those they once ruled. Periods of protracted military occupation and traditional alliances similarly generate and perpetuate long-standing affiliations, if not sympathies, between countries and peoples.[103] Colonisation also led to capitalism's spread around the world, exposing territories to global markets and trade as never before, and encouraging the circulation of people and ideas around empires. Most important, though, is geographic proximity. The closer a country is to either the United States or to the European Union, the stronger its economic, political, civil-society and human relations with them are.[104]

Linkage, therefore, channels influence from place to place around the world. Of course, so-called international effects are rarely that. Ideas, values, programmes and ambitions always originate from somewhere and are almost always more strongly associated with, believed in and adhered to by, some countries over others. As a result, their spread, to the extent that they disseminate at all, is also uneven as they tend to follow the better-established and developed linkage paths. Indeed, linkage is 'rooted in concrete ties – networks; organizations; and flows of people, information, and resources – among states'.[105] And the pressure it helps exert is most effective in those regimes where NGOs have a strong and active presence and which have 'extensive interaction' with Western countries.[106]

Linkage has encouraged democratisation in three '*material* rather than normative or ideational' ways.[107] That is, while it 'may facilitate the diffusion of ideas and norms', its main effect is on dictators' 'interests, incentives, and capabilities'.[108] The first way in which it changes autocrats' behaviour is by generating greater international interest in any abuses they commit.[109] The widespread media activity, frequent intergovernmental interactions, and transnational movement of people and ideas which characterise high linkage all reduce the likelihood of such misdemeanours escaping the West's notice. And the heavy NGO presence and constant communication between expatriate communities and their friends and relations elsewhere mean that even relatively minor transgressions can attract considerable international attention. Moreover, Western governments often feel compelled to respond to such abuses because of the pressure put upon them by the media, human and civil rights groups, and members of the affected diaspora community.[110]

These governments are also more likely to take action if they feel that their interests are under threat. Inevitably, the chances of this happening are higher when the abuses occur in countries with which they have strong links. Conversely, they are less likely to respond if the transgressions take place in regimes with which they have weaker ties. For, in the absence of an extensive and sustained media campaign to expose wrongdoings, the determined activism of civil-society groups to hold those responsible to account, and the concerted efforts of sizeable expatriate communities to make Western political leaders take action, Washington, London, Paris and Brussels are under little pressure to respond and have few reasons to do so.[111]

The second way in which high linkage helps to change autocrats' behaviour is by 'increasing the number of domestic actors with a stake in adhering to regional or international democratic norms'.[112] A defining feature of high linkage is the presence of large numbers of individuals and organisations with strong 'personal, financial, or professional ties to the West'.[113] Moreover, the longer such good relations are maintained, the larger this group of interconnected actors grows. Inevitably, the transnational bonds they share give them a powerful interest in their country's relationship with the West. To the extent that, should it deteriorate significantly because of the actions of their political leaders, they will press them to do whatever is necessary to win back the West's favour.

These concerns are very keenly felt by technocrats with ties to Western universities and international bodies. For these links not only make them more aware of what is happening overseas but encourage them to aspire to secure funding from, and positions in, European and North American institutions.[114] Technocrats tend, therefore, to oppose any actions that might damage or sever these bonds, and call for and support measures intended to improve their country's global standing.[115] Both for and through these actors linkage 'blurs international and domestic politics' by turning Western norms into local demands.[116] And the more members of the ruling elite with vested interests in avoiding international isolation there are, the harder dictators find it to gain and maintain their support for authoritarian rule.[117]

The third way in which linkage helps alter dictators' behaviour is by 'reshaping the domestic distribution of power and resources' to the benefit of pro-democracy forces and detriment of autocrats.[118] The connections that opposition groups and figures forge with like-minded politicians and organisations in the West help protect them from persecution at home. For, by their willingness to take action on their allies' behalf, these influential friends make regimes think twice before arresting or attacking those who oppose them. This leads to the opening up of critical spaces within regimes which dictators cannot easily dismiss or silence, and with which, therefore, they have to engage.[119]

'Western governments, transnational party networks [and] international agencies' may also provide opposition groups with much-needed material support and media access, thereby enabling them to compete better with the autocrats they are trying to oust.[120] While these groups may be given only little or negative coverage by local newspapers, radio stations and television channels, and be unable to draw upon the human, financial and other resources of the state, this outside help allows them to 'mount [more] effective national electoral campaigns' than they would otherwise be able to.[121] Moreover, if such assistance forms part of a programme of 'intense Western engagement', then it may well help rival opposition outfits to collaborate more to the benefit of their broader, shared objectives.[122]

Opposition links to Europe and North America can also lead to a surge in popular support for their cause. Through the Western media, ordinary people are able to learn more about their government's questionable international reputation and the hardships that will befall them should it refuse to respect their civil liberties and human rights, and the high esteem in which Washington, London, Paris and Brussels hold its pro-democracy opponents.[123] These messages can also deter members of the local elite from either remaining in or entering into ruling coalitions with those in power, and have a destabilising effect on the ruling party by 'helping to strengthen reformist tendencies' within it.[124]

On many occasions, however, linkage's impact is hard to identify and measure because it 'influences a variety of state and nonstate actors' and generates 'multiple often decentralized forms of pressure that may operate below the radar . . . of outside observers'.[125] Moreover, it can be difficult to distinguish from leverage, especially when both are high. Indeed, there are instances when linkage can be viewed as a form of leverage, such as when it 'raises the cost of international norm-violating behaviour for individual actors (e.g., lost business, professional, or funding opportunities)' although Levitsky and Way are clear that the two must retain their analytical distinction.[126] Linkage also has a 'cluster' effect as its influence on political outcomes is the result of the 'cumulative impact of a diversity of ties'.[127] That is, its impact is greatest when a regime is connected to the West by numerous ties covering a range of sectors and sections of society rather than perhaps an equal number of links concentrated in just a handful of sectors. And, finally, not all linkage is Western and, where ties to other states are strong, 'they can be expected to shape how governments respond' to European and North American pressure.[128]

When assessing the strength of each regime's links to Europe and North America, Levitsky and Way focus on four types of connection: economic, social, communication and intergovernmental. Economic ties are measured by the amount of trade a regime has with the United States and the European Union's member states for as long as it has been undemocratic. Social ties are measured by the average number of citizens of a regime travelling to, and residing in, the United States and European Union in a year as a percentage of that regime's total population for as long as it has been undemocratic. Communication ties are measured by a regime's annual average per capita transnational voice traffic and Internet access for as long as it has been undemocratic. And, finally, intergovernmental ties are measured by a regime's membership of the Organization of American States (OAS) or potential membership of the European Union.[129]

Each tie for every regime is then given a score of between 1 and 5 'based on its ranking relative to all non-Western countries in the world', with 5 representing the highest quintile and 1 the lowest.[130] These four scores are then converted into an overall mark of between 0 and 1 which determines whether a regime's links to the West are classified as high, medium or low.[131] Though the book adopts Levitsky and Way's three grades and their broad approach to determining them (by assessing the strength of a regime's ties to Europe and North America), it does so by qualitative, rather than quantitative, means. That is, instead of assigning each connection a score and then working out an overall mark, it makes a judgement as to the strength of that particular relation. Furthermore, it makes assessments on each of the six types of connection that Levitsky and Way initially identify (economic, intergovernmental, technocratic, social, information and civil-society) rather than just the four they eventually focus on.[132] Indeed, their decision to ignore technocratic and civil-society ties when calculating the strength of a regime's links to the West is intriguing because it is unexplained. With its qualitative approach to determining linkage and fewer case studies, therefore, the book is perhaps better placed to look at all six ties.

Organisational Power

When leverage and linkage are lower, political outcomes are more heavily influenced by local factors. Two considerations in particular hold the key to whether regimes democratise. The first is the 'balance of power' between dictators and opposition forces.[133] And the second, which greatly determines who gains the upper hand in this relationship, is the willingness and capacity of regimes to defend themselves and resist liberalisation. Indeed, 'authoritarian governments vary considerably in their ability' to do what is necessary to overcome such threats, 'to control civil society, co-opt or divide oppositions, repress protests, and/or steal elections'.[134] In some instances, they are so impoverished and poorly organised, so fundamentally weak, that they are at risk from even small, brief protests. Others, though, are sufficiently well resourced and structured to withstand large and sustained challenges.[135]

When assessing regime strength, Levitsky and Way focus on organisational prowess. They do so in recognition of the manifold difficulties and great costs which authoritarian regimes have to overcome and defray in order to survive. To stay in power, dictators have to dissuade an amorphous and ever-shifting assortment of individuals, groups and communities from challenging their rule. At the same time, they have to persuade a range of figures, organisations and constituencies, on whose support they depend, to remain loyal and committed to their cause.[136] And these challenges are even greater in competitive authoritarian regimes where those in power have to deal with a host of 'actors (parties, media, judges, NGOs) and arenas of contestation (elections, legislatures, and courts) that do not exist . . . or are merely a façade [*sic*]' in full autocracies.[137] In most instances, managing these forces and spaces depends on the development and maintenance of 'organized mechanisms of coordination, monitoring, and enforcement'.[138]

Organisational power is determined by three capabilities of unequal importance: coercive capacity, ruling-party strength and, last and least, control of the economy. The better able a regime is physically to defend itself, the greater its stability and chances of survival. Regimes use two broad types of coercion to thwart their opponents: high- and low-intensity. The first includes measures which, by virtue of their scale or focus or design, are conspicuous. These actions are notable either because they are too large, too aggressive and too public not to be, or because the regime is trying to make a point, to remind its rivals of what it is willing and able to do. High-intensity coercion includes the (often lethal) use of force against crowds of protestors, the assassination of prominent critics, the incarceration of activists and their leaders, and armed attacks against recalcitrant democratic institutions.[139]

In contrast, low-intensity coercion comprises measures that are less conspicuous. These actions are comparatively unremarkable because they are smaller, less violent, cause fewer deaths, or are directed against less noteworthy targets. As a consequence, they are often vital to maintaining competitive authoritarian rule because they do not attract the same level of Western condemnation. Low-intensity coercion takes a range of physical and other forms. Opposition politicians, activists and supporters are routinely monitored and harassed. Their networks are disrupted and meetings broken up. Their offices are vandalised and homes attacked. They are denied access to certain jobs, schools, universities and public services. They are subjected to fallacious investigations, lawsuits, enquiries and probes. By means of the police, armed forces, intelligence and security services, paramilitary groups, tax agencies, courts and other regulatory bodies, life is made as difficult and unpleasant for them as possible to force them to desist and to deter others from following in their path. By these means, regimes hope to bully their rivals into submission and, in so doing, avoid having to use high-intensity coercion against them later.[140]

Coercive capacity has two facets: scope and cohesion. Scope is the 'effective reach of the state's coercive apparatus'.[141] It is determined by the size and competence of the combined coercive means at a regime's disposal. These include both armed and unarmed agencies, state and non-state organisations. They include the military, gendarmerie, police, security services and intelligence agencies. And they sometimes include local political leaders and state functionaries, judges, courts, tax and other regulatory bodies, and paramilitary groups.[142] When a regime's security forces are well funded, trained and equipped, and have proven their ability 'to penetrate society, monitor opposition activity, and put down protest in all parts' of the national territory, then it has high coercive scope.[143] But, if a regime's security forces are small, underfunded, badly trained and inadequately equipped, have little meaningful presence in large swathes of the country, or their personnel are so poorly and erratically paid that they are either unable to do much or are reluctant to obey orders, then it has low coercive scope. Scope has great bearing on a regime's ability to undertake low-intensity coercion. To undertake the full range of low-intensity activities, a regime needs a nationwide infrastructure. Inevitably, a regime's capacity is weaker in those places where this infrastructure is either incomplete or damaged or missing. These areas provide vital spaces in which opposition forces can plan and operate in comparative freedom. Indeed, a regime's resort to high-intensity coercion often indicates the extent to which its low-intensity mechanisms have broken down.[144]

Cohesion is the degree of unity that exists within a state's coercive apparatus. Effective coercion depends on robust chains of command, on orders being followed without question, alteration or delay. Cohesion is high when those in power can expect their subordinates, regardless of rank, to do what they are told. Accordingly, cohesion is low when leaders do not have this confidence, cannot assume that their instructions will be followed. Cohesion is vital to high-intensity coercion. Such activities are conspicuous and likely to result in widespread condemnation both at home and abroad. This censure might be sufficient to trigger or hasten a regime's collapse. This means that those officers and functionaries who engage in high-intensity activities do so at great personal risk. For not only might they be singled out for sanction by the international community but they make themselves dependent on the regime's survival and on those in power taking care of them. Should the regime fall or its government change or its leaders simply prove fickle, then they could be exposed to all manner of retribution. Acts of high-intensity coercion, therefore, pose particular challenges to chains of command. Often, only those leaders with confidence in the cohesion of their security apparatus or who are completely desperate engage in it.[145]

The level of cohesion exhibited by a security apparatus is determined by a range of factors. Crucial is the amount of material care lavished on its members by the regime. If those in power pay their service personnel, police officers and bureaucrats well and on time, then it is more likely to be able to rely on their loyalty. If it does not, however, then it is less likely to be able to depend on them, especially if it asks them to undertake high-intensity coercive actions. Yet cohesion is often strongest when key members of the ruling elite and security apparatus are bound by non-material ties, by shared ethnicity (in a country where such links matter), ideology (usually nationalist or revolutionary), or experience (forged in a war, revolution or liberation movement). When a regime and its security force are led by individuals with direct personal experience of violent conflict, they are 'more likely to possess the cohesion, self-confidence, and "stomach" to use force'.[146]

Strong parties are important to authoritarian regimes as they help contain and resolve intra-elite tensions and conflicts. They provide a mechanism by which leaders can reward (and thus encourage) the loyalty of their supporters. They also offer members of the elite a structure for career advancement, thereby encouraging them to stay within the party and co-operate with one another. For doing so not only holds out the promise of future benefits but defection would put an end to any ambitions an individual might have for as long as the party remained in power. Conversely, when governing parties are weak, they are unable to offer such opportunities, leading to more members of the elite seeking power from outside the regime. Such defections can greatly destabilise a regime.[147] Strong parties also help maintain regime stability through their ability to mobilise and marshal their grass-roots supporters. On occasion, this faculty is used to deploy rank-and-file members alongside security forces to coerce rival parties (disrupt their meetings, intimidate their candidates and followers, damage and destroy their property). And, more broadly, it discourages elite defection by making it harder for individuals to generate support for their cause and construct a popular powerbase.[148]

Strong parties are especially important to competitive authoritarian regimes because of their need to organise and participate in democratic processes. Strong parties are better able to mobilise their members and supporters at election time, to get the vote out in favour of the regime. And they have the means and personnel needed to steal elections, to perpetrate the various forms of fraud that can determine outcomes. Strong parties are also better able to control legislatures and legislative processes. A well-disciplined party with a commanding majority is not only able to decide what laws are, and are not, passed but is more likely to be able to make structural changes to the political system. Through this control, a strong party may well be able to amend the constitution, appoint and dismiss judges and other important functionaries, and oversee and shape the remits of electoral commissions and other vital bodies. And this control has other, zero-sum benefits for the regime. For, by exercising it, a party is able to deny the opposition easy or equal access to this important political space, to use the legislature as a forum in which to debate the regime's policies, and criticise and challenge its actions.[149]

A strong party can improve a regime's control of the legislative process by enhancing its influence over the national assembly and providing a mechanism for managing the succession of its leaders. Strong parties are, by virtue of their greater means, better able to win elections. In so doing, they can help presidents impose their wills on their parliaments. For, without such parties, heads of state often struggle to dominate their national assemblies no matter how popular they are or however strong their personal mandates. By extension, strong parties can deliver greater control between elections and during those periods when the president's popularity is lower. By means of patronage, offers of personal and professional aggrandisement, and ideological appeal, strong parties can prevent much of the factionalism and infighting that occur in their absence. Such sectarianism and wrangling not only weakens regimes but provides opposition forces with opportunities to establish and develop themselves. Strong parties also facilitate succession by recruiting and nurturing a greater number of candidates from whom replacements can be drawn, preventing the defection of defeated candidates by offering them other roles and providing an electoral and political machine that is not dependent on a single individual.[150]

Just as state strength is measured by scope and cohesion, so too is that of parties. Scope is determined by the size of either a party's infrastructure or of the territory in which it has a meaningful presence. High-scope parties are large organisations, have many members, maintain permanent presences across much of the country, and are actively engaged in villages, neighbourhoods and workplaces. Low-scope parties, in contrast, are weak organisations, have few members, and have little active presence outside the major towns and cities, and those regions with close ties to key members of the regime.[151]

Cohesion is determined by a regime's ability to gain and maintain the co-operation of like-minded figures and groups in the government, parliament, and at the regional and local levels. Cohesion is vital to deterring elite defections, especially during times of crisis. Cohesion is high when members of the government and other key political figures habitually support the regime, even when it is under pressure or threat, defections are rare and, if they do occur, have little effect, and internal rebellions are infrequent. Cohesion is low, therefore, when parties have little structure or unity and their leading members derive much of their power and standing from elsewhere. In such circumstances, those in power frequently have to confront challenges to their authority, defections and wider rebellions leading to 'opposition takeovers of the legislature or strong electoral challenges from erstwhile regime insiders'.[152] Cohesion can be achieved by a range of means. Patronage can help maintain elite unity during periods of stability yet is often less effective at times of crisis and especially during economic slumps when there are fewer resources to distribute. Cohesion is usually stronger when it is based on non-material ties, such as ethnicity, ideology or shared experience. Indeed, cohesion is often strongest among individuals who, together, participated in, and won, a profound and violent struggle, a war of liberation or a revolution.[153]

Regimes are also better able to contain and defeat opposition challenges if they exercise discretionary control over their national economies. High control can be an alternative for strong coercive capabilities or parties. High control is achieved when the most important parts of the economy and sources of finance are largely at the disposal of the state. This level of control is often found in countries with incompletely reformed command economies or which depend on rents collected from mineral resources for much of their incomes. By means of taxation, controlling access to credit and licences, and the award of government contracts and concessions, therefore, those in power are able to help and reward their supporters and penalise and weaken their adversaries.[154]

In those countries in which the regime can easily influence the incomes, livelihoods and employment of a large portion of the population, engaging in opposition activity is a difficult, hazardous and potentially expensive decision. Opposition-linked businesses can be denied permits and contracts. Independent media outlets can be starved of advertising, newsprint, ink and other essential materials. And critics of the regime can be dismissed from their jobs or refused access to basic public services. Control of the economy can also be used to deprive opposition parties and groups of the resources they need to mount effective campaigns. For, if the most important parts of the economy are state controlled and the private sector small and poor, few alternative sources of revenue exist for rival parties and groups to tap into. Finally, control of the economy can also be used to deter elite defections by raising to intolerable levels the financial and economic costs for those contemplating it.[155]

Inevitably, a regime's organisational power is only one part of the political equation. The other comprises the strength, unity and determination

of the forces ranged against it. Opposition groups and activists can profoundly influence a regime's direction of travel, whether it becomes more
or less democratic. If these groups are strong, they can deprive the regime
of resources and raise the cost of remaining authoritarian. And, if they are
large, if they represent and can mobilise substantial numbers of people,
they can make the electoral calculation confronting incumbents – whether
to become more repressive or more democratic – much harder. Invariably,
therefore, the stronger and larger a country's opposition is, the greater the
chances of political liberalisation.[156]

Indeed, organisational power and opposition strength are inextricably
bound in a zero-sum relationship. When a regime is powerful, it possesses
the coercive means systematically to undermine and negate its opponents. Conversely, when a regime is weak, opposition forces have greater
opportunity to strengthen, and destabilise and challenge, those in power.
Regimes with high organisational power, therefore, are almost always
confronted by weak oppositions, while those with low power are sometimes, but not as frequently, faced by strong opponents.[157] This explains
why, in 'many seemingly protest-driven transitions, incumbents' inability
to prevent large-scale elite defection . . . or use coercion to crack down
on opposition protest . . . contributed directly to their fall from power. In
effect, protestors knocked down a rotten door.'[158]

Levitsky and Way's assessments of a regime's coercive capacity and
party strength are based on the scope and cohesion of each. They argue
that a regime has high capacity if it has a 'large, well-trained, and well-
equipped internal security apparatus with an effective presence across the
national territory' and 'specialized intelligence or internal security agencies with demonstrated capacity to penetrate civil society and monitor
and repress opposition activities at the village and/or neighborhood level
across the country'; medium capacity if its 'security forces maintain a
minimally effective presence across virtually the entire national territory' and do not appear to suffer from a lack of 'funding, equipment, and
training'; and low capacity if it has an 'unusually small/underdeveloped
security apparatus' which does not provide even a 'minimally effective
. . . presence in significant parts of the national territory' or seems to lack
sufficient 'funding, equipment, and training'.[159]

And they argue that a regime's coercive apparatus has high cohesion
if it shows signs of 'non-material sources of cohesion', such as a 'recent
history of military conflict', including a 'large-scale external war' that
did not end in defeat, an 'intense and enduring military competition or
threat', or a 'successful revolutionary or anticolonial struggle' in which
'leading security officials' participated'; or 'pervasive ethnic ties between

37

[the] incumbent party and security forces, in a society that is deeply divided along those ethnic lines'; or a 'shared ideology in a context in which this ideological cleavage is dominant'; or 'evidence of consistent ability to use high-intensity coercion in [the] recent past;[160] medium coercive cohesion if there is 'no evidence of non-material sources of cohesion' and has not experienced 'insubordination [or] recent defeat in military conflict', and has paid its security personnel fully and on time;[161] and low cohesion if there is 'no evidence of non-material sources of cohesion' and has experienced 'serious insubordination by state security officials, including attempted coups, open rebellion, large-scale desertion, and refusal to carry out major orders' some time during the decade leading up to the period of analysis; or has been defeated recently 'in a major military conflict'; or repeatedly fails to pay its security personnel's wages on time.[162]

Levitsky and Way argue that a party has high scope if it is a 'mass organization that penetrates virtually all population centres down to village and neighbourhood level and/or civil society and/or workplace' and engages in 'significant grassroots activity – during and between elections – across the national territory'; medium scope if it 'possesses a national organization that penetrates most population centres and is capable of carrying out election campaigns and fielding candidates across the national territory'; and low scope if there is either no party at all, or 'little or no party organization outside of the capital/major urban centres'. And they argue that a party has high cohesion if it governs by itself after achieving 'power via violent conflict, including revolution or [a] national liberation struggle in which much of the current leadership participated', or rules alone after participating 'in at least two national multiparty elections' and its members are bound by 'non-material source[s] of cohesion', such as a shared ideology or ethnicity in a context in which this ideological or ethnic cleavage is dominant'; medium cohesion if it rules alone after participating 'in at least two national elections', or is new (so 'has participated in fewer than two national elections') and its members are united by a 'shared ideology or ethnicity in a context in which that ideological or ethnic cleavage is predominant'; and low cohesion if those in power rule without a party, or in collaboration with 'multiple . . . , competing parties', or with a new party (that 'has participated in fewer than two national elections') and whose members are not bound by a non-material source of cohesion.[163]

Finally, Levitsky and Way argue that a regime exercises discretionary control over the economy if the state-owned 'mineral sector accounts for more than 50 percent of export revenue', or the 'centrally planned economy ... does not undergo large-scale privatization'.[164] Each component of state and party strength (scope and cohesion), and the regime's discretionary control of the economy are then awarded a score of 0 (low), 1 (medium) or 2 (high). These five scores (state scope and cohesion, party scope and cohesion, and discretionary economic control) are then added together to give an overall mark which signifies a regime's organisational power. If the mark is between 0 and 2, then a regime's power is low; if it is 3, then a regime's power is medium–low; if 4, then medium; if 5, then medium–high; and if 6 to 8, then high.[165] Again, while this book adopts Levitsky and Way's three grades (low, medium and high) and broad approach to assessing organisational power (by examining each of the three subdimensions and considering the scope and cohesion of the state and party), it does so by qualitative, rather than quantitative, means. That is, it does not assign any scores but makes a judgement as to the strength of each component of each subdimension.

Conclusions

The end of the Cold War led to a profound shift in international attitudes. Whereas once authoritarian rule had been accepted, now it was condemned. Whereas once dictators had been hailed and helped, now they were censured and undermined. Many of those regimes that had sided with the Soviet Union suddenly found themselves without a patron. While many of those that had aligned with the United States soon discovered that they were surplus to requirements and unwanted. In the space of just a few years, democracy was established as the only legitimate form of government. And only those countries which embraced it could expect to receive any assistance from the now dominant West.

Yet authoritarianism's defeat was not total. Full dictatorships survived, including in some of the states that emerged out of the wreckage of the Soviet Union. And democracy's victory was never complete. Not all of the regimes which claimed to be democratic truly were. Nor was their liberalisation either assured or inevitable. At least some of those that were competitive authoritarian became more, not less, repressive. It was in response to these changes and sweeping, end-of-history assumptions that Levitsky and Way devised their model. Their goals were threefold: to develop their concept of competitive authoritarianism; to explain why some regimes embrace democracy while others become competitive authoritarian and others still turn into full dictatorships; and to chart and explain the reasons why regimes develop in the ways that they do (either stay the same, or become more or less democratic).

At the model's core are the three dimensions of leverage, linkage and organisational power. Together they cover the international and domestic factors that help and hinder democratisation. Leverage refers to the ability of Western states and international bodies to compel regimes to become more democratic, and the ability of these countries to withstand this pressure. Critical to a regime's capacity to defy the West is whether it has the backing of a Black Knight patron. Black Knights are great powers, usually Russia or China, that provide significant economic, military and political support to a regime. In so doing, they better enable it to endure any sanctions placed on it by Europe and North America.

Linkage refers to the range of connections, and their individual and collective strength, between Western countries and those elsewhere in the world. The strength of these ties and the main forms they take are mainly determined by history, economics and, above all, geography. Indeed, the closer a country is to Europe and North America the greater the number and density of its ties to them. High linkage encourages democratisation in three material ways: by generating greater international interest in any political or human rights abuses committed and thereby raising the likelihood of Western intervention; by creating more domestic actors with a stake in appeasing the West and avoiding any sanctions it might impose; and by encouraging and strengthening local pro-democracy groups.

Finally, organisational power focuses on domestic factors and refers to the strength of a regime's coercive capabilities and party organisation, and control of the economy. Both coercive and party strength are determined by two criteria: scope and cohesion. Scope is decided by the breadth and depth of a security apparatus's or party's reach within its national territory. Cohesion is decided by the strength of purpose and degree of unity exhibited by a security apparatus or party. Discretionary control of the economy is decided by the amount of influence a regime has over vital sectors of the economy and sources of finance. High control of the economy can sometimes negate the need for a powerful security apparatus or party organisation.

Like leverage and linkage, organisational power can be categorised as high, medium and low. When leverage and linkage are both high, the pressure to democratise is intense and applied consistently. When leverage is low and linkage high, Western pressure is strong but poorly directed. When leverage is high and linkage low, the pressure is inconsistently applied. And when leverage and linkage are both low, the pressure is infrequently and ineffectively applied. When leverage and linkage are lower, domestic factors (organisational power) largely determine political outcomes.

Notes

1. Unsurprisingly, many of these new states emerged out of the wreckage of the Soviet Union and included Armenia, Belarus, Georgia, Moldova, Russia and Ukraine. Levitsky and Way, *Competitive Authoritarianism*, pp. 183–235.
2. Ibid. p. 3.
3. Robert H. Jackson (1990), *Quasi-States: Sovereignty, International Relations and the Third World*, Cambridge: Cambridge University Press, p. 85.
4. Larry Diamond (2008), *The Spirit of Democracy: The Struggle to Build Free Societies throughout the World*, New York: Henry Holt and Company, p. 47.
5. Of the six states which emerged out of the USSR that Levitsky and Way examined, only one (Ukraine) democratised. The remaining five regimes were either stable authoritarian (Armenia and Russia) or unstable authoritarian (Belarus, Georgia and Moldova), Levitsky and Way, *Competitive Authoritarianism*, p. 234.
6. For an excellent history of the Prague Spring, see Kieran Williams's (1997) *The Prague Spring and its Aftermath: Czechoslovak Politics, 1968–1970*, Cambridge: Cambridge University Press.
7. Martin Evans and John Phillips (2007), *Algeria: Anger of the Dispossessed*, New Haven, Connecticut and London: Yale University Press, p. 122; Bruce Maddy-Weitzman (1999), 'The Berber Question in Algeria: Nationalism in the Making?', in Ofra Bengio and Gabriel Ben-Dor (eds), *Minorities and the State in the Arab World*, Boulder, CO: Lynne Rienner Publishers, pp. 31–52, p. 40.
8. Saad Eddin Ibrahim (1995), 'Liberalization and Democratization in the Arab World: An Overview', in Rex Brynen, Bahgat Korany and Paul Noble (eds), *Political Liberalization and Democratization in the Arab World*: volume I, *Theoretical Perspectives*, Boulder, CO: Lynne Rienner Publishers, pp. 29–60, p. 47.
9. Stephen J. King (2009), *The New Authoritarianism in the Middle East and North Africa*, Bloomington, IN: Indiana University Press, p. 8.
10. J. N. C. Hill (2009), *Identity in Algerian Politics: The Legacy of Colonial Rule*, Boulder, CO: Lynne Rienner Publishers, pp. 135–8.
11. Algeria did experience democratic transfers of power at the local (*commune*) and regional (*wilaya*) levels, and was poised to undergo a similar handover at the parliamentary (national assembly) level after the Islamic Salvation Front (Front Islamique du Salut, FIS) won the most votes in the first round of balloting held on 26 December 1991. Yet, before the second round could be held and the FIS's victory completed, the military intervened and cancelled the election. No presidential election (the fourth level of government) was staged at this time.

12. Levitsky and Way, *Competitive Authoritarianism*, p. 17.
13. Ibid. p. 17.
14. Ibid. p. 17.
15. Ibid. p. 17.
16. Ibid. p. 17.
17. Ibid. p. 18.
18. Ibid. p. 18.
19. Ibid. p. 18.
20. Ibid. p. 18.
21. Ibid. p. 19.
22. Ibid. p. 19.
23. Ibid. p. 19.
24. Ibid. p. 19.
25. Ibid. pp. 19–20.
26. Ibid. p. 4.
27. Ibid. p. 4.
28. To be clear, Levitsky and Way do not stipulate among whom this assumption was widely held, whether it was academics, policy-makers or general publics. Yet, regardless of who believed this, one of Levitsky and Way's main motivations was to disprove the notion that all competitive authoritarian regimes will inevitably become democratic. Ibid. p. 4.
29. Ibid. p. 39.
30. Levitsky and Way define 'diffusion' as the '"relatively neutral transmission of information" across borders, via either demonstration effects in neighbouring countries or modelling on successful democracies'; 'direct democracy promotion' as the efforts of Western states, and in particular the United States, to '"promote democracy abroad," via diplomatic persuasion, threats and – in a few cases . . . – military force'; 'multilateral conditionality' as the use of 'external assistance or membership in international organizations' to cajole and coerce regimes into democratising; 'democracy assistance' as Western support for 'civic-education programs, electoral assistance, legal and legislative reform, and independent media and civic organizations'; and 'transnational advocacy networks' as webs of 'human-rights groups, democracy, and election-monitoring NGOs' which draw 'international attention to human-rights violations, electoral fraud, and other violations of international norms' and lobby 'Western governments to take punitive action in response to them'. Ibid. pp. 38–9.
31. Ibid. p. 39.
32. Ibid. p. 40.
33. Ibid. p. 40.
34. Ibid. p. 40.
35. Ibid. p. 7.
36. Ibid. p. 7.
37. Ibid. p. 7.

38. Ibid. pp. 5–6.
39. Ibid. p. 6.
40. Ibid. p. 6.
41. Ibid. p. 7.
42. Ibid. p. 7.
43. Ibid. p. 7.
44. Ibid. p. 8.
45. Ibid. p. 8.
46. Ibid. p. 9.
47. Ibid. p. 9.
48. Ibid. p. 9.
49. Ibid. p. 10.
50. Ibid. p. 10.
51. Ibid. p. 10.
52. Ibid. p. 11.
53. Ibid. p. 12.
54. Ibid. p. 12.
55. Ibid. p. 6.
56. Ibid. p. 6.
57. Ibid. p. 6.
58. Ibid. p. 32.
59. Ibid. p. 32.
60. Ibid. p. 32.
61. Ibid. p. 32.
62. Ibid. p. 32.
63. Indeed, Ben Ali won each of the five presidential elections in which he stood, never once securing less than 90 per cent of the vote. And, on three occasions, he won with 100 per cent of the votes cast.
64. Levitsky and Way, *Competitive Authoritarianism*, p. 20.
65. Ibid. p. 21.
66. Ibid. p. 21.
67. Ibid. p. 22.
68. Ibid. p. 22.
69. Ibid. p. 23.
70. Ibid. p. 23.
71. Ibid. p. 23.
72. Ibid. p. 23.
73. Ibid. p. 24.
74. Ibid. p. 24.
75. Ibid. p. 52.
76. Ibid. p. 53.
77. Ibid. p. 53.
78. Ibid. p. 53.
79. Ibid. p. 53.

80. Ibid. p. 53.
81. Ibid. p. 54.
82. Ibid. p. 53.
83. Ibid. p. 340.
84. Ibid. p. 340.
85. Ibid. pp. 40–1.
86. Ibid. p. 41.
87. Ibid. p. 41.
88. Ibid. p. 41.
89. Ibid. p. 41.
90. Ibid. p. 41.
91. Ibid. p. 42.
92. Ibid. p. 42.
93. Ibid. p. 42.
94. Ibid. p. 42.
95. Ibid. p. 42.
96. Ibid. p. 43.
97. Ibid. p. 43.
98. Ibid. p. 372.
99. Ibid. p. 372.
100. Ibid. p. 373.
101. Ibid. p. 43.
102. Ibid. pp. 43–4.
103. Ibid. p. 44.
104. Ibid. p. 44.
105. Ibid. p. 44.
106. Ibid. p. 44.
107. Ibid. p. 44.
108. Ibid. p. 45.
109. Ibid. p. 44.
110. Ibid. p. 45.
111. Ibid. p. 46.
112. Ibid. p. 47.
113. Ibid. p. 47.
114. Ibid. p. 47.
115. Ibid. p. 47.
116. Ibid. p. 48.
117. Ibid. p. 48.
118. Ibid. p. 44.
119. Ibid. p. 48.
120. Ibid. p. 48.
121. Ibid. p. 48.
122. Ibid. p. 48.
123. Ibid. p. 49.

124. Ibid. p. 49.
125. Ibid. p. 49.
126. Ibid. p. 50.
127. Ibid. p. 50.
128. Ibid. p. 50.
129. Ibid. p. 375.
130. Ibid. p. 375.
131. For example, Croatia, Malaysia and Cameroon have marks of 0.94, 0.59 and 0.25, giving them high, medium and low linkage respectively. Ibid. p. 375.
132. Three of these shared ties have the same labels (economic, intergovernmental and social) applied to them throughout. The fourth, however, was initially described as information before later being called communication. Despite this change in name, this category of connection covers the same types of link; those related to the Internet and telecommunications.
133. Levitsky and Way, *Competitive Authoritarianism*, p. 54.
134. Ibid. p. 54.
135. Ibid. p. 55.
136. Ibid. p. 56.
137. Ibid. p. 56.
138. Ibid. p. 56.
139. Ibid. pp. 57–8.
140. Ibid. p. 58.
141. Ibid. p. 58.
142. Ibid. p. 59.
143. Ibid. p. 59.
144. Ibid. p. 59.
145. Ibid. p. 60.
146. Ibid. pp. 60–1.
147. Ibid. pp. 61–2.
148. Ibid. p. 62.
149. Ibid. p. 63.
150. Ibid. pp. 63–4.
151. Ibid. p. 64.
152. Ibid. p. 65.
153. Ibid. p. 65.
154. Ibid. p. 66.
155. Ibid. pp. 66–7.
156. Ibid. p. 69.
157. Ibid. p. 70.
158. Ibid. p. 69.
159. Ibid. p. 376.
160. Ibid. pp. 376–7.
161. Ibid. p. 377.

162. Ibid. p. 377.
163. Ibid. pp. 377–8.
164. Ibid. p. 378.
165. Ibid. p. 378.

2

Tunisia

Tunisia is unique. Of the four regimes examined by this book, it is the only one to have made the transition from competitive authoritarianism to democracy. And, of the numerous Middle Eastern and North African countries directly affected by the Arab Spring, it is the only one in which pro-democracy protestors have come close to realising their original goals. In the years since the Arab Spring began, large parts of Ben Ali's regime have been dismantled. A new, progressive constitution has been introduced.[1] Opposition parties have been established and legalised.[2] And free and fair elections have been held.[3] In Tunisia alone have the anger and ambitions which drove and, for a time, defined the Arab Spring been harnessed to any satisfactory extent. The country remains the most hopeful point on a regional political map that is, in turns, disappointing and tragic.

That Tunisia's demonstrations proved more successful than those elsewhere speaks of their instinctive originality. Tunisia's protestors were pioneers, the first in the region to react in this way at this time. And, while they certainly came to draw succour from some of the groups and actions they inspired elsewhere, they remain the initiators of this particular round of popular regional protest. Theirs was an organic moment, a passionate and devastating response to the actions of the police, the security forces, the government and the regime. And, in responding this way, they established Tunisia as the unlikely epicentre of the turmoil that quickly escalated into the Arab Spring.

So implausible did Ben Ali's demise seem to country and regional analysts in the months leading up to his fall,[4] that most did not even entertain the possibility that he could be removed in circumstances as fast paced and dramatic as those that transpired, let alone consider and dismiss such notions.[5] Indeed, so stable and secure did his regime appear that the respected London-based think tank, the International Institute of Strategic Studies (IISS), made no mention of Tunisia in its 2010 Strategic Survey,[6] which it published just three months before Mohamed Bouazizi's self-immolation.[7] And the IISS was not alone in failing to anticipate the regime's collapse. As Schraeder and Redissi observed, 'to say that Ben Ali's sudden fall caught specialists by surprise would be an understatement'.[8]

While there are numerous facets to this failure of analysis, most spring from two closely related sources: Ben Ali's success in creating and sustaining a positive image of his regime and the West's willingness to accept it. Cavatorta and Haugbølle argue that three mythologies in particular – Tunisia's supposed economic miracle, Ben Ali's alleged commitment to democratic gradualism and the regime's strict adherence to *laïcité* – 'prevented a clearer understanding of the political and socio-economic situation' from being developed.[9] From the moment he seized power in November 1987, Ben Ali presented his regime as a modernising and democratising force in a country that was favourably disposed to develop in these ways. Paradoxically, he was willing and able to exploit the image of Tunisia established by his predecessor, Habib Bourguiba, whom he ousted from power.[10] In so doing, he purposefully appealed to Europe's and North America's preferences for how they would like Tunisia to develop. This helps explain their long-term indulgence of this regime and hesitant responses to the protests that removed him from power.[11]

And to these three mythologies can be added a fourth; the seeming sturdiness of the regime. By the time Tunisia's protests began, the ruling Democratic Constitutional Rally (Rassemblement Constitutionel Démocratique, RCD) was sufficiently well funded, favoured and organised to be able to dominate mainstream politics.[12] Similarly, the security forces had been given enough resources and support to allow them to penetrate all parts of the country down to the level of the village and neighbourhood.[13] Moreover, in the twenty-five years since Ben Ali had taken power, they had proven their effectiveness time and again. As recently as the winter of 2006–7, they had successfully prevented an attack by an armed Islamist group, killing at least a dozen of its members and arresting hundreds more.[14] Neither Western governments nor country specialists had any reason, therefore, to doubt the ability of these forces to deal with the protests of 2010 and 2011.

By consistently and unquestioningly allowing these mythologies to frame their analyses, scholars failed to question adequately either the '"unbearable lightness of Arab authoritarianism"' or 'the expectations of transitology' as applied to Tunisia.[15] By mostly accepting the regime-backed narrative that the country was modernising on all fronts, and then applying their democratisation models and theories based on this belief, scholars inevitably concluded that Ben Ali's Tunisia was not only as stable as it seemed but that it was steadfastly inching towards the sunlit uplands of full democracy. The aim of this chapter, therefore, is to move beyond these mythologies by using Levitsky and Way's model to explain better what has taken place in Tunisia and its exceptionalism: why it alone, of all the countries in the region affected by the Arab Spring, has made the transition to democracy.

The chapter argues: that Tunisia has high linkage to Europe and to the United States across all six categories of connection; that the West has high leverage over Tunis; and that the Ben Ali regime had high organisational power (with both a strong security apparatus and ruling party). Yet this assessment raises a range of questions. On the one hand, Tunisia seems wholly to conform to Levitsky and Way's model. The country's strong links to Europe and North America and the West's high leverage over the regime made Tunisia susceptible to the extensive pressure Washington, London, Paris and Brussels could bring to bear. And the country's vulnerability to this influence was only heightened by its isolation, by the absence of a Black Knight patron. Indeed, such was the significance of these external factors that they relegated domestic considerations (the scope and cohesion of the security forces and ruling party, and the degree of discretionary control exercised by the government over the national economy) to secondary importance. In these circumstances, the strength of the regime largely did not matter because the West had the means to bring about change.

Yet, on the other hand, elements of Tunisia's transition did not proceed as Levitsky and Way's model seemed to suggest they might. To begin with, why did the regime fall at all? Why had it not adapted to the changing political climate? How had it been able to resist the various forms of pressure the West had supposedly put on it to implement the types of democratic reform which would have addressed at least some of the protestors' grievances? And why did it fall so quickly? In the end, Ben Ali was driven into exile less than a month after Bouazizi's self-immolation. Why did the country's well-resourced security forces fail to protect the regime better? How were these protests different from all the others that they had successfully dealt with?

Indeed, Tunisia is a complex case. And, while Levitsky and Way's model can explain what has happened there, it must be applied with care and subtlety. The West's links to, and leverage over, the country remain high. But neither Europe nor the United States put as much pressure on Tunis as they could have done. Western governments habitually refrained from driving the democratisation agenda as hard as they might, preferring instead either to mollify the regime or prioritise other objectives.[16] These competing goals ensured that individual governments behaved inconsistently towards the regime and failed fully to co-ordinate their efforts with one another. Crucially, therefore, the reduced pressure they exerted was due not to a lack of capacity but of will. Their leverage over Tunis was high but not exploited to its fullest extent.[17]

According to Levitsky and Way, if Western leverage is compromised, then organisational power plays a more decisive role in shaping political outcomes in determining whether a regime stands or falls and, if it does evolve, becomes more or less democratic. In which case, the Ben Ali regime appeared to be well equipped to survive as it was. For, not only had it built up a large and effective security apparatus but the ruling RCD was well organised and enjoyed numerous, significant advantages over its rivals. Yet it had a brittle strength, carefully nurtured and perfectly able to withstand certain types of pressure exerted in particular ways but vulnerable to other seemingly quite manageable forces to the point of fragility.

Many of the flaws and weaknesses which most seriously compromised the regime's organisational power were the result of its own actions. Such were the security forces' efforts to carpet the country with their presence, so that they might be better able to monitor the population and identify and deal with any threats as they emerged, that they eroded their capacity to deal with crises when they did break out.[18] Moreover, Ben Ali's suspicious treatment of the military, born of his determination to keep it out of politics, ensured that it felt little loyalty either to him or to his regime at the critical moment. And, even though the RCD enjoyed significant advantages over other parties, key parts of its support, most notably sections of the middle and upper classes, were disillusioned with the regime.[19] So, while the regime had high organisational power, its effectiveness was negated by its brittleness.

To sustain this analysis and argument, the chapter is organised along the same lines as each of Levitsky and Way's original case studies. This structure is also adopted by each of the following three chapters (on Algeria, Morocco and Mauritania, respectively). The first section examines the strength of Tunisia's links to Europe and North America across the six categories of connection. In so doing, the section identifies and analyses the various mechanisms and facilities through which Tunisia's relations with the EU and US are conducted. Inevitably, given that this is the opening case-study chapter, the section examines these mechanisms in more detail than in chapters 3, 4 and 5. The second section then considers the forms and extent of the West's leverage over Ben Ali's regime and whether it had the backing of a Black Knight patron. The third section then assesses the regime's organisational power. And, finally, the fourth section traces its origins and development, paying particular attention to the period from 2005 onwards.

Linkage

Tunisia has had strong links with the West since independence. Moreover, the number and quality of these ties have increased over the years to the extent that the country now has high linkage to the United States and to the European Union. Intergovernmental relations between the United States and Tunisia take place within a range of policy frameworks, most notably the Middle East Partnership Initiative (MEPI) and the Broader Middle East and North Africa (BMENA) partnership initiative.[20] These frameworks are managed and supported by different US government departments and international bodies. The MEPI is administered by the State Department while the BMENA was launched with the backing of the G8, European Union and Bretton Woods Institutions.[21] And, in response to the protests in Tunisia and elsewhere, the Obama administration (somewhat belatedly) established a number of new mechanisms. In September 2011, the State Department created the office of the Special Coordinator for Middle East Transitions (SCMET) to oversee the distribution of American aid and development funds to Egypt, Libya and Tunisia.[22] And, in 2013, the MEPI was subsumed as part of the SCMET and the special coordinator's area of responsibility extended to incorporate most of the Middle East and North Africa.[23]

The MEPI and BMENA were launched shortly before and after the United States' invasion of Iraq in December 2002 and June 2004 respectively. Their common purpose is to use non-military means to encourage Middle Eastern and North African regimes to democratise their political processes and structures.[24] The MEPI does so by providing financial support to national and regional projects that address at least one of its four core areas of concern, namely, economic liberalisation, education, women's empowerment and human rights more broadly.[25] Under the MEPI's auspices, more than $730 million was distributed to schemes across the region between 2003 and 2012.[26]

Yet these funds represent only a small fraction of the total amount of foreign assistance provided to the region by the United States. A far greater portion of its spending there – between 70 and 80 per cent – went on security-related projects.[27] Neither the amount of assistance given by the United States nor the proportion of those funds it spent on security was greatly affected by the change in administration. In its 2008 and 2009 budgets, the Bush administration allocated $6.5 billion and $7.2 billion in foreign assistance to the Middle East and North Africa. Of this, more than $4 billion each year took the form of Foreign Military Financing (FMF) through which the region's governments were given credit to buy

US military equipment.[28] And, in its 2010 and 2011 budgets, the Obama administration allocated $7 billion and $7.1 billion in foreign assistance of which up to $4.8 billion each year took the form of FMF credit.[29] So, even though the amount of funding the United States provided to promote democracy and good governance in the region grew exponentially from $27.3 million in 2001 to $430 million in 2013, it continued to allocate far greater sums under the FMF programme.[30]

American assistance to Tunisia over this period was initially provided on a similar ratio. In 2007, the Bush administration gave the Ben Ali regime $11 million in security and military assistance,[31] which was the equivalent of slightly more than a fifth of the total MEPI budget for that year. In 2010, the Obama administration raised that amount to $19.9 million or around a third of the (higher) MEPI budget.[32] And, in 2012, it more than doubled the sum to $54.5 million or nearly three-quarters of the (higher still) MEPI budget.[33] Furthermore, Tunisia was consistently given more assistance than any other Maghreb country even though it had a much smaller population and territory to secure, and did not initially face any threats as serious as those confronting some of its neighbours, most notably Algeria. Between 2002 and 2005, Tunis was granted $74.8 million in security assistance while Morocco and Algeria were granted $66.9 million and just $5 million respectively.[34]

Over the past twenty years, the European Union's intergovernmental interactions with Tunisia and the Maghreb's other countries have also been conducted through a range of policy frameworks, including the Euro-Mediterranean Partnership (EMP), the Union for the Mediterranean (UfM), the European Neighbourhood Policy (ENP), and the Partnership for Democracy and Shared Prosperity (PfDSP).[35] The EMP was established in November 1995 under the terms of the Barcelona Declaration which was agreed by the Council of the European Union, the European Commission, the EU's fifteen member states and their twelve Mediterranean partners.[36] The main purpose of the EMP was to promote 'peace, security and shared prosperity' by providing a framework for the management of bilateral and regional relations between the various signatories. The partnership was organised into three areas of co-operation. The first was political and security: the creation of 'a common area of peace and stability underpinned by sustainable development, rule of law, democracy and human rights'. The second was economic: 'the gradual establishment of a free-trade area aimed at promoting shared economic opportunity through sustainable and balanced socio-economic development'. And the third was social and cultural: the promotion of 'understanding and ... dialogue between cultures, religions and people, facilitating exchanges between civil society and ordinary citizens, particularly women and young people'.[37]

In accordance with the terms of the EMP, each partner state has signed an association agreement (AA) with the European Union under which they are committed to engage in ever-greater free trade with Europe (except in certain protected sectors) and co-operate more closely with the partnership's other members. To help fund these reforms, the EU launched the Accompanying Measures (Mesures d'Accompagnement, MEDA) financial programme in 1995. The monies this programme provided were augmented by loans from the European Investment Bank (EIB).[38] Tunisia was the first partner state to sign an association agreement on 17 July 1995.[39] And it signed a free trade agreement with the European Union on 1 January 1998.[40] And between 1995 and 1999, and 2000 and 2006 it received €428 million and €517.6 million respectively in MEDA funding.[41]

In 2008 the EMP was formally rebranded as the UfM.[42] The principal differences between the two were the expansion of the UfM's membership (twenty-eight European Union and fifteen partner states) and the reduction in its focus.[43] This narrowing of interest was perhaps inevitable given that, since 2004, the EU's bilateral relations with the partner states had mostly been managed through the ENP and the association agreements.[44] Yet, even so, the EMP's early ambition remained evident in both the ENP's founding belief that closer integration with Europe would strengthen democracy and human rights in the partner states and embrace of such grand goals as the creation of a Euro-Mediterranean free trade zone.[45]

In accordance with the ENP, most partner states have agreed an action plan with the European Union which sets out their individual 'agenda[s] for political and economic reform' over the next three to five years, 'needs and capabilities' and interests.[46] Each plan also specifies what the European Union hopes to gain by entering into partnership with that country. The measures outlined in the plans are supposed to complement those laid out in the association agreements (for those countries which have them). And, to help ensure that the plans are implemented fully and to schedule, the EU offers support (financial, technical and political),[47] incentives (economic integration and fewer travel restrictions to Europe), and oversight, with the European External Action Service (EEAS) and European Commission publishing annual progress reports on each partner.[48]

Tunisia's action plan with the European Union was agreed in late 2004 and came into force on 4 July 2005.[49] The plan had both a narrower focus and contained more specific requirements than the association agreement. Unlike the agreement, the plan was mainly concerned with strengthening democracy, the rule of law, and human rights in Tunisia. That it did so helps explain the Ben Ali regime's delay in implementing it. The plan's tighter focus was reflected in the more detailed short- and medium-term goals it set the regime and which included developing 'the role of civil society', encouraging 'exchanges of experience between Tunisian and European members of parliament', 'developing structured political dialogue on democracy and the rule of law', providing 'support to political parties so as to further strengthen their involvement in the democratic process', and helping 'the Tunisian authorities in the area of administrative reform, with a view in particular to greater transparency'.[50]

In response to what had happened during the first months of the Arab Spring, the European Union quickly launched a review into the ENP which it published in May 2011 as A New Response to a Changing Neighbourhood.[51] The review's main finding was that the European Union had 'been caught on the wrong side of history, in alliances with autocratic leaders . . . that focussed on energy and security and turned a blind eye to abuses'.[52] To make up for this error of positioning, and recalibrate and relaunch its relationship with the governments and, in particular, peoples of North Africa, the European Union promised to provide more support for democracy and democratisation in the region. Indeed, the new-look ENP would offer 'more money, markets and mobility in return for evidence of political reform'.[53]

In addition to the changes it made to the ENP, the European Union also launched its fourth and most recent policy framework, the Partnership for Democracy and Shared Prosperity (PfDSP) on 8 March 2011.[54] The PfDSP was the first framework both devised by the European Union in the wake of the Arab Spring and which sought to structure and regulate Europe's relations with its North African and Middle Eastern partners on the basis of what they were experiencing.[55] The EU did not intend for the PfDSP to replace either the ENP or UfM, but reframe and rein-vigorate them. The PfDSP's initial function, therefore, was curative and declaratory; to try to repair the EU's strained relations with the region's inhabitants by reaffirming its commitment to democracy, acknowledging its failure to better support the Arab Spring protestors,[56] and pledging to provide them with greater assistance from then on.

The PfDSP's second purpose was to set out the EU's priorities: those areas of reform in which it was most eager for progress to be made and towards which it would direct more of its energies. These included: strengthening the various institutions which together make up and sustain healthy democratic systems; working more closely with the citizenries of partner states and generating greater opportunities for 'people-to-people' contact; and encouraging economic liberalisation and improving those elements of worker welfare and development crucial to economic growth.[57] These priorities were subsequently embraced and endorsed by the ENP. And, to advance them, the European Union established new programmes and made additional money available. Intriguingly, these programmes did not come with their own resources but, instead, drew from the ENP's expanded budget.[58]

In May 2011, the EIB raised its loan ceiling for the Middle East and North Africa from €4 billion to €5 billion, and the European Bank for Reconstruction and Development (EBRD) agreed to extend its coverage to the southern Mediterranean and 'make up to €2.5 billion of public and private sector investment' available each year for 'the establishment and expansion of businesses and the financing of infrastructure'.[59] In September 2011, the European Union established the Support for Partnership, Reforms and Inclusive Growth (SPRING) fund with a budget of €359 million, and the Civil Society Facility (CSF) with an initial annual budget of €26.4 million.[60] And in October 2012, the EU launched the European Endowment for Democracy (EED) with an initial budget of €14 million.[61] To date, Tunisia has been one of the main beneficiaries of SPRING funding receiving €140 million in payments between 2011 and 2013.[62] Egypt and Morocco were given €130 million and €115 million respectively over the same perion.[63]

In addition to the changes it made to the ENP and launch of the PfDSP, the European Union created other new structures in response to the Arab Spring. In July 2011, it appointed a Special Representative (EUSR) for the Southern Mediterranean whose task it was to further the objectives of the ENP in the region.[64] And, between September 2011 and February 2012, the EU convened task forces for Tunisia, Egypt and Jordan 'to coordinate European and international support to allow quicker and more effective assistance',[65] by bringing 'together officials from the EU, members states, the European Investment Bank for Reconstruction and Development, as well as representatives from other international financial institutions and from the private sector'.[66]

It was in this renewed spirit of solidarity with the peoples of North Africa that the European Union signed a privileged partnership agreement with Tunisia's Association Council at the first meeting of the Tunisian task force on 28 September 2012.[67] In accordance with it, the EU pledged to provide over €300 million in grant monies and to return all the 'illicitly acquired assets of the previous regime'.[68] It also promised to encourage the EIB and EBRD 'to bring investment finance to the country'.[69] Through their respective policy frameworks, therefore, both the European Union and the United States have forged extensive links with successive Tunisian governments and acquired significant leverage over them all. Moreover, as a result of the conditions these frameworks have imposed on Tunis and the types of funding they have made available, they have encouraged and facilitated the creation of numerous important economic ties between the country and the West.

Indeed, the value of Tunisia's trade with the United States has increased steadily over the past twenty years. This growth is mainly the result of the various commercial agreements Tunis has made. On 29 March 1995, the country joined the World Trade Organization (WTO). In so doing, it satisfied one of Washington's key requirements for closer economic co-operation. Then, on 2 October 2002, the Ben Ali regime signed a Trade and Investment Framework Agreement (TIFA) with the United States. Under its terms, both Tunis and Washington pledged 'to promote an attractive investment climate and expand trade in products and services'.[70] And, on 9 May 2003, the Bush administration launched the Middle East Free Trade Area (MEFTA) initiative with Tunisia as a prospective member.[71]

The value of Tunisia's imports from the United States has more than doubled over the past two decades. Between 1995 and 1999, their annual average value was $342.03 million.[72] Between 2000 and 2004, they rose slightly to $342.41 million.[73] Then, between 2005 and 2010, they increased markedly to $584.36 million.[74] And, most recently, between 2011 and 2013, they were worth $845.98 million.[75] The rise in the value of Tunisia's exports to the United States has been even more dramatic. Between 1995 and 1999, their annual average value was just $50.75 million.[76] Then, between 2000 and 2004, they grew to $64.58 million.[77] Then, between 2005 and 2009, they increased significantly to $209.04 million.[78] And, between 2010 and 2013, they were worth $347.19 million.[79] As a result of these increases, the United States is now the sixth largest importer of Tunisian goods and third highest exporter to the country, making it Tunisia's third biggest trading partner.[80]

And Tunisia has long sought closer economic relations with the European Union as well. Not only was it the first partner state to sign an association agreement in July 1995 but it began removing tariffs on individual imports from the EU as early as 1996, a full two years before the agreement was ratified and came into force.[81] Since then, and in accordance with the terms of the agreement, Tunis has reduced the import tariffs on more than half the products it said it would and eliminated them entirely for capital goods.[82] These measures, and the broader ambition which sustains them, have helped to establish the European Union as Tunisia's most important economic partner.[83] In 2003, the total value of the country's trade with the EU was €13.5 billion. Over the next decade it grew almost annually so that, by 2013, it was worth €20.5 billion.[84]

More indicative, though, is the amount of business Tunisia conducts with the European Union as a proportion of its total trade. In 2003, the European Union accounted for 79.2 per cent of the country's exports and provided 73.7 per cent of its imports.[85] And, while these figures had fallen by 2013, the EU was still Tunisia's biggest trading partner by a considerable margin, receiving 61.9 per cent of its imports and supplying 65.3 per cent of its exports.[86] In comparison, the country's second highest import and export partners (China and Libya) accounted for 5.4 per cent and 8.1 per cent of trade respectively.[87] Moreover, Tunisia's imports to and exports from the European Union amounted to more than double those of its next nine largest trading partners.[88]

A key condition of Tunisia's membership of the European Union's various policy frameworks is that it opens up its economy to greater private and foreign investment. This requirement was underscored by the EU's insistence that all partner states join the WTO.[89] Indeed, one of the main reasons it sought closer relations with Europe was to increase the amount of Foreign Direct Investment (FDI) in the country. And, while Tunis has been slow to derestrict some sectors, most notably the country's financial services, it has pressed ahead with the privatisation of several large state-owned firms.[90]

In so doing, Tunisia has been able, over the past two decades, to generate increasing amounts of FDI. Between 1995 and 1999, the country attracted an average of $367.8 million in foreign investment each year.[91] Between 2000 and 2004, this grew to an average of $625.2 million a year.[92] Then, between 2005 and 2009, it increased again to an average of $1.9 billion per year.[93] And, between 2010 and 2013, it amounted to an average of $1 billion a year.[94] By opening up the country to outside investment, successive governments have encouraged and facilitated the forging of extensive economic links between their country and Europe and North America. A growing number of Tunisian companies, industries and enterprises, across a range of sectors, along with their owners, managers and workforces now value and depend on customers, suppliers and investors in the West.

And these economic ties are augmented by the remittance payments made by the members of the country's extensive diaspora.[95] When measured by their effect on ordinary Tunisians' daily lives and total value, these disbursements are arguably more important than foreign direct investment in the country. For, between 1995 and 1999, remittances were worth an average of $715.4 million each year.[96] And, between 2000 and 2004, their value grew to an average of $1 billion a year.[97] Then, between 2005 and 2009, their value rose again to an average of $1.7 billion per year.[98] And, most recently, between 2010 and 2013, their worth increased yet again to an average of $2.1 billion a year.[99] These payments ensure that millions of Tunisians have a common vested interest in their country maintaining cordial relations with those in which their friends and relations live and work.

Such is the great size of Tunisia's diaspora that it also performs an important social function as its members form human chains between the country and their new homes in the West. For, as of 2012, there were 20,300 Tunisian citizens living in Canada and 15,308 in the United States; 668,668 in France and 189,092 in Italy; 86,601 in Germany and 24,810 in Belgium and Luxemburg; and 16,667 in the Netherlands and 8,776 in Austria. That is, there were 35,608 Tunisians living in North America and 1,032,412 in Europe out of a total diaspora population of 1,223,213.[100] So, out of the 11.35 per cent of the country's population which lived overseas, 87.3 per cent resided in the West.[101]

This social connection continues to be strengthened by the movement and transfer of other populations. In each of the past ten years, Tunisia has attracted millions of tourists, a majority of whom came from the European Union.[102] This flow of people peaked in 2008 when the country had 7.04 million visitors. And, even in 2011, when the number of tourists travelling to the country was at its lowest owing to the instability and uncertainty caused by the Arab Spring, it still received 4.78 million visitors. And, since then, tourist numbers have risen steadily, with 5.95 million people visiting the country in 2012, 6.26 million in 2013,[103] 6.06 million in 2014,[104] and 0.34 million in January 2015.[105] Tourism is also an important source of revenue and foreign currency earnings for Tunisia, making the country 3.5 billion dinars in 2010, 2.4 billion in 2011, 3.1 billion in 2012, 3.2 billion in 2013,[106] 3.5 billion in 2014,[107] and 206,500 in January 2015.[108]

The improved access to information offered by émigrés and tourists has been greatly enhanced by the rapid spread of Internet and mobile phone use in Tunisia. In 2000, only 2.8 per cent of the country's population had any Internet access.[109] By 2005, it had increased exponentially to 9.7 per cent.[110] By 2010, it had nearly quadrupled to 36.8 per cent. And, most recently, in 2013, it had leapt to 43.8 percent.[111] The rise in mobile phone subscription over this period has been even more remarkable. In 2000, just 1 per cent of the population subscribed to a mobile telephone service.[112] By 2005, this had increased to 57 per cent of the population.[113] By 2010, it had nearly doubled again to 105 per cent. And, by 2013, it had jumped to 116 per cent.[114]

And thousands of Tunisians continue to be educated in the West. Indeed, pursuit of educational opportunities is one of the main reasons why Tunisians emigrate to Europe and North America.[115] Ben Ali, like many of his military and socio-economic peers, attended training courses in both France and the United States.[116] And, in so doing, he made and helped reinforce the now well-established pedagogical pilgrimage to Europe and North America. Spending a little time at a French, German or Canadian school, college or university is an important rite of passage for many middle-class sons and daughters. Attending such institutions and receiving instruction in either French or English are rightly seen as significant advantages in the job market back home. Many of those fortunate enough to be educated in the West quickly assume important, influential and comparatively lucrative posts in either the private or public sectors.

And in response to the Arab Spring, the European Union has supposedly taken steps to make it easier for more young Tunisians to study in Europe. One of the measures it introduced with the launch of the PfDSP was to double (to €30 million) Erasmus Mundus scholarship funding (for the 2011–12 academic year) for Southern Mediterranean students and academic staff 'wishing to spend part of their studies, research or . . . teaching period in the European Union'.[117] And, in May 2013, the European Union made an additional €10 million available through the Erasmus Mundus and Tempus programmes 'to further develop the modernisation of higher education as well as the international cooperation capacity of higher education institutions in Tunisia'.[118]

It was always the EU's intention that the expanded Erasmus Mundus programme would complement its new Civil Society Facility. Launched along with the PfDSP in March 2011, the CSF had an initial budget of €26.4 million to be used 'to strengthen the capacity of civil society' in the southern and eastern partner states.[119] Since then, the EU Delegation in Tunisia has assumed responsibility for fifty-four projects which receive €16 million in funding from various European sources.[120] And the European Union is also developing a new Programme of Support to Civil Society (PASC). With a budget of €7 million, its purpose will be 'to support the capacity building of civil society organisation so that they can better contribute to the development and . . . democratic transition of the country', and 'facilitate dialogue and partnerships between civil society organisation and public actors, and make recommendations for legislative reviews related to the actions promoted by the NGOs as well as their work environment'.[121]

Leverage

The West has high leverage over Tunisia. The country does not have a large or medium-sized economy.[122] It is not a major or intermediate oil producer.[123] It does not possess, or have easy access to, nuclear weapons. And it does not enjoy the backing or protection of a Black Knight patron. It does not have, therefore, the economic means, strategic resources, military capabilities or great power alliances needed effectively to deter, counter, mitigate or resist European and North American influence.

Yet the West's leverage over Tunisia is also compromised and not as great as it might be. The lessening of its influence is mainly because of its long-running security concerns in and for the region. According to Levitsky and Way, Western leverage over a country must be classed as medium if the target state does not satisfy any of the criteria for low-level influence and is a central actor in 'a major security-related foreign-policy issue for the United States and/or EU'.[124] Since the attacks on the World Trade Center and Pentagon on 11 September 2001, European and North American governments have been extremely sensitive to the dangers posed by Islamist terror groups operating in and out of the wider Middle East.[125] As a country in this region in close proximity to Europe, Tunisia continues to be viewed with apprehension and treated with caution.

The West's leverage over Tunisia, however, is still high rather than medium even though its security concerns for the country have seldom been specific and never as great as its fears for other countries in the region. Only recently has Tunisia been identified as the home and main operating base of terrorist factions that pose significant national and international threats. Until then, the country went mostly unnoticed: a small, comparatively quiet corner of an important and worrisome region. Indeed, there seemed to be little of individual import about it beyond its location. This both explains, and is reflected in, its earlier failure to generate similar levels of Western interest and anxiety as Algeria and Egypt, Lebanon and Syria, Iran and Iraq, Afghanistan and Yemen.

More importantly, though, these concerns gave rise to, and still sustain, a series of sapping inconsistencies. Western democracy promotion in the region continues to be marked by at least two important tensions. The first is the divergence between rhetoric and action, between what the United States and European Union say they want and will support and what they actually tolerate and the types of assistance they provide.[126] This divergence has evolved subtlety over time and is slightly different today from how it manifested itself both before and during the Arab Spring. Initially, in the years leading up to the protests, the United States and European

Union claimed to prioritise and be wholly committed to extending and deepening democracy in the wider Middle East. The more democracy there was, so the prevailing wisdom in Washington, London, Paris and Brussels ran, the safer everyone would be.[127]

And, to an extent, the United States and European Union were true to their words. Both placed democracy promotion either at or near the heart of their various policy frameworks for the region and the country. And both buttressed these promises with large amounts of money. Under President George W. Bush, funding for democracy promotion in the Middle East grew exponentially from a paltry $27.3 million in 2001 to $183 million in 2005. And, under President Obama, it continued to rise at a similar rate, climbing to $430 million in 2013.[128] Similarly, the EU was contributing around half of the estimated $2 billion that was spent annually worldwide on democracy-related aid projects, making it the world's largest democracy donor.[129]

Yet this expenditure was but a fraction of what the West spent on security in the region. The size of this funding discrepancy inevitably raised difficult questions about where the United States' and European Union's true priorities lay. Moreover, it cast serious doubt on their claims to be willing and able to hold local security providers to account, to cajole and compel the region's militaries, police forces, security services and intelligence agencies to pay democracy greater respect. The dilemma which gave rise to this funding imbalance undoubtedly helps explain the US's and EU's initial, faltering responses to the Arab Spring. French President Nicolas Sarkozy began by defending Ben Ali before leading the NATO charge against Libya's Gaddafi.[130] And President Obama did not come firmly down on the side of the protestors until 19 May 2011, some five months after the Arab Spring had begun.[131]

Washington's failure to back the protestors more fully sooner also sprang from its misapprehension of at least some of their motives. It viewed their economic grievances in largely local terms, as stemming more from domestic abuses, 'corruption, crony capitalism, a lack of accountability and technical failures', than from any opposition to global market forces.[132] It has, therefore, defined events in Tunisia and elsewhere in terms that make them more compatible with its existing policy frameworks and points of reference. In fact, the existence and configuration of these frameworks have prejudiced its thinking. Washington has broadly accepted their intellectual parameters, allowed its thinking to be shaped and clipped by their goals, requirements and structures. And it was encouraged to do so by expediency, by the automatic and perhaps understandable hope that these mechanisms would suffice and cope, and provide it with the means to respond. Yet, as a result, it has missed some of the nuance, failed to appreciate fully the true extent and complexion of the Tunisian protestors' grievances and the broader changes they unleashed and formed part of. In such circumstances, its response would always struggle fully to match its rhetoric.[133]

This seeming double standard was ruthlessly exposed by the Arab Spring.[134] The European Union, in particular, coyly acknowledged that it should have been more supportive of those demanding political reform.[135] Since then, both the US and EU have tried to stay on the right side of history. And, while they have not been wholly successfully in this endeavour, leading to accusations of backsliding and regression, they remain more aware of the promises they have made and the level of international scrutiny they are under. As a result, one of the main causes of this divergence now is process: failings in the mechanisms by which the United States and, in particular, the European Union try to promote democracy.

Part of the problem for the EU was undoubtedly timing. The Arab Spring began just as one of the worst economic crises to hit modern Europe was starting to bite. Brussels and the national governments had to try to find this extra funding at a time when there was little to be had. Moreover, they had to explain why they were doing so to their own beleaguered electorates who increasingly viewed such spending in zero-sum terms. The outcome, therefore, has been a surreptitious fudge. Ostensibly, the European Union has promised more: extra aid, new loans, additional investment.[136] Yet, so far, it has failed to deliver fully. Moreover, despite these pledges, it is actually committing less than it was before the Arab Spring began,[137] is needed by these countries, and what the Gulf States are providing.[138]

The European Union is also struggling to honour its mobility pledge, to ease the travel restrictions it imposes on North African citizens.[139] The surge in migration to Europe, caused by the unrest in Tunisia, Libya and elsewhere, made it politically difficult for EU governments to relax their visa requirements. So, too, did the continent's rapidly worsening economic outlook. With many of their economies entering recession and a growing number of their citizens out of work, European governments found themselves under mounting domestic pressure to reduce inward migration.

Financial pressures, however, are only one cause of this first discrepancy. The ongoing instability in parts of North Africa and the Middle East is also making it harder for the EU to disburse its funds as recipient states simply do not have the capacity to absorb all the monies it is offering them.[140] And, in an effort to promote democracy better and safeguard its taxpayers' investment, the EU has increased the number of conditions it attaches to the funding it provides, thereby making it harder for recipient countries to access this money easily or quickly. The EU measures its funding cycle in years, not months, leading to a degree of tolerance in Brussels for this current shortfall.[141]

Indeed, Mouhib argues that the EU's very structure ensures that some level of inefficiency and inconsistency in its democracy promotion efforts is unavoidable.[142] The 'autonomy of the different institutional groups' within the European Union dictates that these efforts resemble less a coherent strategy and more a 'complex "political process"'.[143] Fundamentally, there is no consensus within the European Union on what its democratisation policies should be or how they ought to be implemented. Responsibility for external relations, of which democracy promotion in North Africa and the Middle East is clearly part, is divided between the EEAS and the Commission. The former has oversight of the Common Foreign and Security Policy (CFSP), the latter of managing economic relations and the various financial instruments involved in them.[144] This division makes the EEAS responsible for policy formulation and activity programming, and the Commission for policy implementation and the disbursement of funds.[145] A slight disconnect exists, therefore, between those parts of the EU (the EEAS) that devise policy and those (the Commission) that instigate it. And the high degree of autonomy enjoyed by the Commission allows it to 'interpret, adjust and change' both the 'form and substance' of policies if it so wishes.[146] This means that some of the actions the EU takes do not fully conform to what was originally planned.

The complexity of this organisational picture has been added to in the wake of the Arab Spring as, in response to the protests, the European Union established new offices, and reinvigorated and launched new programmes. In July 2011, it appointed Bernardino Léon as its Special Representative for the Southern Mediterranean. Between taking office and the autumn of 2013, Léon participated in a series of succession and other negotiations in Tunisia, Egypt, Jordan and elsewhere. Yet he did not fully co-ordinate his actions with the ENP.[147] Rather, he became another moving part in the EU's vast and intricate foreign policy machine. Despite its renewed efforts to stay on the right side of history and support better those campaigning for greater democracy in North Africa and the Middle East, the European Union is still not living up to its rhetoric.

Another noteworthy cause of this divergence is the growing competition the United States and European Union face as aid providers. Their post-Cold War pre-eminence as the main, or only, sources of significant development assistance is under increasing challenge. Other governments are now also willing and able to offer such help. This broadening of aid provision means that recipient states are not as dependent on the West as perhaps they once were. They are better able to pick and choose what help they accept on the basis of what they will be expected to do in return. They are more able to decline specific aid offers and avoid the attached conditions. Furthermore, Western governments are finding it harder to dispense with such stipulations given the high level of scrutiny paid to their provision by their own populations, the international community and the recipient countries.[148] And their actions in Tunisia and North Africa are subjected to especially close analysis because of their previous support of Ben Ali and the region's other authoritarian regimes, and their subsequent solemn pledges to be a greater friend to local pro-democracy forces.

Indeed, on 7 June 2012, the International Monetary Fund (IMF) agreed to provide the Tunisian government with a $1.75 billion loan. This arrangement had taken months of negotiations to reach. And, to receive it, Tunis had to agree to the IMF's conditions, to overhaul public spending and reform the country's banking sector.[149] In contrast, a week later the Tunisian government announced that it had been given $1.2 billion in new funding by Saudi Arabia's Islamic Development Bank (IDB). No requirements or riders were attached to this loan. Inevitably, therefore, the West's leverage over Tunisia has been weakened. So, while Saudi Arabia might not be Tunisia's Black Knight, its actions are sufficient 'to constrain and limit the effects of Western support for democratic change'.[150]

The second key divergence is between Western governments: the United States and the European Union; the EU and national capitals. To be clear, these governments actually agree on a great deal and interact with the region's countries in similar ways. Moreover, their relations with these countries have developed along largely the same lines. In the years leading up to the Arab Spring, Washington and Brussels, Paris, Rome and Madrid all supported democratisation but were arguably more concerned with maintaining stability which led them to treat Ben Ali and the other authoritarian leaders with leniency and even sympathy. As a result, they responded slowly and hesitantly to the Arab Spring before eventually committing themselves more fully to the cause of democracy and the local actors striving for it. Since then, they have all tried to maintain this commitment but remain fearful of the instability that continues to grip parts of the region, and the insecurity it gives rise to.

Nevertheless, important differences between these governments persist. Prior to the Arab Spring, the European Union provided both the region and Tunisia with far more non-military and democracy-building aid than the United States did. The MEPI's political funding stream for 2006 totalled $43 million which was then distributed between all the participating states. Inevitably, therefore, some countries, such as Algeria, received very little from it if anything at all.[151] In contrast, in 2005–6, the EU gave €30 million to democracy-supporting projects in Tunisia alone.[152] And, more fundamentally, the European Union, unlike the United States, seeks to promote both democracy and its broader values through socialisation, by drawing its Mediterranean neighbours into its institutional framework. By these means, it seeks to expose them to the same norms and expectations that shape and dictate political life in Europe, to normalise attitudes and patterns of behaviour that it identifies as being conducive of democracy.[153]

Undoubtedly the European Union is better placed – geographically, ideologically and institutionally – than the United States to adopt this approach. But, in addition to promoting democratic institutions, processes and rights, the EU is seeking to advance its own influence and interests in the region. This, again, it has in common with the United States although the fact of it is an important cause of divergence as both Brussels and Washington seek to maximise their positions, importance and advantages.[154] National interests are also a vital source of difference within the European Union. Broadly, the northern member states would like to see the EU take a tougher line, be more forthright in its demands, resolute in its actions, uncompromising in its expectations, especially over transition processes, than the southern members.[155] They, perhaps understandably given their front-line location, are 'more risk-averse and less change-prone'.[156]

Certainly, southern European anxiety over the Arab Spring helps contextualise and explain the alternative policy lines taken by some of its governments. By the time the protests began, France, Spain and Italy had all forged close working relationships with Ben Ali, Gaddafi and many of the region's other authoritarian leaders.[157] As part of its action plan, Tunisia was supposed to introduce democratic reforms but was never compelled to do so.[158] Similarly, of the €365 million in bilateral aid France provided North Africa in 2003, only €5 million went to governance projects.[159] Initially, therefore, they opposed Ben Ali's removal though they soon switched their support to the protestors.[160] Despite this Europeanisation of their positions, Paris, Rome and, in particular, Madrid have continued 'to pursue interest-based policies' in the region.[161] That is, they largely devolve 'value-based issues' to the European Union and continue to pursue their own interests bilaterally.[162]

Yet, even with these tensions, inconsistencies and divergences, the West's leverage over Tunisia remains high. The numerous strong links that exist between the country and North America and Europe give Washington, Brussels, Paris and Berlin extensive influence over Tunis. And, more crucially, the country simply does not have the wherewithal to evade, resist or mitigate this pressure. Its economy is too small. It does not possess any strategic resources in sufficient quantities. It does not have any nuclear weapons. And it does not have the backing of a Black Knight power. Certainly, countries such as Saudi Arabia have the ability to undermine Western influence. But none chooses to do so to the extent and with enough consistency to be designated a Black Knight.

Organisational Power

The Ben Ali regime had high organisational power. Not only did it build and maintain a strong ruling party and coercive apparatus but it also exercised considerable control over the country's economy. During his near quarter of a century in office, Ben Ali raised state spending on security every year except one (2005).[163] In truth, he perpetuated a pattern of investment established by his predecessor, Habib Bourguiba. Yet, under Ben Ali, this expenditure grew both as a proportion of total state spending and in monetary terms. Indeed, in 1987, the year in which Ben Ali took over as acting president, the Ministry of Interior's portion of the national budget was raised from 5.7 to 8.2 per cent.[164] And it continued to be increased almost annually until it peaked at 9.7 per cent in 1992 before being lowered to Bourguiba-era levels in 1997.[165]

By the time this reduction was introduced, however, the government's total expenditure was almost four times greater than that which it had been a decade earlier.[166] Moreover, it nearly doubled again between 1996 and 1997,[167] thereby ensuring that, even though the size of the Ministry of Interior's allocation fell as a portion of total public spending, it still received more money in 1997 than it had the previous year. This increase was entirely consistent with Ben Ali's long-term spending priorities. Only in 2001 and 2005 did the Ministry of Interior's budget contract slightly from what it had been in the years before.[168] Indeed, by the time Ben Ali fled office in 2011, the Ministry of Interior's budget was more than six-and-a-half times larger than what it been when he assumed power in 1987. Similarly, the Ministry of Defence's budget had increased more than sevenfold over the same period.[169]

The Ben Ali regime's consistently high level of investment in the security forces enabled them to penetrate almost the entire country down to the level of the neighbourhood and village.[170] Yet, despite their 'omni-presence', they still 'failed to prevent crime in the cities or trafficking in the border regions'.[171] And, perhaps more crucially, they lacked cohesion. This was also true, to an extent, of the military. For neither was bound by strong, non-material ties. Unlike Algeria, Tunisia had not had to fight for its independence. And, since then, it had not had to confront any serious internal or external threats. The members of the security forces and military, therefore, had no glorious reference points or memories to unite them. Nor had they had any real opportunities to acquire the single-mindedness and steely determination that often come from engaging in existential struggles.[172]

More serious still was the lack of cohesion between the security forces and the military. Indeed, the Arab Spring ruthlessly exposed the depth of their disunity. And one of its main causes was the highly partial and partisan policies pursued by Bourguiba and Ben Ali. An important tipping point in their resource allocation came in 1984 when, for the first time ever, the Ministry of Interior was given a bigger share of the national budget than the Ministry of Defence.[173] And for each year from then until Ben Ali fled office, this funding pattern was continued. Furthermore, the amount of extra money the Ministry of Interior was given also grew to the extent that, by 2011, its budget was around one-and-a-half times the size of the Ministry of Defence's.[174]

This sustained favouritism was the mainstay of an enduring strategy to exclude the military from public life. Both Bourguiba and Ben Ali were extremely anxious to avoid becoming politically dependent on it. In addition to controlling its finances, therefore, Bourguiba imposed a raft of other restrictions on its personnel, banning them from either founding or joining political parties [including the ruling Socialist Destourian Party (Parti Socialiste Destourien, PSD)], or participating in any way in policy formation (including defence policy).[175] Rather, he and Ben Ali wanted it to concentrate solely on defending the national territory.[176] Indeed, such was Ben Ali's antipathy towards it that, between 2002 and 2009, he allocated an average of just 1.4 per cent of GDP to defence each year compared to the 3.4 per cent, 3.1 per cent and 2.7 per cent allotted by the governments of Morocco, Algeria and Egypt respectively.[177]

What made Ben Ali's treatment of the armed forces all the more intriguing was his own extensive background in them. He was commissioned into the Tunisian army in 1956 and served in it until 1977. During that time, he held several high-profile and important posts including Director of Military Intelligence (1964–74) and Military Attaché to Morocco (1974–77). But, even after he left, he retained strong ties to it, serving twice as Director of National Security (1977–80 and 1984–85), then as Secretary of State for national security (1985) and subsequently as Minister of the Interior (1986–87).[178] Ben Ali's antipathy towards the military, therefore, was born not of ignorance but familiarity. He well knew what the military and security forces could and could not do, and made his choice accordingly.

The division between the security forces and military broadly corresponded to another crucial fault line: that separating low- and high-intensity coercion. Levitsky and Way are clear that an ability to threaten, intimidate, bully and browbeat is vital to a competitive authoritarian regime's longer-term survival. In part, this is because high-intensity measures are very conspicuous and, therefore, force the regime to take greater risks. And the most serious of these is exposure: doing something that invites sustained Western criticism.[179] Low-intensity coercion, in contrast, is less noticeable and observable. By engaging in it skilfully and effectively, regimes are often able to manage and nullify their opponents for long periods of time without incurring potentially devastating levels of international and domestic wrath.

Ben Ali's security forces were perfectly able to engage in low-intensity coercion. Indeed, it was their proven ability to do so that led many observers initially to dismiss the Arab Spring protestors' chances of success. Precedence suggested that the regime would prevail. But what proved to be beyond them, what they could not adequately engage in, was high-intensity coercion. And their inability to do so was matched by the military's unwillingness to try. After decades of suspicion and marginalisation, its officers and units felt little loyalty to the regime or inclination to defend it.[180] As a result, Ben Ali was unable to take the sorts of measures that might have broken the protestors' resolve and saved his political skin.

No such divisions, or at least none of equal depth and width, pervaded Ben Ali's ruling party, the RCD. Upon inheriting it from his predecessor, he quickly reorganised, reinvigorated and relaunched it as a cohesive and effective political force, one that was better able to motivate and discipline its activists, mobilise large parts of the general population, and counter the arguments and actions of rival parties. He did so by expanding its membership by 50 per cent, attracting scores of new and younger members, co-opting candidates and functionaries from rival parties, as well as technocrats from public institutions, and changing its name from the PSD to the Democratic Constitutional Rally.[181] The induction of these younger members also helped him strengthen his control over it by diluting the influence of its older, Bourguiba supporting cadre, and increasing the number of individuals in its ranks who depended on him for their political positions.[182] And to enhance his control still further, he assumed and exercised the right to select 125 of its governing Central Committee's two hundred members.[183]

And, in an effort to maintain its vitality and prevent it from slipping into lethargy, irrelevance and flabby ineffectiveness, he repeatedly remade these reforms, periodically launched recruitment drives, inducted younger members, changed the make-up of the Central Committee.[184] These measures went hand in hand with his economic reforms and continuing development of his clientelist network.[185] For discipline was encouraged and enforced by economic means. Belonging to the RCD brought benefits or, at the very least, potential benefits. Following Ben Ali's and the Central Committee's directives earned rewards while failure to do so resulted in punishments. Very tellingly, none of the main opposition parties (legal and unrecognised) that confronted Ben Ali was founded by individuals who had left the RCD. Some of its best-known and supported competitors, including the United Popular Movement (Mouvement d'Unité Populaire, MUP), the Socialist Democrats Movement (Mouvement des Démocrates Socialistes, MDS), and the Popular Unity Party (Parti de l'Unité Populaire, PUP), had been established by defectors from its predecessor, the PSD.[186] Indeed, such was its discipline and ability to encourage loyalty and deter adventurism that it did not endure any significant or wholesale defections until the last days of the regime.

Yet, just like the security forces and the military, the RCD's cohesion was based mainly on material ties, to the extent that, once it became apparent that the protests had spiralled beyond Ben Ali's control, the party's other leaders quickly turned against him and his family.[187] With a speed born of both mounting panic and ruthless avarice, they hoped that, in doing so, they would be better able to save the party, themselves and as much as they could of the wealth and as many of the privileges they gained through it. The RCD was outlawed on 9 March 2011.

Throughout its time in power, the Ben Ali regime sought closer economic relations with the West, especially the European Union. This enduring goal led it to sign a series of US- and EU-sponsored agreements designed to facilitate greater economic integration. Under the terms of these accords, the regime pledged to introduce a range of sweeping reforms as well as take other important measures. In addition to joining the WTO, it set about liberalising Tunisia's economy: removing tariff barriers, encouraging overseas investment, selling off state-owned industries, and courting private investors. And it made notable progress in several of these areas. By 1996, it had removed all tariffs on capital goods imported from the European Union. By 2004, it had earned over 1 billion DT from public asset sales.[188] And, by 2010, it was attracting $1.3 billion of FDI in the country.[189]

Yet, despite the introduction of these reforms, which were all intended to reduce the state's direct involvement in the economy, the Ben Ali regime continued to exercise significant control over several key sectors, most notably banking, communications and other service industries. And it did so by two main means, firstly by delaying the implementation of particular policies and changes. Indeed, for all its eagerness to co-operate with the United States and European Union, and general willingness to meet their requirements, the regime was still perfectly prepared to defy them over certain issues, to the extent of missing key targets and deadlines.[190] That it was largely able to do so without serious consequence highlights Ben Ali's shrewd reading of his relations with the West. By repeatedly confirming and demonstrating his desire to work with it, secure in the knowledge that it was equally keen to collaborate with him, he was able to create political space in which to take certain indulgences.

And the second was through his family and friends by ensuring that a large number of those economically important and valuable state-owned companies, corporations, enterprises and assets which were sold off passed into their hands.[191] Indeed, by the time the Arab Spring began, the Ben Ali family and its wider Trabelsi clan owned a vast network of holdings across a range of crucial sectors. Through them, the regime was able to wield considerable economic influence as well as put pressure on individuals and groups that opposed and resisted it.

The Ben Ali regime was assisted in its maintenance of its high organisational power by the enduring weakness of Tunisia's opposition parties.[192] It first achieved ascendancy over them shortly after Ben Ali took office when he persuaded them to sign up to his National Pact. In return for his promise gradually to liberalise the country's politics, they agreed to abstain from destabilising his rule, to refrain from doing precisely what they were supposed to.[193] Yet, more important than the pact's content were the intellectual parameters it helped to establish. For, in agreeing to it, these parties not only allowed themselves effectively to be co-opted by the regime[194] but they also waived their right, at least for a little while, to set the political agenda.[195] By means of the National Pact, therefore, the regime was able to inculcate within its rivals a degree of compliance and timidity that ultimately served to make it more secure.

For much of the period Ben Ali was in power, a number of the legal opposition parties struggled to build popular bases of support, not least because their leaders had little interest in doing so. Rather, they tended to view their respective organisations in highly personalised terms, as mechanisms for promoting their opinions, enacting their wills, making their individual voices heard, and attacking their enemies. Indeed, personal rivalry was often a key motivation for the establishment of these groups. The MUP, MDS and PUP were all founded by disgruntled former members of the PSD who had left because they felt that their ambitions were being thwarted by Bourguiba.[196] Creating their own groups, therefore, was how they sought both to cope with this disappointment and prevent it from happening again. As a result, their parties were seldom rooted in the Tunisian populace. They were not intended, initially at least, to act as 'transmission belts between society and the state'.[197]

Indeed, it was not until the mid 2000s that the mainstream parties were better able to set aside this reticence and their differences, and mount more effective challenges. Two of the most capable opposition movements to confront the regime were the *Rencontre Démocratique* and the *18 October Collectif*. The former was an alliance of four parties – the PUP, the Social Liberal Party (Parti Social Libéral, PSL), the Unionist Democratic Union (Union Démocratique Unioniste, UDU), and the Greens (Parti des Verts pour le Progrès, PVP) – founded to contest the 2004 legislative election. The fashioning of their alliance was eased by their ideological homogeneity because they all promoted broadly leftist programmes, strongly supported *laïcité*, and, by extension, opposed political Islam. Accordingly, they built their union on common ground around three core objectives: defending freedom of expression, association and press; reforming the country's political institutions including its electoral system; and securing the release and exoneration of political prisoners.[198]

More remarkable was the *Collectif* which was established the following year. For, not only did it include three ideologically disparate organisations – the leftist and secular Congress for the Republic (Congrès pour la République, CR) and Progressive Democratic Party (Parti Démocrate Progressiste, PDP), and Islamist Ennahda – but it also survived until the start of the Arab Spring.[199] Its foundation and durability, therefore, showed what was possible, the extent to which fundamentally different groups could work together. Moreover, and just as crucially, it helped dispel at least some (but by no means all) of the concerns secular organisations had about political Islam. Ennahda's seeming willingness to collaborate, commitment to democracy and respect for the various civil liberties associated with it, went some way towards easing the subsequent, difficult and protracted, post-Ben Ali constitutional negotiations.

Yet, even so, despite being more organised, better able to hold the regime to account and mobilise popular support against it, as well as offering real-life examples of the extent to which rival groups could, when willing, co-operate with one another, neither the *Rencontre* nor the *Collectif* initiated or led the protests that removed Ben Ali from power. On the contrary, they were as much taken by surprise by the Arab Spring as the rest of Tunisia's mainstream opposition.[200] Furthermore, their initial responses were as hesitant and equivocal as those of the United States and European Union. The *Collectif* did not quite give the uprising its full support. And the PDP stopped just a little short of demanding Ben Ali's departure.[201] Even at the end, these more cohesive and effective groupings were reluctant to go in for the kill. They remained plagued by uncertainty and continued to treat Ben Ali with the kind of reverence that had so marked and compromised the mainstream opposition movement throughout his time in office: so much so, in fact, that the *Collectif* has not survived. It, like the regime it was forged to oppose, has been swept away by the Arab Spring.[202]

Origins and Evolution of the Regime

It is hard to overstate the profundity of Ben Ali's fall from power. The seeming strength of his regime, the longevity of his rule, the speed with which the protests escalated, their effect on Tunisia's neighbours, and the abruptness of his departure all added to the scale of the surprise. And, for a while, they transformed Tunisia from a political backwater into an epicentre, ground-zero of the remarkable shockwaves that caused such damage to so many of the region's *anciens régimes*. Yet, after this initial upheaval, and largely because the decapitation of the Ben Ali regime was comparatively clinical, global attention quickly turned elsewhere. Inevitably, the political, analytical and popular eye was drawn to the bloody tragedies still unfolding in Libya, Yemen, Syria and Iraq.

Yet Ben Ali's fall did not automatically lead to democracy's triumph. On the contrary, many months of difficult negotiation and hard-fought politicking lay ahead before it was achieved. Rather, his demise was one (albeit very important) milestone on the country's long and tortuous road to democracy. For the first thirty years of independence, Tunisia was stably authoritarian.[203] During that time, it had only one president (Habib Bourguiba) and one electoral political party (the Neo-Destour/PSD).[204] Elections were held regularly but amounted to little more than political pageants, regime-organised exercises in self-affirmation and congratulation. In the four presidential elections which were staged, Bourguiba stood unopposed and never secured less than 100 per cent of the vote. And only once did the Neo-Destour/PSD face (very limited) competition, in the first parliamentary ballot held in November 1959. Indeed, it was the Tunisian

Communist Party's (Parti Communiste Tunisien, PCT) moderate success in the few constituencies in which it was permitted to field candidates that led the regime simply to ban all other parties from competing in future elections.[205]

Under Ben Ali, the country quickly became competitive authoritarian although his commitment to preserving the democratic features of his regime waxed and waned throughout his time in office. After seizing power on 7 November 1987, in a medical *coup d'état*,[206] Ben Ali promised to build 'an advanced, institutionalized political life ... based on the principles of a multiparty system and the pluralism of mass organizations'.[207] Seemingly to those ends, he soon sought closer relations with the country's main opposition groups and leaders. Over the next two years, he granted official party status to the PDP and PSL,[208] pardoned thousands of political prisoners arrested by Bourguiba, and entered into dialogue with Rashid al-Ghannushi,[209] leader of the Islamic Tendency Movement (Mouvement de la Tendence Islamique, MTI), who had himself only recently been released from gaol.[210]

Though Ben Ali did not legalise the MTI (even after it changed its name to Ennahda in order to comply with the new law prohibiting parties from appealing directly to specific religious, ethnic or linguistic communities),[211] he made several other concessions to it.[212] In addition to granting it representation on the country's High Islamic Council (Conseil Islamique Supérieur, CIS) and allowing it to establish its own students union – the General Union of Tunisian Students (Union Générale Tunisienne des Étudiants, UGTE) – he invited it to sign up to his National Pact and participate in the 1989 parliamentary election.[213] The pact, in particular, was widely hailed as an important and positive step towards democracy, as evidence of the regime's commitment to work with the opposition, as a promise too public and profound to be either ignored or neglected.[214]

Under Ben Ali, Tunisia was undoubtedly less authoritarian than it had been when Bourguiba had been in power. Yet it was still never a democracy. Single-party rule was replaced not by political pluralism but by ruling-party hegemony.[215] Indeed, almost as soon as the 1989 ballot was over, Ben Ali reversed or discarded many of his earlier compromises. The Ennahda party, in particular, came in for harsh treatment, its fate sealed by its strong showing in the election.[216] In December 1990, the UGTE's journal, *Al-Fajr*, was banned. Then, in March 1991, the union itself was dissolved.[217] And, in May that year, the Minister of the Interior announced the discovery of an Ennahda-led plot to overthrow the regime. By March 1992, the ensuing crackdown had resulted in the arrest and imprisonment of around eight thousand of the party's members and supporters.[218]

Ben Ali's reaction to the result betrayed his pragmatism, confirmed that his easing of Bourguiba's restrictions had been entirely instrumental.[219] Early supporters of the National Pact were dismayed. Its purpose was not to encourage or empower the opposition but strengthen the regime. For 'virtually all the signatories of the pact represented dependencies of the perennial ruling party: far from a compromise or bargain amongst equals, the pact was an effort to create the appearance of political pluralism in the absence of political actors with autonomous social and economic power'.[220] Once Ben Ali had legitimised his seizure of power and cemented his rule, once his grip on power was secure, 'he discarded the more formidable opponents such as the Islamists'.[221]

This pattern of conciliation and co-optation, concession and repression continued for the duration of Ben Ali's time in power. Elections were held regularly, and often included rival candidates and parties, but were never free and fair. In the 1989 and 1994 presidential elections, not only did Ben Ali stand unopposed but he secured victory in each with 100 per cent of the vote. In the 1999, 2004 and 2009 ballots, he faced competition but still managed to win with 98 per cent, 94.5 per cent,[222] and 89.2 per cent of the vote respectively.[223] And the RCD was similarly successful. It won 154 seats (out of 154) in 1989, 135 seats (out of 154) in 1994, 148 seats (out of 182) in 1999, 152 seats (out of 189) in 2004,[224] and 161 seats (out of 214) in 2009.[225]

The size and sheer implausibility of these winning margins speak clearly of the scale of abuse perpetrated by the regime. Electoral law was overwhelmingly weighted in favour of Ben Ali and the RCD. Typical was the 2008 constitutional amendment which set out the criteria that would-be presidential candidates had to meet to be eligible to stand. Its insistence that each entrant either have the backing of thirty members of parliament or mayors, or have served as the elected leader of a legally recognised party for at least two years proved to be particularly onerous and resulted in the disqualification of most of Ben Ali's putative rivals for the 2009 vote. For, of the country's 189 parliamentarians, only thirty-seven belonged to parties other than the RCD. And, by the time the election was held, only six parties, excluding the RCD, had been granted official status.[226]

The timing of the amendment was also noteworthy. For it was introduced just a few months after Ahmed Nejib Chebbi, former secretary general of the PDP, declared his intention to stand. The amendment barred him from doing so on the grounds that he could not muster sufficient support for his candidacy from the right sources and was not at that time the leader of a recognised party. And it also disqualified another of Ben

Ali's more credible rivals, Mustapha Ben Jaafar. He was the leader of the Democratic Forum for Work and Freedoms (Forum Démocratique pour le Travail et Les Libertés, FDTL) and had been since its legalisation in October 2002. Yet he had been elected to that position only in 2008 which meant that his previous years in charge were declared inadmissible. As a result, he failed to satisfy the amendment's two-year leadership requirement.[227] Not only were Tunisia's electoral laws heavily skewed against opposition candidates and parties to the advantage of Ben Ali and the RCD, therefore, but they were also altered and updated on an entirely ad hoc and self-serving basis. Their purpose was not to strengthen democracy but weaken it, to entrench disparity, to preserve the distribution of benefits and obstacles, to give the regime the greatest chance of victory.

Yet Ben Ali still shied away from dispensing with elections altogether, preferring instead to preserve his regime's democratic facade no matter how gossamer-thin and threadbare it might appear. To the extent that, even though he never evinced any desire to step down as president and clearly had no qualms about abusing the electoral process, he still felt required to repeal the law (which, paradoxically, he had introduced in 1988 shortly after seizing power) limiting the number of terms a president could serve to three.[228] Similarly, even though he categorically refused to face any serious competitors in the 2009 election, he still wanted some to take part, hobbled, hopeless and with virtually no chance of winning for certain but present all the same.

In the end, therefore, three challengers were permitted to participate in the 2009 presidential election. Two of them, Mohamed Bouchiha and Ahmed Inoubli, who led the PDP and UDU respectively, quickly confessed the limits of their ambitions. They declared that their goals were not to challenge Ben Ali but strengthen the electoral process by taking part in it.[229] As a result, their campaigns unfolded largely without incident and ended in the crushing defeats they had been aiming for (Bouchiha won 5 per cent of the vote and Inoubli 3.8 percent).[230] The third contender, Ahmed Brahim, leader of the Movement for Renewal (Mouvement Ettajdid), took a less conciliatory path and was subjected to sustained harassment throughout the election. Just weeks before the polls opened, the authorities confiscated the 10 October edition of his party's weekly newspaper (*Ettarik al-Jadid*) on the grounds that it contained his manifesto which, they claimed, he was not allowed to publish until 11 October. The Ministry of Interior then ordered him, in the interests of public order, to strike five points from his proposed programme, most notably his criticisms of one-party rule.[231] In the final count, Brahim came last with just 1.5 per cent of the vote.[232]

The 2009 parliamentary election was similarly uncompetitive. And, even though the number of seats set aside for opposition parties had been increased to fifty-three (from thirty-seven) since the last ballot in 2004, the RCD still picked up three-quarters of them.[233] The regime's maintenance of this quota not only emphasised the general futility of voting in National Assembly elections but further institutionalised the electorate's lack of choice as, for the most part, it did not matter for whom they voted. The opposition together could not win more than a minority of seats (25 per cent). The RCD would always be preponderant.

Since the Ben Ali regime's demise, Tunisia's elections have improved in quality. The first to be held in the wake of his departure was for the National Constituent Assembly on 23 October 2011. It was 'judged "free and fair" by a range of international observer missions'.[234] The success of this ballot owed much to the painstaking preparatory work under-taken by leading opposition figures and those members of the government who remained in place. In particular, they successfully managed 'the twin dynamics of constitutional change and revolutionary protest' which 'moved together in a dialectical *pas de deux*' and 'saw the impetus for progress alternate between institutional office and the street'.[235]

After an abortive attempt by Ben Ali's last prime minister, Mohammed Ghannouchi, to form a new government comprised almost equally of RCD and opposition party members, a Committee to Defend the Revolution (Conseil de Défense de la Révolution, CDR) was established on 23 January 2011. It included twelve prominent opposition and civil society figures and appropriated for itself two key responsibilities: to keep an eye on the government and continue to press for fundamental political reform. In response, Ghannouchi asked the prominent and respected lawyer, Yadh Ben Achour, to review and revise the country's electoral laws. Along with the members of the CDR, he quickly became part of another new body called the Higher Commission for the Achievement of the Objectives of the Revolution, Political Reform and the Transition to Democracy (Haute Instance pour la Réalisation des Objectifs de la Révolution, de la Réforme Politique et de la Transition Démocratique, HIRORRPTD). With 155 members, the commission was much larger than the CDR and met for the first time on 17 March 2011.[236]

Shortly after the commission was established, Ghannouchi and all the other ministers who had served under Ben Ali resigned from the govern-ment.[237] At this point, responsibility for implementing the reform pro-gramme fell to acting President Fouad Mebazaa. After announcing that the new government would be elected later that year and would assume responsibility for drafting the country's constitution, he disbanded the political police of the General Intelligence Directorate (7 March), dissolved the RCD (9 March) and legalised Ennahda (11 March). Then, on 12 April, he passed by presidential decree the new electoral law written by the commission. In addition to setting out how the assembly would be organised and the rules governing political campaigning and party funding,[238] the law called for the establishment of an independent electoral commission, the Higher Authority for Independent Elections (Instance Supérieure Independante pour les Élections, ISIE).[239]

Though the ISIE initially lacked enough trained members and staff to discharge its duties fully, it quickly established its influence. It insisted that the date of the election be moved from 24 July 2011 to 23 October 2011 to give it more time to prepare. It accredited dozens of new parties, raising their number from just eight to over a hundred. It set the period in which parties were allowed to campaign at three weeks (1 to 21 October 2011). It issued strict guidelines on from whom parties could accept donations and funding. And it restricted the amount of media activity each party could engage in. While these regulations and directives undoubtedly made it hard for parties really to engage with the Tunisian public or mount truly national campaigns, they ensured that none enjoyed an officially sanctioned or condoned advantage over any other. They were a first important step towards creating a far more level electoral playing field.[240]

The election was won by Ennahda which secured 41 per cent of the vote and eighty-nine seats. Short of an outright majority, it entered into coalition with the CR (13 per cent and twenty-nine seats) and FDTL (9 per cent and twenty seats).[241] Despite once again confirming its willingness to co-operate with its secular rivals, which extended to allowing the leader of the CR, Moncef Marzouki, to replace Mebazaa as president, Ennahda's victory triggered a ferocious debate about Islam's role in Tunisian politics and the future provisions of the new constitution,[242] to the extent that the drafting of it became a dominant feature of political life for the next two years. Deadlines for its completion came and went, with the passing of each prompting fresh accusations and recriminations. Yet, as painful as this process undoubtedly was at times, it was arguably as important as what it eventually produced. The sustained involvement of dozens of political parties and civil society groups helped create a legal document and political blueprint in which as wide a cross section of Tunisian society as could have been hoped for had a stake.

A draft of the new constitution was finally submitted to the assembly for approval in December 2013. After a comparatively short debate, it was endorsed by the overwhelming majority of members on 26 January

2014.[243] In accordance with its provisions and in keeping with what had been practised since Ben Ali's fall, power was spread much more equitably across the political system. The president is authorised to appoint the ministers of interior and defence, one-third of the Constitutional Court, call states of emergency and, in exceptional circumstances, dissolve the newly established Chamber of Deputies. He or she is also granted limited legislative powers, including returning draft laws to the Chamber of Deputies for further debate, challenging their legality before the Constitutional Court and calling public referendums. The prime minister is chosen by the governing party or coalition in the Chamber of Deputies and empowered to set the broad policy agenda, create and fill ministerial posts, and call and chair cabinet meetings. And the Chamber of Deputies is charged with scrutinising and, if need be, challenging the actions of the president and premier. It can countermand the president's veto, remove them from office, compel them to give testimony, and control public spending through budget bills. Furthermore, chairmanship of the chamber's important and powerful finance committee can be filled only by someone belonging to a non-governing party.[244]

Yet the effectiveness of these reforms remain, at least in part, unproven. What has been argued over in committee and carefully set on paper still needs to be put into practice and tested in the heat of political battle. The importance of this alignment, of matching deed with word, is provided by the political class's ongoing treatment of the country's media. Under Ben Ali, Tunisia had 'one of the worst media environments in the Arab world'.[245] Those journalists, broadcasters and outlets not co-opted by the regime were either bullied into quiescence or simply silenced. Newspapers, magazines, periodicals and journals had to submit all their copy to the Ministry of Interior for approval. Those that defied the censors either had their offending editions seized or were temporarily closed down. Repeated and serious transgressors were placed under severe financial pressure and even bankrupted as the regime exploited its control over advertising revenue and the printing presses to withhold vital income or demand the immediate payment of all outstanding production costs.[246]

This ability to control the means of production gave the regime unparalleled influence over Tunisia's print media, more than that which it could achieve over the audiovisual sector. The advent of affordable personalised satellite technology, in particular, enabled ordinary people to access information and news broadcast from places over which the regime had no jurisdiction. Nevertheless, Tunis still asserted its control over those public and private stations based within the country. It controlled the two television and nine radio public channels through the Tunisian Television

Establishment (Établissement de la Télévision Tunisienne, ETT) and Tunisian Radio Establishment (Établissement de la Radio Tunisienne, ERT) respectively.[247] And it controlled the growing number of private television and radio stations by strictly regulating the accreditation process. Not only did it never make public the terms on which licences were awarded, thereby preventing open competition for them, but it also only ever granted them to members of the president's Trabelsi clan.[248]

Nor did the Internet offer a virtual haven for journalists. While its content was inevitably far less regulated than that of the country's other media sectors, accessing it in Tunisia was still closely monitored and policed. By operating its own Internet provider,[249] controlling providers' access to band width, monitoring fixed-line traffic, making Internet cafés responsible for what their customers viewed, using online word filters and arresting critical bloggers, the regime limited ordinary people's ability to access other sources of information easily and their willingness to do so.[250] 'Political opposition groups, foreign journals . . . and human rights websites . . . were all habitually blocked, as were YouTube, Facebook and, from 2010, Skype.'[251]

As well as targeting particular publications, stations and websites, the regime ruthlessly pursued individual reporters, editors and owners. It used physical violence, libel actions and other laws to threaten and punish those who crossed it or simply tried to retain their independence.[252] By these means, it was able to inculcate and sustain a strong culture of self-censorship within the country's media. The potential consequences of defiance were numerous and high, both professionally and personally. For the most part, therefore, journalists, editors, owners and publications were cowed into submission. They did not strongly or consistently challenge official statements and explanations. They did not closely investigate the actions and interests of prominent regime members. They gave the RCD's candidates and policies greater and more preferential coverage. And they paid the opposition less attention and were more critical of them. As a result, the media served less to involve ordinary Tunisians in the country's political and decision-making processes, and more to disseminate information that the regime either wanted, or was willing for, them to know.

Yet, crucially, these abuses did not occur because of an absence of guaranteed rights and freedoms. The regime was not able to act as it did because there were no laws in place to stop it. Certainly, there were legal shortfalls and loopholes. Newspapers, magazines, journals and periodicals were subject to the illiberal Press Code (Code de la Presse, CP).[253] But safeguards and provisions did exist. Not least in the form of constitutional guarantees which were supposed to override everything else. Indeed, the problem lay not in what was promised but what was delivered or, more accurately, what media outlets, civil society groups and ordinary Tunisians were able to claim.

So it is with no little trepidation, therefore, that human rights activists and pro-democracy campaigners note and condemn the current gap between pledge and action. Tunisia's new constitution is undoubtedly more liberal and popular than that which it replaced. Articles 31 and 32 guarantee freedom of thought, conscience, expression, publication and access to information.[254] And, since 2010, the country has climbed a full forty places in the Reporters Without Borders' World Press Freedom Index.[255] Yet it still remains rooted in the index's bottom third. Not all of the controls and disciplinary mechanisms that existed under Ben Ali have been completely dismantled.[256] Intimidation is still practised. Journalists and publications continue to be threatened and prosecuted. On 13 September 2013, no less a figure than the President of the National Union of Tunisian Journalists (Syndicat National des Journalistes Tunisiens, SNJT) was arrested for accusing the Public Prosecutor of fabricating evidence. And, though the charge was eventually dropped, his detention bore disturbing similarities with others from the Ben Ali era when it was a crime to criticise prominent political figures.[257]

Ben Ali's treatment of Tunisia's journalists, like his persecution of human rights activists, Ennahda's members, other Islamists and political opponents and, indeed, anyone who was either critical of him or tried to retain their independence, provided clear confirmation of the importance of repression to his rule. Underpinning the authoritarian laws, ignored rights and corrupted judiciary,[258] was the barely concealed threat of state-sanctioned and perpetrated violence.[259] The chain-mail glove of the country's distorted and defiled legal system contained the iron fist of state coercion. Legalised intimidation was buttressed by even harder power.

Conclusions

Discrepancies have defined Tunisia's political development over the past ten years. Clearly Ben Ali was never as committed to democracy, civil liberties and human rights as he said he was. Indeed, this was the very basis of his competitive authoritarian regime. It constructed and maintained a democratic facade comprising unfair elections, ineffective and hollowed-out institutions, solemn yet never honoured promises of liberalisation, and cataclysmic warnings about who could take power if he was ever ousted. These trappings, along with Ben Ali's determination to preserve them, were what prevented his regime from sliding into full dictatorship. And, for nearly two-and-a-half decades, they were sufficient to satisfy the West, help contain domestic opposition and preserve his rule.

Inevitably, therefore, this discrepancy does not explain why the regime fell when it did or why Tunisia, alone of all the countries examined by this book, and which experienced significant Arab Spring unrest, has made the transition from competitive authoritarianism to democracy. Rather, the answer lies in other vital incongruities, between what the United States and European Union said and did, and the amount of democratising pressure they put on Tunis compared to that which they could have exerted. It is these discrepancies that make Tunisia a complex case and hold the key to both Ben Ali's longevity and the country's eventual transition.

From the moment he seized power, Ben Ali sought to fortify Tunisia's already strong links to the West. He eagerly signed up the country to a range of US- and EU-sponsored policy frameworks including the MEPI, BMENA, EMP, UfM, ENP and PfDSP. To qualify to join these schemes, especially those launched and backed by the European Union, he had to introduce a raft of (mostly economic and fiscal) reforms as well as promise to make other (mainly political and legal) changes in due course. In so doing, and as of course was his intention, he strengthened his government's diplomatic relations with its Western counterparts, and brought about and paved the way for Tunisia's closer economic integration with the United States and Europe.

One of the most important economic ties binding the country to the West remains the millions of dollars in remittance payments made each year by the thousands of Tunisians living and working in North America and Europe to friends and relations still in the Maghreb. This large transnational community also continues to play vital social and technocratic roles and act as a significant alternative source of information, albeit one of declining importance. The members of the diaspora, along with the millions of American, Canadian and European citizens who visit the country every year, form a human link between Tunisia and their homes overseas. The rapid expansion in mobile-phone, Internet and social-media use has made it easier for them to provide friends and family members back home with additional and international views on events in their country. And a sizeable minority of them are in the West to study and train, to learn and acquire new skills and knowledge to take back home with them.

The United States and European Union also had high leverage over Tunisia. Crucially, the country did not have a large or medium-sized economy, was not a major or intermediate oil producer, did not possess any nuclear weapons or enjoy the backing of a Black Knight patron. The

West's considerable influence over Tunisia should have negated the Ben Ali regime's high organisational power, its strong and cohesive security forces and ruling party, and ability to control critical parts of the economy. But Washington and Brussels steadfastly refused to bring their true power over Tunis to bear. Not only were they reluctant to do so for fear of creating political instability in the country for Islamists to exploit but they proved unable and unwilling to co-ordinate better with one another what pressure they did apply. Significant inconsistencies existed between what Washington and Brussels, the EU Commission and European national governments did.

As a result, the regime's high organisational power enabled it to nullify its opponents and perpetuate itself for over two decades. And when the end finally came for Ben Ali, it was triggered by domestic not international factors and actors. The regime's prolonged neglect of the military proved crucial. So, too, did its construction of a ruling party out of mainly material ties and allegiances. These pivotal weaknesses ensured that not only could the regime not adequately defend itself against the Arab Spring protests when they broke out but that the broader ruling elite quickly turned against Ben Ali and his family. It was only at this point that the United States and European Union weighed in more heavily on the side of the demonstrators, their high leverage over and links to Tunisia helping ensure the end of competitive authoritarianism and the country's political liberalisation.

Notes

1. Duncan Pickard (2014), 'Prospects for Implementing Democracy in Tunisia', *Mediterranean Politics*, 19: 2, 259–64, p. 260.
2. Rikke Haugbølle and Francesco Cavatorta (2011), 'Will the Real Tunisian Opposition Please Stand up? Opposition Coordination Failures under Authoritarian Constraints', *British Journal of Middle Eastern Studies*, 38: 3, 323–41, pp. 330–40; Andrea G. Brody-Barre (2013), 'The Impact of Political Parties and Coalition Building on Tunisia's Democratic Future', *The Journal of North African Studies*, 18: 2, 211–30, pp. 215–20.
3. Emma C. Murphy (2013), 'The Tunisian Election of October 2011: A Democratic Consensus', *The Journal of North African Studies*, 18: 2, 231–47, pp. 231–2.
4. Ben Ali fled Tunisia on 14 January 2011. Brody-Barre, 'The Impact of Political Parties and Coalition Building', p. 212.
5. Francesco Cavatorta and Rikke Hostrup Haugbølle (2012), 'The End of Authoritarian Rule and the Mythology of Tunisia under Ben Ali', *Mediterranean Politics*, 17: 2, 179–95, p. 180.

6. The annual Strategic Survey is a compendium of all the major incidents and developments that have taken place in the world over the previous year, and analysis of what is likely to happen in the coming months.

7. Bouazizi set himself alight on 17 December 2010. Brody-Barre, 'The Impact of Political Parties and Coalition Building', p. 211.

8. Peter J. Schraeder and Hamadi Redissi (2011), 'Ben Ali's fall', *Journal of Democracy*, 22: 3, 5–19, p. 5.

9. Cavatorta and Haugbølle, 'The End of Authoritarian Rule', p. 180.

10. Noureddine Jebnoun (2014), 'In the Shadow of Power: Civil–Military Relations and the Tunisian Popular Uprising', *The Journal of North African Studies*, 19: 3, 296–316, p. 300; Cavatorta and Haugbølle, 'The End of Authoritarian Rule', p. 189.

11. Federica Bicchi (2014), 'The Politics of Foreign Aid and the European Neighbourhood Policy Post-Arab Spring: "More for More" or Less of the Same?' *Mediterranean Politics*, 19: 3, 318–32, p. 318; Steven Heydemann (2014), 'America's Response to the Arab Uprisings: US Foreign Assistance in an Era of Ambivalence', *Mediterranean Politics*, 19: 3, 299–317, p. 299; Larbi Sadiki (2009), *Rethinking Arab Democratization: Elections Without Democracy*, Oxford: Oxford University Press, p. 120.

12. For example, in the 1990 municipal election, the RCD won 3,716 seats out of 3,750; Sadiki, *Rethinking Arab Democratization*, p. 109.

13. Moncef Kartas (2014), 'Foreign Aid and Security Sector Reform in Tunisia: Resistance and Autonomy of the Security Forces', *Mediterranean Politics*, 19: 3, 373–91, p. 376.

14. Alaya Allani (2009), 'The Islamists in Tunisia between Confrontation and Participation: 1980–2008', *The Journal of North African Studies*, 14: 2, 257–72, p. 266.

15. Cavatorta and Haugbølle, 'The End of Authoritarian Rule', p. 180.

16. Brieg Tomos Powel (2009), 'The Stability Syndrome: US and EU Democracy Promotion in Tunisia', *The Journal of North African Studies*, 14: 1, 57–73, p. 70.

17. Ibid. p. 65.

18. Kartas, 'Foreign Aid and Security Sector Reform in Tunisia', pp. 376–7.

19. Cavatorta and Haugbølle, 'The End of Authoritarian Rule', p. 185.

20. The term Broader Middle East and North Africa (BMENA) partnership initiative has been referred to as the Greater Middle East and North Africa Initiative (GMEI). The two labels and acronyms have occasionally been used interchangeably. Powel, 'The Stability Syndrome', pp. 19 and 60; Patrick Holden (2009), 'Security, Power or Profit? The Economic Diplomacy of the US and the EU in North Africa', *The Journal of North African Studies*, 14: 1, 11–32, p. 19.

21. Powel, 'The Stability Syndrome', p. 60; Holden, 'Security, Power or Profit?', p. 16.

22. Heydemann, 'America's Response to the Arab Uprisings', p. 305.

23. Ibid. p. 305.
24. Powel, 'The Stability Syndrome', p. 60.
25. Holden, 'Security, Power or Profit?', p. 19.
26. More precisely, the MEPI allocated $90 million in the 2003 financial year, $89.4 million in 2004, $74.4 million in 2005, $113.8 million in 2006, $50 million in 2007, $49.5 million in 2008, $50 million in 2009, $65 million in 2010, $80 million in 2011 and $70 million in 2012; Heydemann, 'America's Response to the Arab Uprisings', p. 300.
27. Ibid. pp. 305–6.
28. Ibid. p. 303.
29. Ibid. p. 308.
30. Ibid. p. 307.
31. Powel, 'The Stability Syndrome', p. 69.
32. Kartas, 'Foreign Aid and Security Sector Reform in Tunisia', p. 378.
33. Ibid. p. 378.
34. Powel, 'The Stability Syndrome', p. 69.
35. Ana Echagüe, Hélène Michou and Barak Mikail (2011), 'Europe and the Arab Uprisings: EU Vision versus Member State Actions', *Mediterranean Politics*, 16: 2, 329–35, p. 330.
36. The dozen partners were: Algeria, Cyprus, Egypt, Israel, Jordan, Lebanon, Malta, Morocco, Syria, Tunisia, Turkey and the Palestinian Authority. European Union (1995), 'Barcelona Declaration', 27–8 November, <http://trade.ec.europa.eu/doclib/docs/2005/july/tradoc_124236.pdf> (last accessed 20 March 2015).
37. Ibid.
38. Holden, 'Security, Power or Profit?', p. 22–3.
39. Tunisia's agreement took effect on 1 March 1998. Holden, 'Security, Power or Profit?', p. 22.
40. Mohamed Hedi Bahir, Mohamed Abdelbassef Chemingui and Hakim Ben Hammouda (2009), 'Ten Years after Implementing the Barcelona Process: What can be Learned from the Tunisia Experience', *The Journal of North African Studies*, 14: 2, 123–44, p. 123.
41. European Union (2007), 'Mediterranean Neighbourhood Countries: Commitments and Payments (€ million)', 15 January, available at <http://eeas.europa.eu/euromed/docs/meda_figures_en.pdf> (last accessed 20 March 2015).
42. European Union (2015), 'Euro-Mediterranean Partnership (EUROMED)', available at <http://eeas.europa.eu/euromed/index_en.htm> (last accessed 20 March 2015).
43. The UfM's new partner states were Albania, Bosnia and Herzegovina, Mauritania and Montenegro. And, while it continued to embrace a range of issues, its focus was not as broad as it had been before. Indeed, its key initiatives were mainly environmental, social and infrastructural, and included: 'the de-pollution of the Mediterranean Seas, including costal and protected

marine areas'; 'the establishment of maritime and land highways that connect ports and improve rail connections so as to facilitate movement of people and goods'; 'a joint civil protection programme on prevention, preparation and response to natural and man-made disasters'; 'a Mediterranean solar energy plan that explores opportunities for developing alternative energy sources in the region'; 'a Euro-Mediterranean University'; and 'the Mediterranean Business Development Initiative, which supports small businesses operating in the region by first assessing their needs and then providing technical assistance and access to finance'; Ibid.

44. Holden, 'Security, Power or Profit?', p. 23.
45. Ibid. p. 24.
46. So far, twelve partner states have agreed their action plans. Of the four which have not, Algeria is negotiating its plan with the European Union while Belarus, Libya and Syria are suspended from the ENP. European Union (2015), 'European Neighbourhood Policy (ENP)', <http://eeas. europa.eu/enp/index_en.htm> (last accessed 20 March 2015).
47. One of the main mechanisms used to apportion and distribute these funds is the European Neighbourhood and Partnership Instrument (ENPI); Bicchi, 'The Politics of Foreign Aid and the European Neighbourhood Policy Post-Arab Spring', p. 318.
48. Available at <http://eeas.europa.eu/enp/index_en.htm> (last accessed 20 March 2015). The EEAS was established by the Lisbon Treaty and became formally active on 1 December 2010; Bicchi, 'The Politics of Foreign Aid and the European Neighbourhood Policy Post-Arab Spring', p. 319.
49. Brieg Powel and Larbi Sadiki (2010), *Europe and Tunisia: Democratization via Association*, Abingdon: Routledge, p. 40; Raffaella A. Del Sarto and Tobias Schumacher (2011), 'From Brussels with Love: Leverage, Benchmarking, and the Action Plans with Jordan and Tunisia in the EU's Democratization Policy', *Democratization*, 18: 4, 932–55, p. 932.
50. Available at <http://eeas.europa.eu/enp/pdf/pdf/action_plans/tunisia_enp_ap_final_en.pdf> (last accessed 22 March 2015).
51. Sue Dennison (2013), 'The EU and North Africa after the Revolutions: A New Start of "plus ça change"?' *Mediterranean Politics*, 18: 1, 119–24, p. 119; Bicchi, 'The Politics of Foreign Aid and the European Neighbourhood Policy Post-Arab Spring', p. 323.
52. Dennison, 'The EU and North Africa after the Revolutions', p. 119.
53. Ibid. p. 119.
54. The PfDSP was launched by the European Commission and endorsed by the European Council a few days later. Echagüe, Michou and Mikail, 'Europe and the Arab Uprisings', p. 329; Andrea Teti (2012), 'The EU's First Response to the "Arab Spring": A Critical Discourse Analysis of the Partnership for Democracy and Shared Prosperity', *Mediterranean Politics*, 17: 3, 266–84, p. 272; Bicchi, 'The Politics of Foreign Aid and the European Neighbourhood Policy Post-Arab Spring', p. 323.

55. Teti, 'The EU's First Response to the "Arab Spring"', p. 266.
56. Indeed, the PfDSP opens with the declaration that 'the EU must not be a passive spectator. It needs to support wholeheartedly the wish of the people in our neighbourhood to enjoy the same freedoms that we take as right. European countries have their own experience of democratic transition.' European Commission (2011), 'A Partnership for Democracy and Shared Prosperity With The Southern Mediterranean', 8 March, <http://eeas.europa.eu/euromed/docs/com2011_200_en.pdf> (last accessed 22 March 2015).
57. Ibid.
58. Bicchi, 'The Politics of Foreign Aid and the European Neighbourhood Policy Post-Arab Spring', p. 328.
59. European Commission (2011), 'The EU's response to the 'Arab Spring', 16 December, <http://europa.eu/rapid/press-release_MEMO-11-918_en.htm> (last accessed 27 March 2015).
60. Ibid.
61. European Commission (2013), 'European Endowment for Democracy – additional support for democratic change', 9 January, <http://europa.eu/rapid/press-release_IP-13-17_en.htm> (last accessed 27 March 2015). Even before the post-Arab Spring round of funding pledges, the Middle East and North Africa have been described as '"over-aided," receiving substantially more aid per poor person compared to other regions'. Miguel Pellicer and Eva Wegner (2009), 'Altruism and its Limits: The Role of Civil and Political Rights for American and French Aid Towards the Middle East and North Africa', *The Journal of North African Studies*, 14: 1, 109–21, p. 110.
62. More specifically, Tunisia was given €20 million in SPRING funding in 2011, €80 million in 2012, and €40 million in 2013; Bicchi, 'The Politics of Foreign Aid and the European Neighbourhood Policy Post-Arab Spring', p. 329.
63. Egypt was awarded €90 million in SPRING funding in 2012 and €40 million in 2013. And Morocco was given €80 million in 2012 and €35 million in 2013; ibid. p. 329.
64. The person appointed to this post was Bernardino Léon. And he was charged with 'enhancing the Union's political dialogue, contributing to the partnership and broader relationship with the countries of the Southern Mediterranean region'; 'contributing to the response of the Union to the developments in the countries of the Southern Mediterranean region and, in particular, to strengthening democracy and institution building, the rule of law, good governance, peace and regional cooperation, including through the European Neighbourhood Policy and the Union for the Mediterranean'; and 'enhancing the European Union's effectiveness, presence and visibility in the region and in relevant international forums. Establishing close coordination with relevant local partners and international and regional organisations.' Council of the European Union (2011), 'Council Decision 2011/424/CFSP of 18 July 2011 Appointing a European Union Special Representative

for the South Mediterranean Region', 18 July, <http://eur-lex.europa.eu/LexUriServ/LexUriServ.do?uri=OJ:L:2011:188:0024:0026:en:PDF> (last accessed 23 March 2015).

65. European Commission (2011), 'EU/Tunisia Task Force Agrees Concrete Assistance for Tunisia's Transition', 29 September, <http://europa.eu/rapid/press-release_IP-11-1137_en.htm> (last accessed 23 March 2015).

66. The Tunisian Task Force met on 28 and 29 September 2011, the Egyptian on 14 November 2011 and the Jordanian on 22 February 2012; ibid. European Commission (2012), 'First meeting of EU–Egypt Task Force to support the ongoing reforms in Egypt', 13 November, <http://europa.eu/rapid/press-release_IP-12-1202_en.htm?locale=en> (last accessed 23 March 2015); European Commission (2012), 'First meeting of EU–Jordan Task Force to support the ongoing reforms in Jordan', 21 February, <http://europa.eu/rapid/press-release_IP-12-153_en.htm?locale=en> (last accessed 23 March 2015); Bicchi, 'The Politics of Foreign Aid and the European Neighbourhood Policy Post-Arab Spring', p. 322.

67. European Union (2011), '"A Privileged Partnership" – The EU and Tunisia', 29 September, <http://eeas.europa.eu/top_stories/2011/290911a_en.htm> (last accessed 27 March 2015).

68. More specifically, the EU 'pledged initial support worth over €150 million', to 'provide a €100 million grant in support of €1 billion multi-donor . . . programme', and 'a €57 million . . . grant to reform the water sector'; ibid.

69. Ibid.

70. Government of the United States of America (2002), 'Agreement between the Government of the United States of America and the Government of Tunisia Concerning the Development of Trade and Investment Relations', 2 October, <https://ustr.gov/sites/default/files/uploads/agreements/tifa/asset_upload_file459_9936.pdf> (last accessed 31 March 2015).

71. Office of the United States Trade Representative (2003), 'Middle East Free Trade Area Initiative (MEFTA)', May, <https://ustr.gov/trade-agreements/other-initiatives/middle-east-free-trade-area-initiative-mefta> (last accessed 31 March 2015).

72. More specifically, Tunisia imported $399.99 million worth of goods in 1995, $320.45 million in 1996, $341.09 million in 1997, $289.04 million in 1998, and $359.6 million in 1999. World Bank (2015), 'Tunisia Product Import Trade Value', 31 July, <http://wits.worldbank.org/CountryProfile/Country/TUN/StartYear/1994/EndYear/1998/TradeFlow/Import/Indicator/MPRT-TRD-VL/Partner/USA/Product/all-groups> (last accessed 31 March 2015).

73. More specifically, Tunisia imported $395.12 million worth of goods in 2000, $384.52 million in 2001, $301.87 million in 2002, $270.11 million in 2003 and $360.41 million in 2004; ibid.

74. More specifically, Tunisia imported $329.54 million worth of goods in 2005, $431.41 million in 2006, $647.23 million in 2007, $748.76 million in 2008, and $764.84 million in 2009; ibid.

75. More specifically, Tunisia imported $905.24 million worth of goods in 2010, $881.77 million in 2011, $798.56 million in 2012, and $798.35 million in 2013; ibid.
76. More specifically, Tunisia's exports to the US were worth $69.06 million in 1995, $75.39 million in 1996, $37.46 million in 1997, $28.42 million in 1998, and $43.42 million in 1999. World Bank (2015), 'Tunisia Product Export Trade Value', 31 July, <http://wits.worldbank.org/CountryProfile/Country/TUN/StartYear/1994/EndYear/1998/TradeFlow/Export/Indicator/XPRT-TRD-VL/Partner/USA/Product/all-groups> (last accessed 31 March 2015).
77. More specifically, Tunisia's exports to the US were worth $42.07 million in 2000, $63.49 million in 2001, $53.59 million in 2002, $48.50 million in 2003, and $115.28 million in 2004; ibid.
78. More specifically, Tunisia's exports to the US were worth $95.45 million in 2005, $262.67 million in 2006, $167.23 million in 2007, $323.05 million in 2008, and $196.83 million in 2009; ibid.
79. More specifically, Tunisia's exports to the US were worth $388.53 million in 2010, $276.58 million in 2011, $326.20 million 350 in 2012, and $397.45 million in 2013; ibid.
80. European Commission (2015), 'European Union, Trade in goods with Tunisia', 10 April, available at <http://trade.ec.europa.eu/doclib/docs/2006/september/tradoc_122002.pdf> (last accessed 30 March 2015).
81. Bahir, Chemingui and Hammouda, 'Ten Years after Implementing the Barcelona Process', p. 124.
82. Ibid. p. 128.
83. Powel, 'The Stability Syndrome', p. 65.
84. In 2004, the total value of EU–Tunisia trade was €14.3 billion, in 2005 €14.8 billion, in 2006 €16.3 billion, in 2007 €18.5 billion, in 2008 €19.4 billion, in 2009 €17.1 billion, in 2010 €20.6 billion, in 2011 €20.9, and in 2012 €20.7. Available at <http://trade.ec.europa.eu/doclib/docs/2006/september/tradoc_122002.pdf> (last accessed 29 March 2015).
85. Bahir, Chemingui and Hammouda, 'Ten Years after Implementing the Barcelona Process', p. 125.
86. Available at <http://trade.ec.europa.eu/doclib/docs/2006/september/tradoc_122002.pdf> (last accessed 30 March 2015).
87. Ibid.
88. The biggest importers of Tunisian goods after the EU in 2013 were: China (5.4 per cent), Algeria (4.4 per cent), Libya (4.0 per cent), Turkey (3.8 per cent), the United States (3.5 per cent), Ukraine (1.3 per cent), Brazil (1.2 per cent), Russia (1.2 per cent) and India (1.2 per cent). Together, these countries received 26 per cent of all Tunisia's exports. And the greatest exporter to Tunisia after the EU in 2013 were: Libya (8.1 per cent), the United States (4.1 per cent), Algeria (2.6 per cent), Canada (1.8 per cent), Egypt (1.7 per cent), Turkey (1.6 per cent), South Korea (1.3 per cent), Morocco (1.2

per cent) and China (1.0 per cent). Together, these countries provided 23.4 per cent of all Tunisia's imports; ibid.

89. Clause (a) of the Barcelona Declaration's section on Economic and Financial Partnership: Creating an Area of Shared Prosperity confirms that 'the parties have set 2010 as the target date for the gradual establishment of this [free trade] area which will cover most trade with due observance of the obligations resulting from the WTO'. Tunisia was the second North African partner state to join the WTO. The first was Morocco a few months earlier on 1 January 1995. Then Egypt became a member shortly afterwards on 30 June 1995. Both Algeria's and Libya's membership applications are ongoing; World Trade Organization (2015), 'Members and Observers', April 2015, <https://ec.europa.eu/research/iscp/pdf/policy/barcelona_dec laration.pdf> (last accessed 5 July 2015).

90. Bahir, Chemingui and Hammouda, 'Ten Years after Implementing the Barcelona Process', pp. 129 and 140.

91. More specifically, the country attracted $264 million in FDI in 1995, $238 million in 1996, $339 million in 1997, $649 million in 1998, and $349 million in 1999; World Bank (2015), 'Foreign Direct Investment, Net Inflows', <http://data.worldbank.org/indicator/BX.KLT.DINV.CD.WD/ countries?page=3> (last accessed 30 March 2015).

92. More specifically, the country attracted $752 million in FDI in 2000, $451 million in 2001, $790 million in 2002, $540 million in 2003, and $593 million in 2004; ibid.

93. More specifically, the country attracted $712 million in FDI in 2005, $3.23 billion in 2006, $1.51 billion in 2007, $2.60 billion in 2008, and $1.52 billion in 2009; ibid.

94. More specifically, the country attracted $1.33 billion in FDI in 2010, $432 million in 2011, $1.55 billion in 2012, and $1.05 billion in 2013; ibid.

95. Office des Tunisiens à l'Etranger (2012), 'Répartition de la Communauté Tunisienne à l'Étranger', <http://www.ote.nat.tn/fileadmin/user_upload/ doc/Repartition_de_la_communaute_tunisienne_a_l_etranger__2012.pdf> (last accessed 30 March 2015).

96. More specifically, these remittances amounted to $679 million in 1995, $735 million in 1996, $684 million in 1997, $718 million in 1998, and $761 million in 1999; World Bank (2015), 'Personal Remittances, Received', <http://data.worldbank.org/indicator/BX.TRF.PWKR.CD.DT/countries? page=3> (last accessed 30 March 2015).

97. More specifically, these remittances amount to $795 million in 2000, $927 million in 2001, $1.07 billion in 2002, $1.25 billion in 2003, and $1.43 billion in 2004; ibid.

98. More specifically, these remittances amounted to $1.39 billion in 2005, $1.51 billion in 2006, $1.71 billion in 2007, $1.97 billion in 2008, and $1.96 billion in 2009; ibid.

99. More specifically, these remittances amounted to $2.06 billion in 2010,

$2.00 billion in 2011, $ 2.26 billion 2012, and $2.29 billion in 2013; ibid.

100. Available at <http://www.ote.nat.tn/fileadmin/user_upload/doc/Repartition _de_la_communaute_tunisienne_a_l_etranger__2012.pdf> (last accessed 31 March 2015).

101. Tunisia's population in 2012 was 10,777,500; World Bank (2015), 'Total Population', <http://data.worldbank.org/indicator/SP.POP.TOTL/coun tries/TN?display=graph> (last accessed 21 March 2015).

102. Eurostat (2015), 'Tourism statistics – North Africa and Eastern Mediterranean', 30 January, <http://ec.europa.eu/eurostat/statistics-explain ed/index.php/Tourism_statistics_-_North_Africa_and_Eastern_Mediter ranean> (last accessed 1 April 2015).

103. Republic of Tunisia, Ministry of Tourism and Handicrafts (2015), 'Tourism in Figures', <http://www.tourisme.gov.tn/en/achievements-and-prospects/ tourism-in-figures/figures-2013.html> (last accessed 1 April 2015).

104. Available at <http://ec.europa.eu/eurostat/statistics-explained/index.php/ Tourism_statistics_-_North_Africa_and_Eastern_Mediterranean> (last accessed 1 April 2015).

105. Available at <http://www.tourisme.gov.tn/en/achievements-and-prospects/ tourism-in-figures/stat-15.html> (last accessed 1 April 2015).

106. Ibid.

107. Ibid.

108. Ibid.

109. World Bank (2015), 'Internet Users', <http://data.worldbank.org/indicator/ IT.NET.USER.P2?page=1> (last accessed 9 July 2015).

110. Ibid.

111. Ibid.

112. World Bank (2015), 'Mobile Cellular Subscriptions', <http://data.world bank.org/indicator/IT.CEL.SETS.P2/countries?page=2> (last accessed 9 July 2015).

113. Ibid.

114. Ibid.

115. See, for example, the figures for Germany over the past few years. Nora Ragab, Elaine McGregor and Melissa Siegel (2013), *Diaspora Engagement in Development: An Analysis of the Engagement of the Tunisian Diaspora in Germany and the Potentials for Cooperation*, Deutsche Gesellschaft für Internationale Zusammenarbeit (GIZ) GmbH, p. 14.

116. Jebnoun, 'In the Shadow of Power', p. 301.

117. Available at <http://europa.eu/rapid/press-release_MEMO-11-918_en. htm> (last accessed 16 April 2015); Ragab, Elaine McGregor and Melissa Siegel (2013), *Diaspora Engagement in Development*, p. 13.

118. European Commission (2013), 'Increased Education Opportunities between Tunisia and EU', 14 May, <http://europa.eu/rapid/press-release_IP-13- 421_en.htm> (last accessed 16 April 2015).

119. Available at <http://europa.eu/rapid/press-release_MEMO-11-918_en. htm> (last accessed 16 April 2015).
120. European Commission (2015), 'European Neighbourhood Policy and Enlargement Negotiations: Tunisia', 8 April, <http://ec.europa.eu/enlargement/neighbourhood/countries/tunisia/index_en.htm> (last accessed 16 April 2015).
121. Ibid.
122. In 2013, Tunisia's GDP was $46.99 billion; World Bank (2015), 'Tunisia', <http://data.worldbank.org/country/tunisia> (last accessed 14 April 2015). According to Levitsky and Way, a country has a large economy if its GDP is at least $100 billion, and a medium-sized one if its GDP is between $50 billion and $100 billion; Levitsky and Way, *Competitive Authoritarianism*, p. 372.
123. During the course of 2013, Tunisia pumped an average of 63,290 barrels of crude oil a day; US Department of Energy (2014), 'Tunisia', October, <http://www.eia.gov/countries/country-data.cfm?fips=ts> (last accessed 14 April 2015). According to Levitsky and Way, major oil-producing countries pump at least a million barrels of oil a day in an average year, and intermediate ones between 200,000 and a million barrels per day. Levitsky and Way, *Competitive Authoritarianism*, p. 372.
124. Levitsky and Way, *Competitive Authoritarianism*, p. 372.
125. Holden, 'Security, Power or Profit?', p. 14; Michelle Pace (2009), 'Paradoxes and Contradictions in EU Democracy Promotion in the Mediterranean: The Limits of EU Normative Power', *Democratization*, 16: 1, 39–58, p. 43.
126. Powel, 'The Stability Syndrome', p. 65; Pellicer and Wegner, 'Altruism and its Limits', p. 110.
127. Powel, 'The Stability Syndrome', p. 60; Holden, 'Security, Power or Profit?', p. 16.
128. Heydemann, 'America's Response to the Arab Uprisings', p. 307.
129. Powel, 'The Stability Syndrome', p. 63.
130. Echagüe, Michou and Mikail, 'Europe and the Arab Uprisings', pp. 332–3.
131. Heydemann, 'America's Response to the Arab Uprisings', p. 309.
132. Ibid. p. 314.
133. Ibid. p. 314.
134. Bicchi, 'The Politics of Foreign Aid and the European Neighbourhood Policy Post-Arab Spring', p. 319.
135. Echagüe, Michou and Mikail, 'Europe and the Arab Uprisings', p. 330.
136. Bicchi, 'The Politics of Foreign Aid and the European Neighbourhood Policy Post-Arab Spring', p. 322.
137. Ibid. p. 325.
138. Dennison, 'The EU and North Africa after the Revolutions', p. 120.
139. Ibid. p. 121.
140. Bicchi, 'The Politics of Foreign Aid and the European Neighbourhood Policy Post-Arab Spring', p. 328.

141. Ibid. p. 328.

142. Leila Mouhib (2014), 'EU Democracy Promotion in Tunisia and Morocco: Between Contextual Changes and Structural Continuity', *Mediterranean Politics*, 19: 3, 351–72, p. 352.

143. Ibid. p. 352.

144. Bicchi, 'The Politics of Foreign Aid and the European Neighbourhood Policy Post-Arab Spring', p. 320.

145. Ibid. p. 320.

146. Mouhib, 'EU Democracy Promotion in Tunisia and Morocco', p. 354.

147. Bicchi, 'The Politics of Foreign Aid and the European Neighbourhood Policy Post-Arab Spring', p. 322.

148. Heydemann, 'America's Response to the Arab Uprisings', p. 302.

149. Ibid. p. 304.

150. Ibid. p. 312.

151. Holden, 'Security, Power or Profit?', p. 26.

152. Powel, 'The Stability Syndrome', p. 64.

153. Ibid. p. 65.

154. Holden, 'Security, Power or Profit?', p. 26.

155. Bicchi, 'The Politics of Foreign Aid and the European Neighbourhood Policy Post-Arab Spring', p. 322.

156. Ibid. p. 322.

157. Echagüe, Michou and Mikail, 'Europe and the Arab Uprisings', pp. 331–3.

158. Mouhib, 'EU Democracy Promotion in Tunisia and Morocco', p. 366.

159. Richard Youngs (2008), 'Is European Democracy Promotion on the Wane', Centre for European Policy Studies, May, <http://aei.pitt.edu/9373/2/9373.pdf> (last accessed 24 April 2015), p. 12.

160. Echagüe, Michou and Mikail, 'Europe and the Arab Uprisings', p. 330.

161. Ibid. p. 334.

162. Ibid. p. 334.

163. Based on the combined budgets of the Ministries of Interior and Defence. Hachim Bou Nassif (2015), 'A Military Besieged: The Armed Forces, the Police, and the Party in Bin 'Ali's Tunisia, 1987–2011', *International Journal of Middle East Studies*, 47: 1, 65–87, p. 75.

164. The Ministry of Interior oversaw and managed all the main, non-military security agencies and bodies including variously 'the State Security Service . . ., General Directorate of National Security, General Directorate of Public Security, General Directorate of Special Services, General Directorate of Intervention Units, Directorate of Borders and Aliens, Director of Technical Services, Central Directorate of Counterterrorism, and General Intelligence Directorate known as la police politique'; Jebnoun, 'In the Shadow of Power', p. 301.

165. Nassif, 'A Military Besieged', pp. 74–5.

166. In 1987, Tunisia's national budget was 2.24 billion DT and in 1996 4.77 billion DT; ibid. p. 75.

167. In 1997 the country's national budget had risen to 8.01 billion DT; ibid. p. 75.

168. The ministry's budget fell from 623.54 million DT in 2000 to 621.98 million DT in 2001 before rising to 650.59 million DT in 2002, and from 739.45 million DT in 2004 to 718.36 million DT in 2005 before growing significantly to 817.80 million DT in 2006; ibid. p. 75.

169. In 1987, the Ministry of Interior's budget stood at 184.11 million DT and the Ministry of Defence's at 112.82 million DT. By 2011 they had risen to 1.24 billion DT and 828.85 million DT respectively. Ibid. p. 75.

170. Kartas, 'Foreign Aid and Security Sector Reform in Tunisia', p. 376.

171. Ibid. p. 376.

172. Levitsky and Way, *Competitive Authoritarianism*, p. 61.

173. In 1984, the Ministry of Interior was allocated 6 per cent of the national budget, which amounted to 93.40 million DT, and the Ministry of Defence 5.9 per cent or 92.17 million DT; Nassif, 'A Military Besieged', p. 74.

174. In that year, the Ministry of Interior received 6.5 per cent of the national budget, which amounted to 1.24 billion DT. In comparison, the Ministry of Defence was awarded 4.3 per cent or 828.85 million DT; ibid. p. 75.

175. Jebnoun, 'In the Shadow of Power', p. 299.

176. Ibid. p. 299.

177. Tunisia spent 1.6 per cent of GDP on defence in 2002, 2003, 2004, 2005 and 2006, and 1.4 per cent in 2007, 2008 and 2009. Fluvio Attinà (2015), 'Mediterranean Security Revisited', in Patricia Bauer (ed.), *Arab Spring Challenges for Democracy and Security in the Mediterranean*, Abingdon: Routledge, 120–36, p. 126.

178. Jebnoun, 'In the Shadow of Power', p. 301; Nouri Gana (2013), 'Tunisia', in Paul Amar and Vijay Prashad (eds), *Dispatches from the Arab Spring: Understanding the Arab Spring*, Minneapolis, MN and London: University of Minnesota Press, pp. 1–23, p. 4.

179. Levitsky and Way, *Competitive Authoritarianism*, p. 59.

180. George Joffé (2011), 'The Arab Spring in North Africa: Origins and Prospects', *The Journal of North African Studies*, 16: 4, 507–32, p. 519.

181. The new name was adopted in February 1988. Dirk Vandewalle (1988), 'From the New State to the New Era: Toward a Second Republic in Tunisia', *Middle East Journal*, 42: 4, 602–20, p. 614.

182. Emma C. Murphy (1997), 'Ten Years on – Ben Ali's Tunisia', *Mediterranean Politics*, 2: 3, 114–22, p. 119.

183. Bradford (1998), 'The Political Economy of Structural Adjustment in Tunisia and Algeria', *The Journal of North African Studies*, 3: 3, 1–24, p. 4.

184. Ibid. p. 4–5.

185. Ibid. p. 8.

186. Rikke Haugbølle and Francesco Cavatorta (2011), 'Will the Real Tunisian Opposition Please Stand Up? Opposition Coordination Failures under

Authoritarian Constraints', *British Journal of Middle Eastern Studies*, 38: 3, 323–41, p. 330.

187. Joffé, 'The Arab Spring in North Africa', p. 519.
188. Bahir, Chemingui and Hammouda, 'Ten Years after Implementing the Barcelona Process', pp. 128 and 140.
189. In contrast, it had amounted to just $91.7 million when Ben Ali had seized power in 1987 <http://data.worldbank.org/indicator/BX.KLT.DINV. CD.WD/countries?page=5> (last accessed 07 May 2015).
190. Bahir, Chemingui and Hammouda, 'Ten Years after Implementing the Barcelona Process', p. 129.
191. Cavatorta and Haugbølle, 'The End of Authoritarian Rule', p. 185.
192. Haugbølle and Cavatorta, 'Will the Real Tunisian Opposition Please Stand Up?', p. 326; Dillman 1998: 8)
193. Cavatorta and Haugbølle, 'The End of Authoritarian Rule', p. 187.
194. Dillman (1998), 'The Political Economy of Structural Adjustment', p. 4.
195. Haugbølle and Cavatorta, 'Will the Real Tunisian Opposition Please Stand Up?', p. 326.
196. Ibid. p. 330.
197. Ibid. p. 330.
198. Ibid. p. 335.
199. Ibid. p. 336.
200. Michelle Pace and Francesco Cavatorta (2012), 'The Arab Uprisings in Theoretical Perspective – An Introduction', *Mediterranean Politics*, 17: 2, 125–38, p. 129.
201. Haugbølle and Cavatorta, 'Will the Real Tunisian Opposition Please Stand Up?', p. 339.
202. Ibid. p. 340.
203. Levitsky and Way, *Competitive Authoritarianism*, p. 37.
204. Officially it was called the New Liberal Constitutional Party but was popularly known as the Neo-Destour party; Clement Henry Moore (1965), *The Dynamics of One-Party Government*, Berkeley and Los Angeles, CA: University of California Press, p. 8. It changed its name to the PSD in 1964; Dirk Vandewalle (1988), 'From the New State to the New Era: Toward a Second Republic in Tunisia', *Middle East Journal*, 42: 4, 602–20, p. 604.
205. Other parties did exist and some, like the MDS, were legalised. But they were not permitted to compete in parliamentary elections; Keith Callard (1960), 'The Republic of Bourguiba', *International Journal*, 16: 1, 17–36, p. 22.
206. Ben Ali invoked Article 57 of the constitution which states that 'in the event of the incapacity of the head of state [Bourguiba] to fulfil his duties the prime minister [Ben Ali] will be immediately invested with the function of the presidency for the remainder of the term of the national legislature'. L. B. Ware (1988), 'Ben Ali's Constitutional Coup in Tunisia', *Middle East Journal*, 42: 4, 587–601, p. 592. On the night of 6 November 1987,

therefore, Ben Ali had seven doctors declare Bourguiba medically unfit and removed him from power; Willis, *Politics and Power in the Maghreb*, p. 96.

207. Noureddine Jebnoun (2014), 'Ben Ali's Tunisia: The Authoritarian Path of a Dystopian State', in Noureddine Jebnoun, Mehrdad Kia and Mimi Kirk (eds), *Modern Middle East Authoritarianism: Roots, Ramifications, and Crisis*, Abingdon: Routledge, pp. 101–22, p. 103.

208. Haugbølle and Cavatorta, 'Will the Real Tunisian Opposition Please Stand Up?', pp. 330–2.

209. Larbi Sadiki (2002), 'Political Liberalization in Bin Ali's Tunisia: Façade Democracy', *Democratization*, 9: 4, 122–41, p. 132.

210. Andrew Borowiec (1998), *Modern Tunisia: A Democratic Apprenticeship*, Westport, CT: Greenwood, pp. 44–5.

211. The new law was introduced on 12 May 1988; ibid. p. 45.

212. In protest at this decision, Ghannushi went into exile in May 1989. He did not return to Tunisia until 2011. Willis, *Politics and Power in the Maghreb*, pp. 167 and 196.

213. Allani, 'The Islamists in Tunisia', p. 263.

214. Lisa Anderson (1991), 'Political Pacts, Liberalism, and Democracy: The Tunisian National Pact of 1988', *Government and Opposition*, 26: 2, 244–60.

215. Sadiki, 'Political Liberalization in Bin Ali's Tunisia', p. 128.

216. Against the odds and to Ben Ali's surprise it 'received up to 25 per cent of the vote'; ibid. p. 125.

217. Allani, 'The Islamists in Tunisia', p. 265.

218. Willis, *Politics and Power in the Maghreb*, p. 168.

219. Sadiki, 'Political Liberalization in Bin Ali's Tunisia', p. 132.

220. Lisa Anderson (1999), 'Politics in the Middle East: Opportunities in the Quest for Theory', in Mark A. Tessler, Jodi Nachtwey and Anne Banda (eds), *Area Studies and Social Science*, Bloomington, IN: Indiana University Press, 1–10, p. 4.

221. Sadiki, 'Political Liberalization in Bin Ali's Tunisia', p. 125.

222. Stephen J. King (2009), *The New Authoritarianism in the Middle East and North Africa*, Bloomington, IN: Indiana University Press, p. 176.

223. Powel and Sadiki, *Europe and Tunisia*, p. 53.

224. King, *The New Authoritarianism*, p. 175.

225. Laurel E. Miller, Jeffrey Martini, F. Stephen Larrabee, Angel Rabasa, Stephanie Pezard, Julie E. Taylor and Tewodaj Mengistu (2011), *Democratization in the Arab World: Prospects and Lessons from Around the World*, Santa Monica, CA: RAND Corporation, p. 67.

226. Human Rights Watch (2009), 'Tunisia: Elections in an Atmosphere of Repression', Human Rights Watch, 23 October, <http://www.hrw.org/news/2009/10/23/tunisia-elections-atmosphere-repression> (last accessed 19 May 2015), p. 1.

227. Ibid. p. 1.

228. This law was repealed in 2002; Dafna Hochman Rand (2013), *Roots of the Arab Spring: Contested Authority and Political Change in the Middle East*, Philadelphia, PN: University of Pennsylvania Press, pp. 58–9.
229. Ibid. p. 62.
230. European Forum for Democracy and Solidarity (2009), 'Tunisian President Ben Ali Wins Presidential Poll for the Fifth Time', 26 October, <http://www.europeanforum.net/news/756/tunisian_president_ben_ali_wins_pres idential_poll_for_the_fifth_time> (last accessed 19 May 2015).
231. Human Rights Watch, 'Tunisia', p. 1.
232. Available at <http://www.europeanforum.net/news/756/tunisian_presi dent_ben_ali_wins_presidential_poll_for_the_fifth_time> (last accessed 19 May 2015).
233. Christopher Alexander (2010), T*unisia: Stability and Reform in the Modern Maghreb*, Abingdon: Routledge, p. 62.
234. Murphy, 'The Tunisian Election of October 2011', p. 231.
235. Ibid. p. 233.
236. Ibid. pp. 233–4.
237. Ghannouchi resigned on 27 February 2011; ibid. p. 234.
238. More specifically, the new assembly would have 217 members representing thirty-three electoral districts; Tunisia's large diaspora would be divided into six constituencies and represented by eighteen members of parliament; half of all candidates named on the lists would have to be women; one candidate on each list would have to younger than thirty; and all former RCD judges, local officials, regional governors, senior civil servants and military personnel would be barred from standing; ibid. p. 235.
239. Ibid. p. 235.
240. Ibid. pp. 236–7.
241. The CR was legally recognised as a party on 8 March 2011 and had previously co-operated with Ennahda as part of the *Collectif*. The FDTL had been legalised in 2002; Brody-Barre, 'The Impact of Political Parties and Coalition Building', pp. 212–13 and 217–18.
242. Marzouki was elected president by the Constituent Assembly and formally entered office on 13 December 2011; Gana, 'Tunisia', p. 241.
243. Pickard (2014), 'Prospects for Implementing Democracy', p. 259.
244. Ibid. p. 261.
245. Freedom House (2010), 'Tunisia', <https://freedomhouse.org/report/free dom-world/2010/tunisia#.VV4aAhtFCM8> (last accessed 21 May 2015), p. 1.
246. George Joffé (2014), 'Government–Media Relations in Tunisia: A Paradigm Shift in the Culture of Governance?', *The Journal of North African Studies*, 19: 5, 615–38, pp. 618–19.
247. The ETT and ERT were both established on 7 November 2006 and replaced the Tunisian Television Broadcaster (Radiodiffusion–Télévision Tunisienne, RTT) which had been found in 1957; ibid. p. 620.

248. Ibid. p. 620.
249. The country's first commercial provider – Planet Tunisie – was owned by Ben Ali's daughter, Cyrine Ben Ali; ibid. p. 621.
250. Responsibility for managing and supervising the Internet was assumed by the Tunisian Internet Agency (Agence Tunisienne d'Internet, ATI); ibid. p. 621.
251. Ibid. pp. 621–2.
252. Ibid. p. 619.
253. The CP was issued in 1975 and amended in 1988, 1993 and 2001; ibid. p. 619.
254. Ibid. p. 615.
255. In 2010, Ben Ali's last full year in power, Tunisia was ranked 164th out of 178 countries. In 2015, it was graded 126th out of 180 countries; Reporters Without Borders (2011), 'Press Freedom Index 2010', <http://en.rsf.org/press-freedom-index-2010,1034.html> (last accessed 18 May 2015).
256. Joffé, 'Government-Media Relations in Tunisia', p. 628.
257. Reporters Without Borders (2013), 'Journalists' Work Hampered by Abusive Prosecutions and Arrests', 17 September, <http://en.rsf.org/tunisie-journalists-work-hampered-by-17-09-2013,45177.html> (last accessed 18 May 2015).
258. Amira Aleya-Sghaier (2014), 'The Tunisian Revolution: The Revolution of Dignity', in Ricardo René Larémont (ed.), *Revolution, Revolt, and Reform in North Africa: The Arab Spring and Beyond*, Abingdon: Routledge, 30–52, p. 44.
259. Ibid. p. 37.

3

Algeria

Algeria is perplexing. Like Tunisia, it has defied expectations. Yet it has done so in very different ways. For, unlike its near neighbour, it has not succumbed to dramatic or fundamental political change. Certainly, it was affected by the Arab Spring. Its protests were sufficiently large, frequent and angry to frighten the regime into making several noteworthy concessions. Opposition parties were promised more media coverage. A new job-creation scheme was launched. And most significant of all, the nineteen-year-long state of emergency was lifted.[1] Yet the regime did not fall. President Abdelaziz Bouteflika not only survived but went on to win an unprecedented fourth term in office. Algeria is puzzling, therefore, not for how it has changed but the reasons why it has remained the same.

Paradoxically, some of the main factors that were initially highlighted as likely reasons why Algeria would soon follow Tunisia down the path of decisive unrest were quickly recast as impediments to its political transformation. Commenting on the growing expectations of specialists that Bouteflika's regime would be one of the next to fall, James Gelvin notes the high level of expert emphasis placed on Algeria as a trendsetter.[2] The country, so the argument ran, had been here before. In the late 1980s it had been one of the very few Arab states to form part of the so-called Third Wave of democratisation that had been triggered by the end of the Cold War. In June 1990 and December 1991 it had held free and fair multiparty elections which had been won by the opposition Islamic Salvation Front (Front Islamique du Salut, FIS).[3] By the time the Arab Spring began, therefore, Algeria had already experimented with democracy. Its citizens had demanded and won greater political freedoms once before. Moreover, they had done so in a way similar to that in which Tunisians had during the Arab Spring. They had experience of pressuring their government into introducing democratic reforms.

Furthermore, Algerians bore many of the same burdens in 2011 that had prompted them to act before and which had driven their neighbours to oust Ben Ali.[4] Conditions in the country, therefore, appeared propitious to decisive unrest. Gelvin argues that four factors in particular encouraged this perception.[5] The first was the government's abandonment of its 'ruling bargain' with the people whereby, in return for withholding their political rights, it promised to satisfy their basic material needs.[6] This social contract had been systematically eroded since the early 1980s as successive governments had rejected Arab socialism in favour of greater economic liberalisation.[7] The second was the demographic youth bulge which made it hard for many young adults to find gainful or legal employment,[8] and prompted thousands to try each year to migrate illegally to Europe.[9] The third was the rapid rise in food prices which drove down standards of living.[10] And the fourth was the air of crisis which seemed to hang over the regime as it remained locked in battle, as it had been for the past twenty years, with a range of armed Islamist factions.

Yet these precedents, similarities and appearances were deceiving. The regime did not succumb but emerged from the Arab Spring largely unscathed. Indeed, of all the region's republics, Algeria was one of the least affected by the protests.[11] As a result, the scholarly debate has turned to explaining why this was, to identifying and analysing the causes of the country's exceptionalism. Among the factors most frequently highlighted are the size, strength and determination of the Algerian military and security forces. Their role was both vital and varied. They defended the regime. They policed and contained the protestors. They protected 'key urban areas – in central Algiers around the Parliament, the Senate, and other government buildings and left the rest to the rioters'.[12] In so doing, they helped stop the demonstrations from either metastasising into something more dangerous to the government or easily sweeping Bouteflika from power.

The military's and security forces' willingness to defend the regime inevitably gave it confidence. It was not abandoned by the army as Ben Ali and Mubarak were. It was not attacked by mutinous units as Gaddafi was. Bouteflika's long-standing compact with the military held firm.[13] So armed, both psychologically and materially, it simply had to keep its nerve. And it could also draw comfort from the considerable experience its defenders had accumulated over the past two decades. They had successfully dealt with numerous serious threats. By the time the Arab Spring began, they had been slowly strangling the life out of several terror groups, most notably al-Qaeda in the Islamic Maghreb (AQIM), for a number of years. Paradoxically, this threat was itself the result of their earlier success against various insurgent factions, including the Armed Islamic Group (Groupe Islamique Armé, GIA), the Islamic Salvation Army (Armée Islamique du Salut, AIS) and the Salafist Group for Preaching and Combat (Groupe Salafist pour la Prédication et la Combat, GSPC). Indeed, the pressure they had brought to bear had helped force these factions to recalibrate their armed campaigns and confront the regime in less direct, more asymmetric ways.[14]

Just as crucially, the country's armed and security forces demonstrated a capacity to learn and evolve. Throughout the early and mid 1990s, they successfully adapted to the rapidly growing insurgency for which they were initially ill-prepared.[15] And, more pertinently, by the time the Arab Spring protests began, they had identified and absorbed many of the most important lessons from the Black October riots of 1988. Arguably, the army's response to these demonstrations had contributed greatly to the chain of political events that had led first to the multiparty elections of June 1990 and December 1991, its subsequent intervention in the nascent democratic process, and the ensuing serious violence from which the country has yet to emerge fully. Unsurprisingly, the most vital lessons were how best to manage a series of large, well-coordinated protests. In 2011, therefore, the military and security forces did not respond with anything like the same level of brutality that they had in 1988. In so doing, they ensured that their actions 'did not become the cause of further protests (as had happened in Tunisia)', to the extent that 'even radical acts, such as a self-immolation on January 12, failed to reignite the contestation'.[16]

Yet, paradoxically and perhaps fortuitously, the military and security forces were still able to draw some benefits from their past actions and, in particular, the fearsome reputations they had rightly earned as a result of what they had done. For, almost as soon as the Arab Spring protests began in Algeria, the local press made a connection with the Black October riots.[17] While this invocation certainly did not deter the tens of thousands of demonstrators who repeatedly took to the streets of Algiers, Oran and the country's other major urban centres throughout early 2011 and, with far less frequency, in 2012 and 2013, it helped to establish the early psychological context. Algeria's Arab Spring did not take place in an historical vacuum. The shadow of the recent past loomed large for everyone. And no one wanted to return to the excessive violence and widespread bloodshed of before.

The strength and coherence of Algeria's security apparatus are undoubtedly integral to the country's experiences and political development over the last few years. Indeed, Algeria has high organisational power. Yet this alone cannot explain what has happened there, particularly the United States' and European Union's responses to the Bouteflika regime *after* they sought to reposition themselves on the right side of history.[18] Crucially, why did they not put more pressure on Algiers to democratise? Why, given everything that had happened in the country and wider region, did they not press for greater liberalisation during the build-up to the

2014 presidential election, especially after Bouteflika confirmed that he would stand for a fourth term? Why were they seemingly content to allow Algeria to remain competitive authoritarian?

As with Tunisia, the West's failure to put more democratic pressure on the Bouteflika regime was due to both reluctance and poor co-ordination. Despite everything that had happened and all they had said, the United States and European Union remained unwilling to force the issue. And what pressure they were prepared to bring to bear was marked by many of the same inconsistencies that had diluted their influence over Tunis. Yet, important differences in their interactions with the two regimes remained. Though the West was anxious to avoid destabilising Ben Ali for fear of encouraging and enabling Islamist groups to gain greater power and influence, it was also prepared to accept (if not believe) the promises he made slowly to liberalise the country's politics. Its dealings with Algiers, in contrast, continue to be dominated by security concerns to the general exclusion of most other issues. Terrorism and energy, fighting al-Qaeda and safeguarding the flow of Algerian gas, are uppermost in its thoughts.

And there is another crucial difference – capability. The West did not put as much pressure on the Ben Ali regime as it could have done. It does not possess the same level of influence over Algiers. For the United States' and European Union's linkage to Algeria is but medium and their leverage over the ruling elite only low. Accordingly, their capacity to demand change, to press for democratisation, is reduced. This makes Algeria a more conventional case for Levitsky and Way's model. Washington's and Brussels' weaker ties to, and influence over, Algiers mean that the regime's high organisational power plays a more decisive role in determining its political development. Algeria has remained competitive authoritarian because that is what those in power want and are able to achieve. They currently have the means to withstand any democratising pressure put on them by internal and external forces.

To sustain this analysis and argument, and facilitate Algeria's comparison with its neighbours, the chapter is organised along the same lines as each of Levitsky and Way's original cases and this volume's other country studies. The first section assesses the strength of Algeria's links to the United States and the European Union across the six categories of connection. The second considers how much leverage each has over the country and whether they must compete with a Black Knight patron. Section three then evaluates the regime's organisational power, the strength and cohesion of its ruling party and coercive forces. And, finally, the fourth section charts the regime's origins and development, especially since 2005.

Linkage

The strength of Algeria's links to North America and Europe vary significantly across the six categories of connection. In some – technocratic, social, information and civil society – the ties are strong. Yet, in the remaining (arguably most important) two – economic and intergovernmental – these bonds are weaker, thereby ensuring that the country's overall linkage to the West is medium rather than high. The reasons for this discrepancy are rooted in Algeria's past and, as such, raise important and challenging questions about some of Levitsky and Way's underlying assumptions. For they argue that strong linkage is determined by 'historical factors, including colonialism, military occupation, and . . . alliances' and, above all, 'geographic proximity'.[19] The nearer a country is to either Europe or North America, and the closer its past association with them, the more likely it is to have strong links to the EU and US today. Indeed, powerful bonds to one often precipitate closer ties to the other.

This certainly explains those strong links that Algeria currently has to the United States and to various European countries. That so many of its citizens live in, rely on, and look to Spain, Italy, Germany and, above all, France for jobs, training, news, and opportunities is the result of numerous, powerful historical factors. This trans-Mediterranean population, along with the aspirations and impulses which created and sustain it, inevitably account for the close human ties forged between Algeria, these countries and the European Union more broadly. Yet these factors have an additional, more divisive, dimension. For it is Algeria's shared history with France that makes it such a wary and, at times, reluctant political, military and economic partner. It is this shared history that is preventing the creation of stronger intergovernmental and economic links today.

While important, this lesson does not fundamentally compromise Levitsky and Way's model. Nor does it completely invalidate their specific claim. History and geography, even when they have given rise to difficult and painful encounters, invariably create and sustain robust bonds between a country and the United States or European Union. Rather, it represents an important caveat: that sometimes such shared pasts, which were frequently enabled by geographic proximity, can generate and perpetuate, by various cultural means over several generations, powerful emotions that can complicate relations today. As will be shown, Algeria *could* have stronger economic and intergovernmental ties to Europe than those that it presently has. The opportunities and mechanisms to enhance them exist while the EU's appetite to forge them is hearty. Algiers's continuing, albeit slowly softening, reluctance to do so is due to its colonial experiences, and the national myths, attitudes, expectations and demands they sustain. History and geography are not neutral forces that only encourage greater linkage. They are complex processes that can separate as well unite.

Like Tunisia, Algeria is a member of both the MEPI and BMENA policy frameworks. While the MEPI is currently supporting four local and three regional projects with Algeria-specific dimensions,[20] Algiers does not receive nearly as much aid and development funding as its neighbours.[21] Between 2009 and 2014, Washington planned to give Algeria $40.83 million of financial assistance but Tunisia $358.62 million.[22] Moreover, between 2009 and 2015, the United States did not provide Algiers with any Foreign Military Financing credits but gave Tunis $142.17 million worth.[23]

Algeria's relations with the European Union are also not as close as those of its near neighbour. While Tunisia's attitude towards, and interactions with, the European Union have long been willing and enthusiastic, Algeria's have been hesitant and circumspect. Initially, Algiers was eager to join the EMP. It saw the new framework as a golden opportunity to rehabilitate its international reputation in the wake of its suspension of the democratic process in January 1992, subsequent persecution of FIS members and supporters, and launch of its uncompromising armed campaign against the various insurgent factions it had done so much to create and provoke.[24] Yet this early enthusiasm quickly dissipated in the face of EU reluctance to include 'specific counter-terrorism provisions' in the country's association agreement[25] to the extent that, in 1997, President Liamine Zéroual suspended the AA negotiations, thereby effectively throwing Algeria's EMP application into abeyance. These talks did not start again until 2000 and were only truly revitalised when international events and attitudes shifted in Algeria's favour. Following the terror attacks on the World Trade Center and Pentagon on 11 September 2001, the European Union finally relented and agreed to include the provisions Algiers wanted.[26] The AA was duly signed on 22 April 2002 and finally came into force on 1 September 2005, nearly a decade after the EMP's initial launch. In contrast, Tunisia's and Morocco's agreements were signed on 17 July 1995 and 26 February 1996, and took effect on 1 March 1998 and 1 March 2000 respectively.[27]

The warning signs for the EU, therefore, were plainly visible. Algeria was not to be persuaded, pressured, cajoled or browbeaten as perhaps its neighbours might. Even when the regime was at its most isolated and vulnerable – when global oil and gas prices were at their lowest in a generation,[28] when it confronted a large and determined insurgency that had the backing of many ordinary Algerians,[29] when it stood on the brink of being cast from power,[30] was being kept at arm's length by most Western governments at a time when it needed their help most of all – it held fast to its demands. And, in the end, it prevailed and Brussels compromised.

Algiers's determination only to join the EU's frameworks when it was in its clear interests to do so, and on terms which it deemed acceptable, was inevitably buttressed by its experiences in negotiating the AA. By resolutely matching the European Union's sustained opposition to the terrorism provisions it had initially proposed, it had eventually prevailed and gained the settlement it had originally wanted. Paradoxically, Algiers cited the successful conclusion and imminent implementation of its AA as a reason why it did not need or want to join the ENP.[31] Rather than encourage Algiers to join other frameworks and seek closer relations with Europe, as Brussels had hoped, the agreement of the AA saw it lapse into reticence. Of all the EU's southern Mediterranean partners, Algeria was the only one not to sign up to the new framework.

As well as being unnecessary, Algiers decried the ENP as Eurocentric and unhelpful. It argued that the framework spoke primarily of and to the EU's new-found obsession with security and good governance,[32] and, as a result, did not pay adequate attention to either the wider region's urgent socio-economic concerns or advancing Algeria's strategic objectives.[33] Not until 2012, therefore, did the Algerian Association Council (AC) (the body charged with leading and conducting negotiations with the EU) acquiesce to open talks with Brussels over the country's action plan (AP).[34] Just as with the AA, progress has been slow and no agreement has yet been reached. In contrast, Tunisia and Morocco both consented to join the ENP almost as soon as it was launched (in May 2004), signed their APs shortly after (on 9 December 2004),[35] and implemented them seven months later (on 4 and 27 July 2005 respectively).[36]

While Algeria has, with the recasting of the EMP, joined the UfM, it remains a cautious and only tentatively engaged member. As the product of mainly French diplomatic efforts, the framework was duly treated with considerable wariness by Algiers. It alone of all the southern Mediterranean partners evinced little desire to take 'an active part in the UfM's institutional arrangements'.[37] During the 'fierce deal-making that preceded the setting up of the secretariat', it declined either to bid to host the new institution or lobby to fill any of the executive positions that were being created.[38] Moreover, it has displayed a similar level of circumspection towards some of the framework's programmes and initiatives, including those with goals it broadly supports. Despite its desire to develop the country's solar energy potential, it has responded cautiously to the framework's Mediterranean Solar Plan.[39] Again, Algeria was the only southern Mediterranean partner to display such reticence.

In the light of its diminished involvement in the European Union's various policy frameworks, Algeria has not received as much investment through their associated financial mechanisms as either of its immediate neighbours. Under the EMP's accompanying MEDA programme, the country was given €164 million and €338.8 million in funding between 1995 and 1999, and 2000 and 2006 respectively. This compared unfavourably to the €428 million and €517.6 million, and €660 million and €980.1 million, granted to Tunisia and Morocco over the same the periods.[40] And, given Algeria's far more circumspect involvement with the ENP framework, to the extent that it opened negotiations over its AP only in 2012, it has received significantly less European Neighbourhood and Partnership Instrument (ENPI) investment than either of its neighbours. Between 2007 and 2013, the country was awarded €366.1 million in ENPI funds compared to the €775 million and €1.3 billion given to Tunisia and Morocco respectively.[41] These disbursements include the €35 million, €140 million and €115 million granted to Algeria, Tunisia and Morocco under the SPRING programme.[42]

In addition to concluding its association agreement and opening negotiations on its action plan, Algiers signed a Memorandum of Understanding (MOU) with the European Commission on 7 July 2013 on establishing a Strategic Energy Partnership (SEP) with the EU.[43] Talks between the two sides had begun in 2006 but had quickly stalled as Bouteflika's government had objected to Brussels's attempts to use its own 'market regulatory norms' as the basis of their agreement.[44] Algiers had also been frustrated by the EU's overly technocratic focus, its seeming obsession with rules and guiding principles that not even all its member states and institutions believed in or adhered to.[45]

While the signing of the MOU was a noteworthy step forward, it represented slight return on seven years of talks. More importantly, the SEP has still not been concluded nor seems likely to be any time soon.[46] As with all Algeria's negotiations with the European Union, these discussions have proved as difficult as they have been protracted. That both parties are still committed to them testifies to the importance Algiers and Brussels place on what they are trying to achieve and of energy to their relationship. For each side depends on the other. Algeria is one of the European Union's most important energy providers. In 2013, the country was the EU's eighth largest source of oil (3.9 per cent),[47] fourth of natural gas (22 per cent) and second of Liquefied Natural Gas (LNG) (22 per cent).[48] And its importance to particular member states is even greater still. In 2013, it was the largest supplier of natural gas to both Portugal (24.4 terawatt hours, TWh) and Spain (192 TWh), and the third and fourth biggest to Italy (132.3 TWh) and France (59.1 TWh) respectively.[49]

The European Union is, by a considerable margin, Algeria's most important energy customer. In 2013, Europe imported 72 per cent of the country's crude oil and 75 per cent of its natural gas.[50] And its export capacity to the bloc will soon increase once work on the new Galsi pipeline to Italy and Spain has been completed.[51] Hydrocarbons dominate Algeria's balance of trade with the European Union. Between 2010 and 2014 the total value of the EU's imports from the country was €164 billion of which €139.32 billion comprised mineral fuels, lubricants and related materials.[52] Furthermore, in 2013, the European Union took 65 per cent of all Algeria's exports and provided it with 52.2 per cent of its imports. In that year, the country conducted more trade with the EU (59.1 per cent) than the rest of the world combined.[53]

While clearly not on the same scale, Algeria's trade with the United States has grown in value over the past two decades and is similarly dominated by hydrocarbons.[54] Between 2010 and 2013 the total value of US imports from Algeria was $45.01 billion of which $44.98 billion comprised fuels.[55] Much of this bilateral trade is conducted under the TIFA Algeria signed with the United States on 13 July 2001.[56] Like Tunisia's agreement, it commits Algiers and Washington to 'take appropriate measures to encourage and facilitate the exchange of goods and services and to secure favorable conditions for long-term development and diversification of trade between their respective nationals and companies' including establishing a bilateral 'Council on Trade and Investment . . . to hold consultations . . . ; . . . identify agreements appropriate for negotiation; and . . . identify and work toward the removal of impediments to trade and investment'.[57] The United States is also actively encouraging and supporting Algeria's efforts to join the WTO. Once it has done so, it will be able to participate more fully in the United States MEFTA initiative.

The value of Algeria's exports to the United States have grown exponentially over the past two decades. Between 1995 and 1999, their annual average value was $1.75 billion.[58] Between 2000 and 2004, they nearly quadrupled to $4.23 billion.[59] And then, between 2005 and 2010, they more than tripled again to $14.57 billion,[60] before decreasing to $9.98 billion between 2010 and 2013.[61] The increase in the value of its imports from the United States has been less dramatic but more consistent. Between 1995 and 2004 their annual average value was $1 billion.[62] Between 2005 and 2009 they rose slightly to $1.44 billion.[63] And then, between 2010 and 2013, they nearly doubled to $2.11 billion.[64] By 2013, therefore, the United States was Algeria's second largest export market (8.1 per cent) and third biggest import partner (4.3 per cent).[65]

Algeria has also been able to generate increasing amounts of FDI over the past twenty years. Between 1996 and 1999, it attracted $357 million of overseas investment on average each year.[66] Between 2000 and 2004, this amount grew significantly to $793 million per year.[67] Then, between 2005 and 2013, it more than doubled again to $2.01 billion a year.[68] These figures do not include the considerable sums sent into the country each year by the tens of thousands of Algerians living abroad. For decades now, this expatriate population has provided vital financial support to an even larger number of people living in Algeria. Between 1995 and 1999, remittances were worth an average of $982 million a year.[69] And between 2000 and 2004 their value grew to an average of $1.34 billion per year.[70] Then, between 2005 and 2009, their value fell markedly to an average of $142 million a year.[71] And, most recently, between 2010 and 2013, their worth increased a little again to an average of $205 million per year.[72] Even allowing for the significant decline in their value over the past decade, these payments still ensure that millions of ordinary Algerians have a powerful financial interest in their country maintaining cordial relations with those in which their friends and relatives live and work.

The diaspora also plays an important social role as part of the vast transnational network of people and communities which connects Algeria to other, mainly Western, countries. For, as of 2012, there were an estimated 961,850 Algerian citizens (or 2.9 per cent of the country's total population) living abroad. Of these, most (721,796) were based in France. But many were also living in Spain (60,207), Canada (33,575), Italy (23,278), Britain (22,000) and the United States (17,068). Taken together, there were 950,641 Algerians (or 98.8 per cent of the total diaspora population) living in Western countries.[73] In recognition of their great number and significant financial contribution, these émigrés are allowed to elect eight of the Algerian parliament's 389 members.[74] While the political effect of this right may be limited, especially under the current regime, it still performs an important social function by helping to bind those living overseas to the country they have left behind.

A significant number of those Algerians who travel overseas do so to further their educations. In the 2013/2014 academic year, there were 21,935 Algerian nationals registered at French universities alone. And Algerians have comprised the third largest foreign continent in French universities in each of the last six academic years.[75] Most of those who study in France and elsewhere in the West make their own arrangements to do so. Only a tiny fraction participates in the exchange programmes run by either Brussels or Washington, such as the EU's Erasmus and Tempus Mundus schemes,[76] or the MEPI's Student Leaders Programme (SLP) and Leaders for Democracy Fellowship (LDF) initiative.[77] Indeed, to date, only fifty MA students, one PhD candidate and sixteen scholars from Algeria have taken part in the Erasmus programme.[78]

The majority of those who study in Europe and North America, therefore, are from wealthy families. Attending a Western college or university has become an important coming-of-age experience for many affluent young Algerians. By virtue of the educations they receive and qualifications they are awarded, and having the socio-economic backgrounds that allow them to study abroad in the first place, they are well placed to secure rewarding and responsible jobs in either the public or private sectors once they return home. In this way, Algeria's long-standing and strong technocratic links with the West, and especially with France and Europe, are maintained.

Algeria's émigré communities are also important sources of alternative news and additional information. They can share Western media coverage of global affairs with their contacts in North Africa. They can explain to their friends and relations how events in Algeria are viewed and interpreted in the rest of the world. They can better enable Algerians to question and challenge the regime's arguments and claims. The improved access to information offered by the diaspora has been greatly enhanced by the rapid spread of Internet and mobile phone use in Algeria. In 2000 only 0.5 per cent of the country's population had access to the World Wide Web.[79] By 2005, it had increased exponentially to 5.8 per cent.[80] By 2010, it had more than doubled again to 12.5 per cent. And, most recently, in 2013, it had jumped to 16.5 per cent.[81] The rise in mobile phone subscriptions over this period has been even more dramatic. In 2000, virtually no Algerian subscribed to a mobile telephone service.[82] By 2005, this had risen to 40 per cent of the population.[83] By 2010 it had more than doubled again to 88 per cent. And, by 2013, it had jumped to 101 per cent.[84]

The movement of so many Algerians, both to and through Europe and North America, has inevitably encouraged and led to the establishment of a range of transnational civil society groups.[85] And, within Algeria, the European Union continues to make funding available through the ENPI, CSF and other initiatives to a range of civil society groups and projects. For example, in June 2015, the EU Delegation in Algiers invited organisations working with young people to compete for up to €4 million of funding offered by the European Union's Youth Support Programme.[86] There are now, therefore, a growing number of civil society groups, both in and connected to, Algeria which, either through their members, activities, target constituencies or sources of funding, have strong and important links to Europe.

Leverage

The West's leverage over Algeria is not only low but cannot, unless there is a profound and very unlikely shift in circumstances, be higher. For the country meets two of the three criteria Levitsky and Way set for determining regime ability to withstand outside pressure.[87] It has a large economy with an estimated GDP of \$214.1 billion.[88] And it is a major energy producer, extracting 1.2 million barrels of crude oil and 6.4 trillion cubic feet of natural gas a day during the course of an average year.[89] Indeed, the only criteria it does not meet is possession of nuclear weapons. It does not need, therefore, the backing of a Black Knight patron (which it does not have) effectively to deter, resist and mitigate the limited democratising pressure the United States and European Union are willing and able to bring to bear.

Moreover, what leverage Washington and Brussels do possess is rendered less effective by their inconsistent use of it. Their failure to press Algeria more rigorously is due mainly to the country's importance as a security provider and the assessment this has led them to make about how best to treat Algiers to ensure that their interests are met. For, crucially, Algeria has been at the forefront of the fight against Islamist terrorism in the Maghreb and wider Western Mediterranean for nearly two-and-a-half decades.

Ranged against the country's successive military-backed governments over this period have been an assortment of violent factions, including the Armed Islamic Movement (Mouvement Islamique Armé, MIA), the Movement for the Islamic State (Mouvement pour l'État Islamique, MEI), the GIA, the AIS, the GSPC and AQIM. The campaigns these groups continue to wage (for they have never united and pursued a common set of aims) have made Algeria both the site for, and epicentre of, much of the Islamist violence that has plagued the region. In addition to the scores of attacks carried out by these groups, they have also enabled (through the provision of money, weapons, training and encouragement) like-minded factions in other parts of Africa and elsewhere to take up arms. And, in so doing, they have compelled Algeria's military and security forces to grow, learn, adapt and improve. Not only has Algeria witnessed much of the worst Islamist violence to take place in the region over the past twenty or so years, and is home to some of the largest and longest-established terror groups operating in the Maghreb which are, in turn, helping factions elsewhere to carry out their own attacks, but its armed and security forces are the most experienced and best adapted of any in North Africa to wage a sustained counterterrorism campaign. In more ways than one, therefore, Algeria is, and will remain at, the heart of the struggle against Islamist terrorism in the region for the foreseeable future.

And the country's importance as a bulwark against Islamist terrorism has only increased since the start of the Arab Spring. The political upheaval that was unleashed by the various iterations of the Jasmine Revolution has created significant opportunities for AQIM and its fellow travellers to exploit. Libya's reduction to a state of failure has been particularly significant. The Council of Deputies' authority is either challenged or simply ignored, to the extent that there is currently no single nationally and internationally recognised government exercising a monopoly over the legitimate means of coercion throughout the whole of the country's territory. As a result, the borders are not secure or properly policed. Many of the weapons and pieces of equipment belonging to Gaddafi's assorted armed forces are unaccounted for.[90] So, too, are some of the munitions France, Qatar, the United Arab Emirates and other international actors have provided their respective local allies over the past five years.[91]

Unsurprisingly, some of these missing arms have made their way, by various routes, into the hands of AQIM fighters.[92] Algiers has responded by intensifying its efforts to isolate the six hundred to nine hundred militants at large in the mountainous and heavily wooded area of Kabylia, and deploying an extra sixty thousand troops along its eastern border.[93] Others of the region's countries have also been adversely affected by Libya's failure. Mali's protracted civil war was exacerbated by the return of around three thousand of Gaddafi's Tuareg auxiliaries still in possession of most of their arms and equipment.[94] Tunisia has similarly been flooded with weapons precipitating the sharp increase in the number of terror attacks carried out both on its territory and by its citizens. Up to three hundred of its nationals fought for AQIM against French forces in northern Mali between January and March 2013. A majority of the militants who seized the Tigantourine gas facility near Ain Amenas in southern Algeria on 16 January 2013 were Tunisian citizens.[95] And the devastating gun attacks at the Bardo Museum in Tunis on 18 March 2015 and on a tourist beach in Sousse on 26 June 2015 were carried out by Tunisian fighters belonging to AQIM and Islamic State (IS) respectively.

Many of the region's other governments, however, are not able to respond as effectively to the Islamist terror threat as Algiers. The Council of Deputies does not control and, therefore, cannot adequately police large parts of Libya. Bamako's authority over Mali's northern territories was tenuous long before the start of the civil war in January 2012 and is only weaker now. Nouakchott has enjoyed some recent successes against AQIM units operating within Mauritania but has needed extensive help from France to achieve them.[96] And Tunis is struggling to maintain the fragile political consensus so crucial to the forging of the country's new democratic settlement, and rehabilitate the armed and security forces. Indeed, all of Algeria's neighbours must confront this growing terror threat at precisely the time circumstances have rendered them less able to do so. Algiers is better placed to respond not only because of its extensive counterterrorism experience but because it has been less disturbed by the Arab Spring.

Yet Algeria's role as a key security provider is marked by a surprising paradox. For, even though Western governments acknowledge it as such, they do not provide it with nearly as much help and support as they do Tunisia. Most military-related aid is furnished by the United States and individual European countries rather than by the European Union. To date, Algiers has been given far less funding for peace and security projects by Washington than its neighbour. And, whereas Tunis has been granted millions of dollars in Foreign Military Financing credits by the United States, Algeria has received none. This discrepancy cannot easily be attributed to capability and necessity alone, to Washington channelling funds to where it believes they are needed most. For, while Tunisia's military was starved of resources by Ben Ali, and is, as a result, desperately trying to make up for lost time and modernise, its security forces were generously provided for. Moreover, the scale of the Islamist terror threat confronting Tunis has not, until very recently, been as great as that facing Algiers. Put starkly, no Tunisian government, past or present, has had to deal with a comparable level of threat for the same amount of time that the Bouteflika regime has. In terms of capability and necessity, therefore, Tunisia has received levels of military and security assistance from the United States and other Western governments that Algeria has long had a stronger operational claim to.

That this is so casts the United States' and European Union's Algeria dilemma in a slightly unedifying light. On the one hand, they appear eager for the Bouteflika regime to succeed, to wage an effective counterterrorism campaign against AQIM. Yet, on the other, they seem reluctant to back this aspiration with the types and levels of support they have provided other similar regimes, some of which have faced far less serious threats. Indeed, the West is acting like Algiers's unwilling accomplice. Western governments want the Bouteflika regime to remain sufficiently strong and capable to deal with the danger but do not want to be seen to be helping it too much or in certain, mainly security related, ways.

This seeming contradiction is partly informed by the persistence of the dark reputation the country's armed and security forces acquired while fighting the insurgency of the 1990s. Though the US, French and other Western governments were not displeased by the Algerian military's prevention of the FIS's almost certain victory in the legislative election,[97] they and their citizenries grew increasingly alarmed by the rapidly rising level of violence and growing number of reports accusing the army and security forces of failing to minimise civilian casualties,[98] abusing the human rights of suspects and prisoners,[99] and even perpetrating some of the war crimes attributed to the Islamists.[100] In response, Washington and the European Union quietly distanced themselves from Algiers and placed restrictions on the amounts and types of weapons that could be exported to the country.[101] This pressure was to prove instrumental in driving the Zéroual regime to seek membership of the EMP.

By the time that it did, however, the West's united front had already started to fragment as individual governments questioned the wisdom of seeking to isolate the country. One of the first to break ranks was France which, by virtue of the strength of its hostility to the FIS, was broadly sympathetic to what the Algerian military had done.[102] The last vestige of the Élysée Palace's ostensible early concern for the behaviour of Algeria's armed and security forces was torn away by the GIA's hijacking of Air France flight 8969 on Christmas Eve 1994,[103] and subsequent bombing of the Paris Metro on 25 July, 17 August and 17 October 1995 and a Jewish school in Lyon on 7 September of that year. Yet, even before then, it had started to provide Algiers with increasing amounts of material support. In November 1994, it announced that it had recently sold Algiers some decidedly military-looking equipment.[104] The following year it encouraged the European Union to invite the Zéroual regime to join the EMP.

In December 2002, President Bush lifted the United States' own embargo on the sale of military equipment to Algeria, thereby bringing an end to the West's limited and half-hearted efforts to sanction the country's armed forces.[105] Almost from the moment these measures were introduced, they were challenged, rejected and emasculated by a succession of Western governments for reasons of national security. In so doing, the West not only reduced democracy and security to an unforgiving binary, whereby the achievement of one was assumed to come at the expense of the other, but also made clear which of these outcomes it prized most highly. Moreover, in making this compromise, in not pressing Algiers harder to reform, the West sided with a regime it had previously criticised yet had, in part, given up trying to change. International circumstances, not modifications of behaviour, made the West back Algiers. As a result, Western governments feel compelled to support the Bouteflika regime but at something of a distance.[106]

Algeria is also a vital energy provider to several EU countries. France, Italy, Portugal and Spain, in particular, all depend heavily on Algerian gas, to an extent that the European Commission is anxious to conclude a Strategic Energy Partnership with Algiers better to safeguard supply. Yet the European Union's concerns are not solely the result of its high reliance on Algeria. They have been given additional weight by the recent political, economic and attitudinal shifts the EU believes it has identified taking place within the Bouteflika regime and wider country. More specifically, it fears the reawakening of Algerian resource nationalism which would probably lead the regime to limit foreign involvement in the country's energy sector. It is alarmed by the rapid growth in domestic energy demand which could reduce the amounts of oil and gas available for export. It is wary of the Algerian oil and gas company Sonatrach's new business strategy which may result in European companies and investors being increasingly excluded from the Algerian market.[107] And it is mindful, paradoxically, of the fall in global gas prices which could drive Algiers to explore either establishing or joining an OPEC-style cartel with greater urgency.[108]

Confirmation of Algeria's special significance as a security provider, the dilemma this creates and sustains in Western capitals, and the EU's inconsistent application of its own rules and principles are provided by the country's protracted application to join the World Trade Organization. The Barcelona Declaration affirmed the signatories' commitment to create a free-trade area by 2010 'with due observance of the obligations resulting from the WTO'.[109] This clause coyly expressed a crucial and fully understood expectation: that all partner states would actively seek to join the WTO. That Algeria is the only North African partner not yet a member is entirely in keeping with its broader approach to the European Union. It has repeatedly demonstrated its willingness to adopt a unique position, to take a separate line in its dealings with Brussels. More instructive is the length of time its WTO application has taken so far. The country's membership working party was established on 17 June 1987 but did not meet until more than a decade later on 22 April 1998.[110] Perhaps unsurprisingly, therefore, its application has taken nearly thirty years and is still ongoing. Algiers is seemingly in little rush to expedite the process or satisfy this key requirement of the Barcelona Process. And the European Union is sufficiently accepting of the country's slow progress not only to allow it to join the EMP/UfM but actively solicit its membership of the ENP and seek closer working relations with it on other matters.

Börzel and van Hüllen attribute the EU's seeming double standards to a 'substantive inconsistency' within the ENP.[111] Certainly, the start of the Arab Spring was a damning indictment of the framework, not because it opposed the democratic changes being demanded by so many Tunisians, Algerians, Moroccans and others but because it had clearly failed to deliver them itself. For the framework's primary purpose had been (and remains) to help the European Union promote good governance in the Mediterranean with the same effectiveness and success that it had achieved in Central and Eastern Europe. The onset of the protests, therefore, provided stark confirmation that it had failed to achieve what it had been set up expressly to accomplish.

Indeed, the ENP was created with a fundamental flaw, a structural weakness that greatly impaired its ability to bring about political change in North Africa. For, unlike in Europe, it could not encourage its reforms with the offer of EU membership. Deprived of this ultimate inducement, it had to trust to the appeal of those lesser benefits which could be accessed by closer (but not complete) integration with the European Union.[112] These enticements were far from inconsequential. Yet the European Union struggled to make the most of them owing to its ineffective 'use of conditionality and capacity building'.[113] As a result, it failed to push the southern Mediterranean partners quite as hard as it could to become more democratic.

According to Börzel and van Hüllen, the EU's failure to achieve more, however, was not because it lacked internal cohesion or 'actorness'.[114] The European Commission and member states consistently spoke with 'one voice' in their dealings with the southern Mediterranean partners.[115] Rather, this failure was because of the EU's inaccurate or unrealistic assumption about the compatibility of its political goals. For it believed that democratic and effective governance were complementary, that by promoting one it could strengthen the other even in the short term.[116] Yet, the moment it began negotiating individual action plans with each partner state, it effectively abandoned this principle.[117] Instead of treating democratic and effective governance as mutually reinforcing, it cast them as mutually exclusive. As a result, these negotiations became marked by a paradoxical inversion. The more authoritarian a regime was, and in need of having outside democratising pressure put upon it, the less willing the European Union was to press it to change for fear of the instability that could be unleashed by doing so.[118] Time and again, the EU gave priority to effective over democratic government.

Organisational Power

Overall, the Bouteflika regime has high organisational power although its capacity varies across the three subdimensions. The bedrock of its strength is the country's armed and security forces. These are large, well funded and cohesive, and have a meaningful presence across much of the country. And, though the regime does not exercise total control over them – final authority still rests with their commanding officers – it has sufficient influence to be able to rely upon them when it needs to. The regime also controls the most important parts of the Algerian economy, namely, the oil and gas sectors. While successive governments have allowed, and even encouraged, greater private and foreign involvement in other hitherto state-owned industries, they have jealously guarded their domination of these two.

Ostensibly, the only restriction on the regime's organisational power is the absence of a dominant ruling party. Bouteflika currently has the backing of the two largest parties in parliament – the National Liberation Front (Front de Libération National, FLN) and the National Rally for Democracy (Rassemblement National Démocratique, RND) – yet neither of them commands a majority. Such a situation was unknown in Ben Ali's Tunisia where the ruling RCD always held far more seats than all the other parties combined. The FLN's and RND's failure to achieve a comparable level of primacy is in part due to the existence of the other. Ultimately, though, the regime has never allowed either of them to achieve the sort of pre-eminence that the FLN used to enjoy prior to President Benjedid's abolition of one-party rule in 1989.

Since then, no government has tried to recreate the status quo ante. In truth, it would have been politically difficult for it to do so. Yet there was much more they could have done short of that. They could have manipulated the electoral process to ensure that either the FLN or RND enjoyed the same level of dominance as the RCD. They could have turned one or other of them into a mass-membership organisation capable of mobilising large swathes of the population. Certainly, this was one of the functions the FLN used to perform under President Boumedienne. But, to date, no government has seriously attempted any of this.

Their disinclination to do so reveals much about Algeria's competitive authoritarian order, the strength of the Bouteflika regime, the complexion of inter-institutional rivalries within it and the potency of the non-violent opposition. The regime neither needs nor wants a dominant ruling party to achieve high organisational power, in part because the demise of the single-party order removed one of the triumvirate of institutions that had ruled the country from independence to 1989.[119] With it gone, the power and influence of the other two members of the triad were inevitably enhanced. And, while this may not be to Bouteflika's personal disadvantage – because he has one less institution to play off against the others – the military does not lament its passing as a rival. That the regime does not seem to need such a party speaks volumes about the weakness of the opposition forces ranged against it. It has not had to create one because the current arrangements are sufficient to give Bouteflika and the ruling elite the level of control over the political process they crave. As a result, the regime's party strength must be graded medium rather than high.

Algeria's security apparatus is just as divided as Tunisia's was under Ben Ali. Deep and bitter rivalries separate its constituent parts, most notably the army and the Department of Intelligence and Security (Département du Renseignement et de la Sécurité, DRS). Indeed, the competition between them helps explain their involvement in the political process as each seeks to safeguard its interests against the other.[120] Yet, unlike Ben Ali, Bouteflika has been careful not to choose sides. He has tried to retain the support and goodwill of both. In December 2010, his government announced that it was giving most of the country's 170,000 police officers both a 50 per cent pay rise and back pay for the previous three years. Exactly a year later, it announced a similar deal for members of the military, increasing some salaries by as much as 40 per cent and again offering three years of back pay.[121] Not only was Bouteflika mindful to be generous to the armed and security forces at a time when the regime was under pressure but he also ensured that they were treated fairly equally.

This apparatus has high scope and high cohesion based on non-material ties. During his sixteen years in office, Bouteflika has maintained military spending at a consistently high level. In so doing, he has perpetuated a pattern of investment established by his predecessors. Between 1995 and 2004, both President Zéroual and he spent an average of 3.5 per cent of the country's GDP on the armed forces each year.[122] Between 2005 and 2009 he reduced this investment slightly to an average of 3.02 percent of GDP per annum,[123] before raising it substantially to an average of 4.58 per cent of GDP a year between 2010 and 2014.[124] Yet, even with these fluctuations, defence spending has increased almost every year for the past two decades.[125] And it has grown exponentially since the start of the Arab Spring, to the extent that, in 2014, Algeria spent more on its military ($11.8 billion) than Morocco ($4 billion), Libya ($3.3 billion), Tunisia ($906 million) and Mauritania ($150 million) combined ($8.35 billion).[126]

The Bouteflika regime's heavy investment in the armed and security forces has enabled them to penetrate most of the country down to village and neighbourhood levels. This presence has been built up over the past two decades in response to the threat from Islamist insurgents and terrorists. There are still parts of the country in which the military has no permanent presence, most notably in Kabylia and the Sahel. These are the areas in which the majority of the remaining Islamist fighters are based. Yet almost all these places are remote, inhospitable and sparsely populated. And they are also fluid: their borders are not fixed or static. Rather their locations change depending on where the military and the militants are operating. Their existences are not evidence of the armed forces' lack of scope. Such is Algeria's great size, it would be virtually impossible to maintain a permanent military presence everywhere at all times. More noteworthy is the ability of these forces to move into such spaces at will. Indeed, there is no part of the country they cannot occupy and hold should they need to.

The high scope of these forces is confirmed by their ability to conduct low-intensity operations. Even though the state of emergency has been lifted, the regime continues to deter and disrupt public meetings and protests. During the 2014 presidential election campaign, the police arrested hundreds of opposition members who demonstrated against Bouteflika's re-election.[127] Rival parties, candidates and supporters are also harassed and treated unfairly by other state institutions and bodies. The courts are not wholly independent and are regularly used to punish and silence critics of the regime, including human-rights activists.[128]

This heavy investment has also helped give Algeria's armed and security forces strong cohesion. It has ensured that they are well equipped, thoroughly trained, and have robust command and control structures. And these forces are also bound by other even more powerful non-material ties born of two critical and violent experiences. The first is the war of liberation which remains Algeria's most important national myth. Even today, some fifty years since its conclusion, and despite the youthfulness of the greater part of the population, it provides the overarching historical, emotional and psychological context in which public life is conducted. The constitution quickly identifies 'the 1st of November 1954 . . . [as] a turning point . . . [in Algeria's] destiny and . . . long resistance to [the] aggression carried out against its culture, . . . values and . . . identity' before rooting the country's 'current struggles . . . in the glorious past'.[129] The war is a hallowed memory and those who fought in it highly revered. Indeed, so great are the 'material benefits and prestige attached to . . . veteran status' that the number of people claiming to be ex-combatants leapt from 24,000 in 1962 to 420,000 in 1999.[130] And, through bodies such as the National Organisation of the Children of Mujahidin (Organisation Nationale des

Enfants de Moudjahidine, ONEM), even those born after the war are eager to associate themselves with it.[131]

The enduring strength of this myth is perhaps unsurprising given that the country continues to be run by men who fought in the war. Not only do they partly owe their positions to having done so but, as ex-combatants, they are helping to maintain the war's political importance through their veneration of it and by the fact of their being in power. They have influence because they are veterans and they have then used this influence to preserve and exalt the memory of the conflict. The president, army's Chief of Staff (General Ahmed Gaid Salah) and head of the DRS (General Mohamed Mediène) are former combatants, as were all their predecessors. Crucially, therefore, Algeria's government and security apparatus have long been led by men who know how to win and hold on to power. Moreover, the great trials they had to overcome to acquire it have both proven and strengthened their resolve to retain it.

Their willingness and ability to preserve their authority have also been tested and enhanced by their second, more recent, violent experience – the protracted armed struggle against Islamist insurgents and terrorists. Unlike before, when they were the insurrectionists trying to capture the state, Bouteflika and the other veteran leaders have had to defend what they hold from determined and capable foes who have tried to exploit the revolutionary tradition they helped establish and promulgate.[132] While the insurgents came desperately close to victory in the mid 1990s,[133] the regime fought back to reduce steadily both the size and seriousness of the threat. In so doing, Algeria's leaders showed once again that they have the know-how and determination to do what is necessary to stay in power. Moreover, the continued existence of a dogged rump of groups and fighters has helped them justify their high defence spending and curtailment of certain political and civil rights. In addition to strengthening the armed and security forces' non-material cohesion, this second violent experience has provided a fig leaf of legitimacy for the maintenance of competitive authoritarian rule.

The strength of the armed and security forces' cohesion is confirmed by their ability to conduct high-intensity coercion. Indeed, it was by carrying out such operations that they first triggered the chain of events that led President Benjedid to introduce his democratic reforms, and later caused the start and rapid expansion of the Islamist insurgency. Their brutal behaviour during the 1988 Black October riots arguably left the government with little option but to take bold and decisive action, while their subsequent efforts to destroy the FIS drove thousands of the party's supporters to take up arms against the state. Since then, they have continued to engage in high-intensity coercion. And, even though their conduct has been heavily criticised at times, the threat to the Algerian state from Islamist militants is now much lower than it used to be. And, perhaps more crucially, the armed and security forces themselves have endured. They have not collapsed or been defeated or fragmented into warring clans.

Both the FLN and RND have broad but brittle scope. They are the country's two largest parties, fielding candidates and winning votes across its territory. Yet, the RND does not have deep roots in society while the FLN's are not as strong as they once were. It was founded in 1954 by the so-called 'nine historics' as a revolutionary vanguard.[134] Its pivotal role in winning independence for Algeria led to its installation as the country's only legal political party. By the time President Benjedid revoked this privilege in 1989, however, it had lost much of its early mystique and support. Brutal confirmation of its decline was provided by the 1990 and 1991 elections when, despite enjoying numerous unfair advantages over its rivals, it was soundly beaten. After several years removed from power, it has successfully re-established itself as a party of government.

It was during the FLN's short period in the political wilderness that the RND emerged. It was established on 6 January 1997 by Abdelak Benhamouda to give President Zéroual the type and level of control that the FLN no longer could.[135] More specifically, it was created to help manage and manipulate the soon-to-be-reestablished National Assembly. It continues to perform this function for Bouteflika, as well as provide him with an affiliation and platform when standing for election. The RND by origin and the FLN through choice, therefore, are 'personal vehicles' for elite politicians.[136] As such, they do not seek to facilitate, or even greatly encourage, the electorate's 'integration and mobilization', its involvement in the political process. Nor do they try to 'articulate and aggregate' its interests, to discover, collate and channel popular concerns. And they do not 'formulate much public policy', suggest or help develop many new laws.[137]

Confirmation of the regime's considerable influence over the National Assembly was provided by the November 2008 parliamentary vote on the abolition of the constitutional limit on the number of terms an individual could serve as president. This amendment was proposed by Bouteflika's supporters as a prelude to him standing for re-election. That the regime felt compelled to seek the National Assembly's approval could be seen as evidence of the value it placed on due process. Certainly, this decision indicated its desire to at least be seen to be abiding by the constitution. More telling, though, was the passing of the motion by a simple show of hands without any prior public consultation. The regime solicited parliament's approval because it wanted to maintain its democratic facade. It did not, however, want a proper debate or to be challenged. And, in this, the National Assembly duly obliged.[138]

The RND's cohesion is based mainly on material ties. As an establishment party, its primary purpose is to serve the regime. It has little function or sense of identity beyond that. It does not represent anything especially important or profound, proclaim or occupy a distinct ideological or political position that is likely to generate and retain a large and devoted constituency of followers. Moreover, it has no non-material ties to speak of and upon which it can draw. Inevitably, some of its members and leaders share common pasts fighting either the French or Islamists. Yet, they did not do so on behalf of the RND. Such links, therefore, are almost entirely incidental to the party. What it does have, though, is access to power and patronage. Its rewards for supporting the regime are a bit part in government, money and opportunities. This is what it can offer its members.

The FLN, in contrast, has a rich and illustrious history. It will forever be venerated as the agent of Algeria's liberation. Yet the power of this past to bind and motivate its members will inevitably decrease as their numbers decline in comparison with those born after independence. And this trend is exacerbated by the loss of its privileged status. Now, there are other parties to join, some of which have comparable, or even better, access to those in power. By extension, the FLN can no longer guarantee its members the benefits that it once did. Moreover, belonging to it is not as important as it used to be. Membership is not essential for accessing certain opportunities, for the party's renaissance was not instigated by the regime. Rather, the FLN has sought to re-establish itself as a party of government. It is a supplicant to those in power.

The country's programme of economic liberalisation over the past twenty-five years has been marked by at least two inconsistencies. The first is the degree of enthusiasm with which successive regimes have pursued it. They have long viewed such reforms with distaste, suspicion and even hostility. President Benejdid's initial decision to start selling state-owned assets to private and foreign investors was driven more by necessity than any deep-felt desire to recast the country's economy. He, the High State Council (Haut Comité d'État, HCE) and President Zéroual were subsequently compelled to make these changes, first to qualify for the emergency loans they desperately needed from the IMF and World Bank, and later to satisfy the terms of the agreements they had signed with these bodies.[139]

The general antipathy felt by successive governments towards making these reforms is mainly born of their shared and abiding desire to exercise as much control over the economy as they can. The country's harrowing

experiences in freeing itself from French rule created and sustain a powerful cultural impulse to prize and defend all forms of national independence. The second inconsistency, therefore, is the regime's determination
to retain this control while encouraging greater outside involvement in
the economy. Together, these discrepancies have helped give Algeria's
liberalisation programme a patchy complexion. Over the years, successive governments have implemented the associated reforms with varying
degrees of urgency and rigour. By extension, some of the changes they
have made have proved to be more effective than others, leading to peri-
odic jumps in foreign investment. Often, one of the key influences on government behaviour has been the state of the country's finances – its level
of indebtedness and export earnings from oil and gas sales.

Since Bouteflika took office, Algeria's fiscal situation has stabilised.
The size of its debt has fallen substantially from 65 per cent of GDP in
1998 (the year before he took office),[140] to just 4.5 per cent in 2015.[141] And
its hydrocarbon export earnings have increased exponentially from $9.7
billion in 1998,[142] to $63.8 billion in 2013.[143] Together, these develop-
ments have enabled Bouteflika to retain control of the most important parts
of the economy and reverse some of the liberalising reforms introduced
previously. In 2006 he made a series of amendments to the Hydrocarbon
Act which governs the country's oil and gas industries.[144] In addition to
revoking some of the concessions the act had awarded foreign firms operating in these sectors, he gave Sonatrach the right to take a controlling
stake in all future oil and gas projects undertaken in the country.[145] Then,
in 2009, he extended this obligation to the rest of the economy, passing a
law requiring all companies to be at least 51 per cent Algerian owned.[146]

Algeria's lowly position in the World Bank's 2015 Doing Business
Index, therefore, is not only unsurprising but provides clear confirmation
of the limited effect the liberalisation programme has had.[147] Despite the
declared commitment of successive governments to encourage greater
private and foreign investment, and the changes they have implemented,
the economy has still only been partially reformed. Substantial portions of
it remained unchanged. Some of the old command structures, along with
the impulses that gave rise to them, survive intact. Moreover, and more
crucially, the country depends on the state-controlled oil and gas sectors
for 95 per cent of its export revenue.[148]

The regime also uses its control of large parts of the economy to discipline and shape the behaviour of thousands of people it employs. During
the 2009 presidential election, over eight thousand bodies – including
trade unions and occupational associations – all publicly declared their
support for Bouteflika. Many of the members of these groups subsequently

claimed that they had been compelled to do so upon pain of receiving official reprimands, losing their jobs, being denied promotions or having their careers blighted in some other way.[149] In addition to helping the regime resist external democratising pressure, therefore, its control of the economy gives it decisive influence over the livelihoods of hundreds of thousands of Algerians which it uses to defend and perpetuate competitive authoritarianism.

The Bouteflika regime continues to benefit from the collective weakness of the country's opposition parties. Indeed, its ascendancy over them has been little affected by the Arab Spring. Like Ben Ali, Bouteflika and his predecessors have established a series of political and psychological parameters that limit and constrain their rivals' behaviour and imagination. Unlike Ben Ali, they have done so by more brutish means. They have made no offer of a National Pact. They have proved reluctant to compromise. They have not tried to placate. The military's intervention in the democratic process confirmed both the limits of its patience and the lengths it was willing to go to. The HCE's outlawing of the FIS showed what happened to groups and organisations that challenged the established order. And Zéroual's and Bouteflika's repeated refusals to lift the ban, despite being petitioned to do so by other opposition parties, demonstrated the long-term consequences of crossing the regime. It did not forget and it did not forgive.[150]

In return for not declaring them illegal and persecuting their members, the regime is prepared to suffer the existence of these parties. In truth, it needs them to help maintain its democratic facade. Yet, as it has made clear, it is not particularly concerned which parties perform this function, just that they do not threaten the established order. Regardless of whatever criticisms they make of the regime and its works, therefore, their participation in political life legitimises what it has done and continues to do. They have effectively surrendered the right to make the political running. They are willing to abide within the limits the regime has set and which support a partially competitive (that is, not completely) democratic order. They have allowed themselves to be co-opted.

Many of Algeria's opposition parties suffer from other debilitating weaknesses. The Socialist Forces Front (Front des Forces Socialistes, FFS) is well established with a loyal and substantial following. But its close association with the Kabyle community means that it struggles to attract much support among the Arab majority and build a national presence. As the other main Berber party, the Rally for Culture and Democracy (Rassemblement pour le Changement et la Démocratie, RpCD) faces similar challenges and is also completely dominated by its founder and head, Saïd Sadi.[151] Similarly, the Justice and Development Party (Parti de la Justice et du Développement, PJD) is simply a vehicle for advancing the political ambitions of its leader, Abdallah Djaballah. And, while the Workers' Party (Parti des Travailleurs, PT) claims long and illustrious antecedents – arguably stretching all the way back to Algeria's first nationalist organisation, Messali Hadj's North African Star (Étoile Nord Africaine, ENA) – it struggles to attract much support outside the country's small and relatively privileged urban working and intellectual classes.

Little wonder, then, that, when the first protests broke out in the country in 2011, these parties played largely peripheral roles. For, just as in Tunisia and Morocco, the demonstrations were mainly orchestrated and led by unofficial groups and organisations. Even later on, only a minority joined the National Coordination for Change and Democracy (Coordination Nationale pour le Changement et la Démocratie, CNCD), the umbrella body that was created to try to expand and better manage the demonstrations. One of the few parties to do so was the RpCD, and its influence was not entirely constructive. Its attempts to use the body to help nationalise Sadi's reputation led to the CNCD being seen as a mainly Kabyle entity which further undermined the participating groups' faltering efforts to forge a common platform.[152] The reluctance of most mainstream parties to get more directly involved in the demonstrations highlighted just how ignorant they were of grass-roots grievances and the strength of their disinclination to challenge the regime outside the ascribed channels and conventions.

Origins and Evolution of the Regime

Under Bouteflika, Algeria has completed its transition to competitive authoritarianism. After its brief experiment with democracy, it reverted to being a dictatorship, ruled by the military dominated HCE. Yet, rather than either perpetuate the army's overt and highly divisive involvement in government or resurrect Algeria's pre-1989 authoritarian order, those in power decided to take the country's politics in a new direction. Arguably, the first step towards this goal was Zéroual's election as president in 1995. In practical terms, his appointment to this post changed little, as power continued to be distributed along much the same lines as before. As chairman of the HCE, he was already the country's most high-profile politician and acting head of state. The abolition of the ruling council did not lead to any significant reduction in the military's influence and authority. And, while the ballot was commended by international observers as mostly free and fair, its outcome was never in doubt.

Nonetheless, the election mattered both for presentational reasons and because it helped launch the country's current electoralist order. While

Zéroual's de facto powers may have remained largely unchanged, the re-establishment of the presidency resurrected a pivotal pre-coup institution, thereby paving the way for the normalisation and civilianisation of political life. Though the armed forces' power and influence were mostly unaffected, the HCE's abolition reduced their political exposure and eliminated a body that served as a painful and damaging reminder of their abuse of the democratic process. And, even though the result of the election was never truly in doubt, the staging of it provided the regime with a degree of legitimacy and restarted the electoral process.

Since then, the regime has held regular presidential (1999, 2004, 2009 and 2014) and parliamentary elections (1997, 2002, 2007 and 2012). Some of these votes have been freer and fairer than others. Often, the amount of fraud practised by the regime has reflected the amount of importance it attaches to achieving a particular outcome and sense of what it needs to do to secure the result it wants. This helps explain why many of the most serious concerns raised by domestic and international observers have been about the conduct of presidential elections. As the ostensible means of determining who holds the country's most important political office and, in so doing, becomes its greatest dispenser of patronage, they are deemed to be of far greater consequence than those to decide which party holds the most seats in the National Assembly.[153] Their outcomes, therefore, have been left less to chance.

Arguably the freest and fairest presidential ballot held since the restoration of the electoral process was the 1995 vote.[154] The international observers' praise for its conduct appeared justified by the result. For, unlike Ben Ali's winning margin the year before (94.5 per cent), Zéroual's was not a total affront to credibility (61 per cent). Similarly, the share of the vote secured by the second-placed candidate, Mafoud Nahnah for Society for Peace (Mouvement de la Société pour la Paix, MSP) (25.6 per cent), seemed plausible.[155] The regime's decision not to interfere in this election as much as it would in future ballots reflected both its confidence in Zéroual's victory and reluctance to jeopardise its relaunch of the electoral process by getting caught manipulating the first vote it had staged in nearly seven years.

Since then, however, the regime has showed less restraint. In 1999, Bouteflika stood unopposed after the other six candidates all withdrew hours before the polls opened in protest at how the election had been conducted and what they foresaw as the inevitable outcome.[156] In 2004, 2009 and 2014, he faced competition but still managed to win with 85 per cent, 90.2 per cent and 81.5 per cent of the vote.[157] The popular Algerian newspapers *El Watan* and *Le Matin* described the 2004 result as 'worthy of Kim Il Sung' and 'Brezhnevian'.[158] So serious was the malfeasance witnessed by Western observers in 1999 and 2004, that the European Union, United States, United Nations and Organization for Security Co-operation in Europe (OSCE) refused to send any monitors to oversee the 2009 and 2014 elections which were also marked by extensive fraud.[159] In 2009, there were credible allegations of widespread vote buying, repeat voting, ballot-box stuffing and thefts.[160] And, in 2014, the regime was accused of inflating the electoral register by three million names in order 'to facilitate ballot-stuffing and multiple voting'.[161] As Freedom House noted in its 2015 country report, 'each of Bouteflika's four elections to the presidency has been tainted by accusations of fraud'.[162]

Though less dramatic than Bouteflika's victories, the FLN's and RND's triumphs have been remarkable and important. Since 1997, they have come first and second in every election held and, between them, never occupied less than half the seats in parliament.[163] Together, they have dominated the reformed National Assembly and, in so doing, enhanced the regime's control over it. Their electoral successes have also been subject to censure. While not every election they have done well in has been as roundly criticised as those that Bouteflika has won, domestic and international observers have still raised serious concerns about some. They condemned the 1997 vote as 'seriously flawed'.[164] And, even though foreign monitors declared the 2012 ballot 'largely free and fair', opposition candidates and some local human rights groups dismissed it as 'fraudulent'.[165]

In addition to practising fraud during elections, the regime continues to assume numerous unfair advantages between them. It has routinely made arbitrary and ad hoc use of the country's electoral and other laws to prevent candidates and parties from competing, and disadvantage and undermine their campaigns. After his commendable performance in the 1995 presidential election, Mafoud Nahnah was barred from standing in 1999 on the grounds that he could not prove his participation in the war of liberation.[166] Not only does this remain the sole occasion on which this qualification has been applied but no subsequent runner-up has come close to winning as large a share of the vote as he did.[167] The regime responded to Nahnah's success by denying him the chance to repeat it and has seemingly succeeded in preventing anyone else from doing the same.

To stop the FLN from adopting Ali Benflis as its candidate in the 2004 presidential election, Bouteflika won a court order banning it from holding its nominating conference. When it did so anyway on 30 December 2003, Bouteflika successfully petitioned the Court of Algiers to freeze its assets. Then, on 22 January 2004, he encouraged his own supporters in the party to hold a separate convention at which they switched the party's nomination from Benflis to him.[168] In the end, they both stood as FLN candidates. Benflis finished a distant second with 6.4 per cent of the vote.[169]

Then, in the run-up to the 2009 election, Bouteflika gained several significant advantages over his rivals by breaking a number of electoral laws. Not only did he begin campaigning long before the start of the official three-week electioneering period and make extensive use of public money and materials but he also promised lucrative government contracts to private businessmen in return for their financial support. The regime also ensured that his campaign was given both greater and more favourable media coverage. The Algerian League for the Defence of Human Rights (Ligue Algérienne pour la Défense des Driots de l'Homme, LADDH) estimated that 27.6 per cent of press and as much as 88.5 per cent of television coverage of the election was sympathetically focused on him.[170]

Under Bouteflika, the regime has closely controlled party registration and participation. Between April 1999 and April 2011, the Ministry of the Interior rejected every one of the dozens of applications it received from groups requesting accreditation. As a result, no new party was granted formal recognition by the regime in twelve years.[171] And, of those that were sanctioned, not all were permitted to take part in elections. Only those groups which the regime deemed reliable, posed little threat to its favoured candidates and were willing to abide by its debilitating rules were allowed to do so. Certain minority parties, for reasons that were never fully explained, were exempt from these requirements. Otherwise, a party had to have won at least 3 per cent of the vote in the last election and be able to field candidates in no fewer than twenty-five *wilayas* (administrative districts) to qualify to participate. Inevitably, these measures disadvantaged the smaller and newer parties which had neither the resources nor pedigrees to meet these conditions.[172]

And, although, in the wake of the Arab Spring, the regime has tried to convince the Algerian public of its greater commitment to competition and political openness by relaxing the electoral code, the changes it has introduced pose little threat to either its power or the established, competitive authoritarian order. Typical is its relaxation of the criteria for registering political parties. In the 2012 parliamentary election, the field increased by nearly a third as twenty-one new parties joined forty-four established ones on the ballot.[173] Yet, rather than leading to any significant loosening of the regime's grip on either the election or the National Assembly, this expansion had barely any effect, for most of these groups were not only tiny but had broken away from 'existing parties – especially the FLN and the RND – or [were] vehicles for self-promotion by personalities and businessmen close to the regime'.[174] As such, they posed virtually no danger to the regime nor prevented the two establishment parties from once again winning a collective majority. Instead, these groups have slightly weakened the established parties and mostly been incorporated within the regime's expanded patronage network.[175]

The regime also uses the law and litigation to try to control the country's media. In June 2009, it passed new cybercrime legislation which has greatly enhanced its ability to monitor and regulate what takes place online. All service providers operating in the country are now obliged to block access to any website the government deems a danger to 'public order and decency'.[176] By 2010, this requirement had been extended to include certain content on some opposition parties' websites. And perhaps more significantly, the regime has established a new national Internet-monitoring centre which observes and follows all of the country's Internet traffic.[177] By these means, the regime has been able to find, arrest and charge a number of bloggers for material they have posted online.[178]

Then, in April 2011, in a move intended to appease the Arab Spring protestors, the government announced the decriminalisation of certain press offences. Yet, such was the wording of this amendment, it has actually increased both the regime's ability to block reporting on any topic deemed a threat to the country's security and economic interests,[179] and journalists' exposure to outside pressure, by introducing custodial sentences for the non-payment of any fines they incur during the course of their work.[180] Similarly, in January 2014, the government passed a new law which authorised the establishment of privately owned television channels, and imposed additional restrictions on what they could broadcast, most notably, news that has not been cleared by the censors.[181] Moreover, even with this reform, the regime still dominates the country's broadcast media.[182]

Journalists, reporters, editors and outlets are also routinely prosecuted under the country's defamation laws. Dating from 1990, this legislation makes insulting Islam and questioning or challenging the nation's unity criminal offences. Amendments to them introduced in 2001 have extended the list of proscribed subjects to include the president, parliament, courts and military. Anyone convicted of saying, writing or even drawing something derogatory about these institutions can be imprisoned for up to five years. Publicly disparaging the armed forces and senior political figures is also illegal under the 2005 Charter for Peace and National Reconciliation (Charte pour la Paix et la Réconciliation Nationale, CPRN) and carries the far more serious charges of aiding and abetting terrorism.[183]

Yet the law is not the only way in which the regime disciplines the media. Because most of the country's newspapers depend on the state both to print their copy and for advertising revenue,[184] it can put significant economic pressure on any that displease it.[185] Even those publications which use private presses are not necessarily any better able to resist this interference as the regime habitually harasses the printing companies on which they rely.[186] By these means, and the DRS's sustained harassment of individual journalists and editors, the regime tries to enforce self-censorship. Little wonder that Algeria was ranked 119th out of 180 countries in the 2015 Reporters Without Borders press freedom index.[187]

Conclusions

Algeria has defied expectations. Shortly after the Arab Spring began, it was identified by specialists, eager to make amends for their collective failure to predict what was happening in Tunisia, as one of the next most likely countries to succumb to the rising tide of unrest. Its recent past as the region's trailblazer was highlighted as evidence of the Algerian people's predisposition to democracy. These suspicions were strengthened by the government's rushed and nervous response to the demonstrations and riots that broke out in Algiers, Tizi Ouzou and elsewhere. The Arab Spring protestors managed to achieve in just a few weeks what the country's mainstream parties and politicians had failed to accomplish in nearly twenty years: the lifting of the state of emergency.

Yet the regime did not fall nor, crucially, has it changed very much. While its response to the demonstrations was undoubtedly apprehensive, the concessions it has offered and reforms it has made have not greatly weakened its grip on power. This much was confirmed by Bouteflika's re-election in April 2014. That Algeria continues to be governed by the same president who was in office at the time the protests began is not the most telling outcome of this election. More significant, is what the regime was able to achieve in the circumstances that existed. For, against a backdrop of unparalleled regional upheaval, it succeeded in engineering the re-election of a candidate who was seventy-seven years old, had already completed three full terms in office, had held a senior political post for much of the past half century,[188] and was so ill that most of his campaigning had to be carried out by proxies.

In many ways, in fact, Bouteflika is the antithesis of the type of leader most of the Arab Spring protestors wanted to see in power. For fifty years he has helped build, strengthen and sustain the very order they were seeking to dismantle. Unlike Tunisia, Algeria has remained competitive authoritarian. It holds regular, multiparty elections which are seldom free and fair. Regime-backed candidates invariably prevail because of the significant advantages they enjoy over their rivals. While opposition parties have opportunities to compete, they are very unlikely to cause any political upsets. For the electoral playing field is tilted decisively in the regime's favour. This gerrymandering takes place both between and during elections.

The European Union and United States are able to bring only limited democratising pressure to bear. Their links to the country are medium and leverage over its regime low. In this, Algeria provides an important addendum to Levitsky and Way's model. For, according to them, its close proximity to Europe and long, shared history with France should have made the forging of strong links and high leverage more likely. Yet, in actual fact, this common past born, at least in part, of propinquity, sustains a fierce cultural and political determination to defend the country's independence and preserve its freedom of manoeuvre. Furthermore, both the EU and the US have long prioritised issues of security over those of governance and human rights in their dealings with Algeria. The West, therefore, has neither the means nor the inclination to try to make Algeria democratise. As a result, domestic factors are decisive.

The Bouteflika regime has high organisational power. The armed and security forces each has extensive scope and strong cohesion. They are large and well funded. They have penetrated the most important parts of the country down to the level of the village and neighbourhood. They are able to enter and occupy the remaining areas largely at will. They have proven their abilities to conduct high- and low-intensity operations. The heavy financial investment made in them by successive governments ensures that they are well equipped, thoroughly trained and have robust command and control structures. These bonds are buttressed by more important and hard-forged non-material ties. For, like the government, each is led by men who fought in the war of liberation. And, since the early 1990s, they have confronted and steadily gained the upper hand over a committed Islamist foe.

The regime also exercises discretionary control over the most important parts of the country's economy. Despite the sustained, albeit at times reluctant, commitment of successive governments to attract greater private and foreign investment, the crucial oil and gas sectors are still dominated by Sonatrach. In addition to generating most of Algeria's export and foreign currency earnings, these industries help the regime to resist and mitigate any democratising pressure put on it by the West. They also grant it direct economic influence over thousands of ordinary Algerians. The regime exploits its position as employer to shape the political behaviour of the country's public-sector workers, to discipline them into voting for its preferred candidates and parties.

Indeed, the only shortcoming in the regime's organisational power is the medium strength of its ruling parties. Both the FLN and RCD have broad scope. The FLN has a long and illustrious history with which to attract voters and supporters, and develop non-material ties. Nevertheless, both it and the RCD lack strong cohesion. And the regime has declined to elevate either of them to the same position that the RCD occupied in Tunisia under Ben Ali. Certainly, they enjoy preferential treatment compared to other parties. But they do not dominate parliament or the political system. Only together do they hold a (far from large) majority of seats. Instead of creating a single overbearing party, the regime courts them both and, in so doing, limits its dependence on each of them.

Notes

1. The state of emergency had first been declared on 9 February 1992 by the High State Council (Haut Comité d'État, HCE), the five-man committee which assumed power shortly after President Benjedid had been forced to resign by the military. It was finally ended on 24 February 2011; J. N. C. Hill (2009), *Identity in Algerian Politics: The Legacy of Colonial Rule*, Boulder, CO: Lynne Rienner Publishers, pp. 150 and 139; Frédéric Volpi (2013), 'Algeria versus the Arab Spring', *Journal of Democracy*, 22: 3, 104–15, p. 108.
2. James L. Gelvin (2012), *The Arab Uprisings: What Everyone Needs to Know*, Oxford: Oxford University Press, p. 93.
3. John P. Entelis (2011), 'Algeria: Democracy Denied, and Revived?' *The Journal of North African Studies*, 16: 4, 653–78, p. 658.
4. Joffé, 'The Arab Spring in North Africa', p. 509.
5. Gelvin, *The Arab Uprisings*, pp. 94–6.
6. Iván Martín (2003), 'Algeria's Political Economy (1999–2002): An Economic Solution to the Crisis?', *The Journal of North African Studies*, 8: 2, 34–74, p. 34; Salah E. Zaimeche and Keith Sutton (1998), 'Persistent Strong Populations Growth, Environmental Degradation, and Declining Food Self-Sufficiency in a Rentier Oil State: Algeria', *The Journal of North African Studies*, 3: 1, 57–73, p. 65.
7. Gilbert Achcar (2013), *The People Want: A Radical Exploration of the Arab Uprising*, London: Saqi, p. 94; Entelis, 'Algeria', p. 657.
8. Achcar, *The People Want*, pp. 36–7; Entelis, 'Algeria', p. 662.
9. In 2011, the year in which the Arab Spring began, 40 per cent of the Algerian population was below the age of fifteen and 70 per cent below thirty; Entelis, 'Algeria', p. 662; Susan Slyomovics (2013), 'Algeria', in

Vijay Prashad (ed.), *Dispatches from the Arab Spring*, Minneapolis, MN and London: University of Minnesota Press, pp. 122–34, p. 127.

10. According to the Food and Agricultural Organization of the United Nations (FAO), between July 2010 and the start of the Arab Spring, the price of maize rose by 74 per cent, of wheat by 84 per cent, of sugar by 77 per cent and of cooking oil by 57 per cent; Joffé, 'The Arab Spring in North Africa', p. 509.

11. As Volpi astutely observes, the region's monarchies have been better able to withstand the transformative pressures released by the Arab Spring; Volpi, 'Algeria versus the Arab Spring', p. 104.

12. Ibid. p. 107.

13. Yet, even so, this alliance has not been without its difficult moments. At the start of his second term in office (2004–9), Bouteflika sought to civilianise his rule. In August 2004, he forced General Mohamed Lamari, 'one of the leaders of the military group that ordered the cancellation of the 1991–92 parliamentary elections', to resign as Chief of Staff. And, in August 2005, he eased General Larbi Belkheir (retired) out of his post as director of the presidential office; Entelis, 'Algeria', p. 661; Miriam R. Lowi (2009), *Oil Wealth and the Poverty of Politics: Algeria Compared*, Cambridge: Cambridge University Press, p. 182.

14. Between 2007 and 2010, 1,200 AQIM fighters surrendered and 250 were killed. And, between 2008 and 2011, eighty-one of its leaders gave themselves up; Djallil Lounnas (2014), 'Confronting Al-Qa'ida in the Islamic Maghrib in the Sahel: Algeria and the Malian Crisis', *The Journal of North African Studies*, 19: 5, 810–27, p. 819.

15. Miriam R. Lowi (2005), 'Algeria, 1992–2002: Anatomy of a Civil War', in Paul Collier and Nicholas Sambanis (eds), *Understanding Civil War*, Washington DC: World Bank, 221–46, pp. 234–5; Martin Evans and John Phillips (2007), *Algeria: Anger of the Dispossessed*, New Haven, CT and London: Yale University Press, p. 254.

16. Volpi, 'Algeria versus the Arab Spring', p. 107.

17. Ibid. p. 107.

18. Dennison, 'The EU and North Africa after the Revolutions', p. 119.

19. Levitsky and Way, *Competitive Authoritarianism*, p. 44.

20. US Department of State (2015), 'Middle East Partnership Initiative Local Grants Program Algeria 2015: Current Local and Regional Grants', <http:// photos.state.gov/libraries/algeria/401501/pao2015/MEPI_Local_Grant_ Algeria.pdf> (last accessed 9 July 2015).

21. The United States distinguishes between planned, obligated and spent funding. The book uses the planned figures as they indicate more clearly the United States' intentions.

22. US Government (2015), 'Foreign Assistance', available at <http://beta. foreignassistance.gov/> (last accessed 8 July 2015).

23. US Department of State (2015), 'Foreign Military Financing Account

Summary', <http://www.state.gov/t/pm/ppa/sat/c14560.htm> (last accessed 8 July 2015).

24. Hakim Darbouche (2010), '"Energising" EU–Algerian Relations', *The International Spectator*, 45: 3, 71–83, p. 73.

25. Hakim Darbouche (2008), 'Decoding Algeria's ENP Policy: Differentiation by Other Means', *Mediterranean Politics*, 13: 3, 371–89, p. 375.

26. Darbouche, 'Decoding Algeria's ENP Policy', p. 375; Yahia H. Zoubir (2004), 'The Resurgence of Algeria's Foreign Policy in the Twenty-First Century', *The Journal of North African Studies*, 9: 2, 169–83, p. 176.

27. Holden, 'Security, Power or Profit?', p. 22.

28. Entelis, 'Algeria', p. 656; George Joffé (2002), 'The Role of Violence within the Algerian Economy', *The Journal of North African Studies*, 7: 1, 29–52, p.38; 2002: 38; Zaimeche and Sutton, 'Persistent Strong Populations Growth', p. 64.

29. Lowi, 'Algeria, 1992–2002', p. 232; Luis Martinez (2004), 'Why the Violence in Algeria?' *The Journal of North African Studies*, 9: 2, 14–27, p. 15.

30. Hakim Darbouche and Yahia H. Zoubir (2009), 'The Algerian Crisis in European and US Foreign Policies: A Hindsight Analysis', *The Journal of North African Studies*, 14: 1, 33–55, p. 44; Martinez, 'Why the Violence', p. 19.

31. Tanja A. Börzel and Vera van Hüllen (2014), 'One Voice, One Message, but Conflicting Goals: Cohesiveness and Consistency in the European Neighbourhood Policy', *Journal of European Public Policy*, 21: 7, 1033–49, p. 1036.

32. Darbouche, 'Decoding Algeria's ENP Policy', p. 377.

33. Darbouche, '"Energising" EU–Algerian Relations', p. 75.

34. Börzel and van Hüllen, 'One Voice, One Message, but Conflicting Goals', p. 1036.

35. Holden, 'Security, Power or Profit?', p. 24.

36. Raffaella A. Del Sarto and Tobias Schumacher (2011), 'From Brussels with Love: Leverage, Benchmarking, and the Action Plans with Jordan and Tunisia in the EU's Democratization Policy', *Democratization*, 18: 4, 932–55, p. 950; Commission of the European Communities (2006), 'ENP Progress Report: Morocco [COM (2006) 726 final]', 4 December, Brussels, p. 2.

37. Darbouche, '"Energising" EU–Algerian Relations', p. 76.

38. Ibid. p. 76.

39. Ibid. p. 77.

40. Available at <http://eeas.europa.eu/euromed/docs/meda_figures_en.pdf> (last accessed 6 July 2015).

41. European Commission (2015), 'European Neighbourhood Policy and Enlargement Negotiations', 8 April, <http://ec.europa.eu/enlargement/neighbourhood/countries/algeria/index_en.htm> (last accessed 6 July 2015.

42. Bicchi, 'The Politics of Foreign Aid and the European Neighbourhood Policy Post-Arab Spring', p. 329.

43. European Union (2013), Mémorandum d'entente sur l'établissement d'un Partenariat Stratégique entre l'Union européenne et la République algérienne démocratique et populaire dans le domaine de l'énergie', 7 July, <http://ec.europa.eu/energy/sites/ener/files/documents/20130707_signed_mou_fr.pdf> (last accessed 6 July).

44. Darbouche, '"Energising" EU–Algerian Relations', p. 81.

45. Ibid. p. 81.

46. As of 5 May 2015, the European Commission confirmed that it was in 'political dialogue on energy matters' with Algiers; European Commission (2015), 'EU and Algeria to Cooperate on Energy', 5 May, <https://ec.europa.eu/energy/en/news/eu-and-algeria-cooperate-energy> (last accessed 7 July 2015).

47. Available at <http://ec.europa.eu/eurostat/statistics-explained/index.php/Energy_production_and_imports#Import> (last accessed 7 July 2015).

48. Eurogas (2014), 'Statistical Report 2014', December, <http://www.eurogas.org/uploads/media/Eurogas_Statistical_Report_2014.pdf> (last accessed 7 July 2015), p. 7.

49. Ibid. p. 6.

50. US Department of Energy (2014), 'Country Analysis Brief: Algeria', 24 July, <http://www.eia.gov/beta/international/analysis_includes/countries_long/Algeria/algeria.pdf> (last accessed 7 July 2015), p. 7.

51. The Galsi pipeline will have a capacity of 282 billion cubic feet per year (bcf/y) and will be the fourth to connect Algeria to the European Union. The other three are the Trans-Mediterranean/Enrico Mattei line (1,340 bcf/y), the Maghreb–Europe/Pedro Duran line (390 bcf/y) and the Medgas line (280 bcf/y); ibid. p. 13; Gawdat Baghat (2010), 'The Geopolitics of Energy: Europe and North Africa', *The Journal of North African Studies*, 15: 1, 39–49, pp. 46–7.

52. European Commission (2015), 'European Union, Trade in goods with Algeria', 10 April, available at <http://trade.ec.europa.eu/doclib/docs/2006/september/tradoc_113343.pdf> (last accessed 7 July 2015), p. 8.

53. Ibid. p. 9.

54. Government of the United States of America (2001), 'Agreement between the Government of the United States of America and the Government of the People's Democratic Republic of Algeria Concerning the Development of Trade and Investment Relations', 13 July, <http://www.bilaterals.org/IMG/pdf/US-Algeria_TIFA_2001_.pdf> (last accessed 31 August 2015).

55. World Bank (2015), 'United States Products by Sector Import Trade Value', 1 August, <http://wits.worldbank.org/CountryProfile/Country/USA/StartYear/2009/EndYear/2013/TradeFlow/Import/Indicator/MPRT-TRD-VL/Partner/DZA/Product/sector> (last accessed 8 July2015).

56. US Department of State (2006), 'Algeria 2006 Investment Climate Statement', <http://2001-2009.state.gov/e/eeb/ifd/2006/61956.htm> (last accessed 8 July 2015).

57. US Government (2001), 'Agreement between the Government of the United States of America and the Government of the People's Democratic Republic of Algeria Concerning the Development of Trade and Investment Relations', 13 July, <https://ustr.gov/sites/default/files/uploads/agreements/tifa/asset_upload_file631_7732.pdf> (last accessed 8 July 2015).

58. More specifically, Algeria's exports to the United States were worth $1.56 billion in 1995, $1.70 billion in 1996, $2.22 billion in 1997, $1.52 billion in 1998 and $1.75 billion in 1999; World Bank (2015), 'Algeria All Products Export Trade Value', 1 August, <http://wits.worldbank.org/CountryProfile/Country/DZA/StartYear/1994/EndYear/1998/TradeFlow/Export/Indicator/XPRT-TRD-VL/Partner/USA/Product/Total> (last accessed 7 July 2015).

59. More specifically, Algeria's exports to the United States were worth $3.42 billion in 2000, $2.67 billion in 2001, $2.59 billion in 2002, $4.90 billion in 2003 and $7.57 billion in 2004; ibid.

60. More specifically, Algeria's exports to the United States were worth $10.59 billion in 2005, $14.85 billion in 2006, $18.09 billion in 2007, $18.95 billion in 2008 and $10.36 billion in 2010; ibid.

61. More specifically, Algeria's exports to the United States were worth $13.82 billion in 2010, $15.12 billion in 2011, $10.77 billion in 2012 and $5.34 billion in 2013; ibid.

62. More specifically, Algeria's imports from the United States were worth $1.41 billion in 1995, $931 million in 1996, $920 million in 1997, $991 million in 1998, $769 million in 1999, $1.04 billion in 2000, $1.03 billion in 2001, $1.16 billion in 2002, $709 million in 2003 and $1.08 billion in 2004; World Bank (2015), 'Algeria All Products Import Trade Value', 1 August, <http://wits.worldbank.org/CountryProfile/Country/DZA/StartYear/1994/EndYear/1998/TradeFlow/Import/Indicator/MPRT-TRD-VL/Partner/USA/Product/Total> (last accessed 7 July 2015).

63. More specifically, Algeria's imports from the United States were worth $1.36 billion in 2005, $1.42 billion in 2006, $2.13 billion in 2007, $2.19 billion in 2008 and $2.01 billion in 2009; ibid.

64. More specifically, Algeria's imports from the United States were worth $2.12 billion in 2010, $2.17 billion in 2011, $1.76 billion in 2012 and $2.37 billion in 2013; ibid.

65. Available at <http://trade.ec.europa.eu/doclib/docs/2006/september/tradoc_113343.pdf> (last accessed 7 July 2015), p. 9.

66. More specifically, the country attracted $270 million in FDI in 1996, $260 million in 1997, $606 million in 1998 and $291 million in 1999. Available at <http://data.worldbank.org/indicator/BX.KLT.DINV.CD.WD/countries?page=3> (last accessed 7 July 2015).

67. More specifically, the country attracted $280 million in FDI in 2000, $1.10

billion in 2001, $1.06 billion 2002, $633 million in 2003 and $881 million in 2004; ibid.

68. More specifically, the country attracted $1.15 billion in FDI in 2005, $1.84 billion in 2006, $1.68 billion in 2007, $2.63 billion in 2008, $2.74 billion in 2009, $2.3 billion in FDI in 2010, $2.57 billion in 2011, $1.50 billion in 2012 and $1.68 billion in 2013; ibid.

69. More specifically, these remittances amounted to $1.12 billion in 1995, $880 million in 1996, $1.06 billion in both 1997 and 1998, and $790 million in 1999. Available at <http://data.worldbank.org/indicator/BX.TRF.PWKR.CD.DT/countries?page=3> (last accessed 8 July 2015).

70. More specifically, these remittances amounted to $790 million in 2000, $670 million in 2001, $1.07 billion in 2002, $1.75 billion in 2003 and $2.46 billion in 2004; ibid.

71. More specifically, these remittances amounted to $170 million in 2005, $189 million in 2006, $99 million in 2007, $103 million in 2008 and $150 million in 2009; ibid.

72. More specifically, these remittances amounted to $196 million in 2010, $202 million in 2011, $214 million in 2012 and $209 million in 2013; ibid.

73. Proportionally, therefore, 75 per cent of all Algeria's émigrés live in France, 6.3 per cent in Canada, 2.4 per cent in Italy, 2.3 per cent in Britain and 1.8 per cent in the United States; Migration Policy Centre (2013), 'Algeria', June, <http://www.migrationpolicycentre.eu/docs/migration_profiles/Algeria.pdf> (last accessed 8 July 2015), p. 1.

74. European Institute for Research on Mediterranean and Euro-Arab Cooperation (2015), 'Algeria, Elections and Parliament', <http://www.medea.be/en/countries/algeria/algeria-elections-and-parliament/> (last accessed 9 July 2015).

75. Institute of International Education (2015), 'International Students in France', available at <http://www.iie.org/Services/Project-Atlas/France/International-Students-In-France> (last accessed 4 September 2015).

76. The Tempus scheme seeks 'to promote the reform and modernisation of higher education in the Partner Countries; . . . enhance the quality and relevance of higher education to the world of work and society . . . ; . . . increase the capacity of higher education institutions . . . to cooperate internationally . . . ; . . . foster the reciprocal development of human resources; [and] . . . enhance mutual understanding between the peoples and cultures of the EU and . . . Partner Countries'. Its goals are intended to complement those of the Erasmus Mundus programme which aims to enhance the quality of 'European higher education'; promote 'the European Union as a centre of excellence in learning around the world'; and promote 'intercultural understanding through cooperation with Third Countries'. European Commission (2013), 'Tempus IV (2007–13): Overview of the Programme', 12 December, available at <http://eacea.ec.europa.eu/tempus/programme/about_tempus_en.php> (last accessed 14 July 2015) and European Commission (2013),

'About Erasmus Mundus 2009–13', 12 December, available at <http:// eacea.ec.europa.eu/erasmus_mundus/programme/about_erasmus_mundus_ en.php> (last accessed 14 July 2015).

77. The SLP and LDF both strive to 'enhance cultural understanding, international collaboration, democratic institution building, knowledge sharing, and economic development between US and Middle East/North Africa-based students, entrepreneurs, lawmakers, and civil society leaders'. The SLP and LDF are open to applicants from all partner countries (of which there are fourteen) and offer places to 120 and up to twenty-five young people each year respectively. US Government (2015), 'The U.S.–Middle East Partnership Initiative (MEPI): MEPI Student Leaders Program', 1 August, available at <http:// mepi.state.gov/opportunities/mepi-exchange-programs/student-leaders. html> and <http://mepi.state.gov/opportunities/mepi-exchange-programs/ leaders-for-democracy-fellowship.html> (last accessed 1 August 2015).

78. Available at <http://eacea.ec.europa.eu/erasmus_mundus/programme/about_ erasmus_mundus_en.php> (last accessed 14 July 2015).

79. Available at <http://data.worldbank.org/indicator/IT.NET.USER.P2?page= 2> (last accessed 9 July 2015).

80. Ibid.

81. Ibid.

82. Available at <http://data.worldbank.org/indicator/IT.CEL.SETS.P2/countries?page=2> (last accessed 9 July 2015).

83. Ibid.

84. Ibid.

85. Paul A. Silverstein (2004), Algeria in France: Transpolitics, Race, and Nation, Bloomington, IN: Indiana University Press, pp. 220–36.

86. EU Neighbourhood Info Centre (2015), 'Algeria: €4 million Available to Support Civil Society Youth Actions in Annaba, Bechar, Khenchela and Oran', 5 May, <http://www.enpi-info.eu/medportal/news/latest/40765/ Algeria:-%E2%82%AC4-million-available-to-support-civil-society-youth-actions-in-Annaba,-Bechar,-Khenchela-and-Oran> (last accessed 10 July 2015).

87. Quickly to recapitulate, if a country has a large economy (with a GDP of at least $100 billion), or is a major oil producer (pumping more than a million barrels a day in an average year), or has or can access nuclear weapons easily, then Western leverage over it can only be low. Indeed, the target state needs only to satisfy one of these criteria for this to be so. Levitsky and Way, *Competitive Authoritarianism*, p. 372.

88. World Bank (2015), 'Algeria', <http://data.worldbank.org/country/algeria> (last accessed 3 July 2015).

89. Available at <http://www.eia.gov/beta/international/analysis_includes/coun tries_long/Algeria/algeria.pdf> (last accessed 3 July 2015), pp. 6 and 10.

90. Like Ben Ali, Gaddafi treated Libya's military with suspicion. As the leader of the small group of army officers which had seized power from King Idris

in 1969, he fully understood the military's importance to his regime's survival. To prevent it from doing to him what he had done to his predecessor, he imposed strict limits on the activities its members could engage in. And, to dilute its influence still further and provide him with an alternative source of coercive power, he established a militia made up of Tuareg tribesmen from northern Mali Joffé; 'The Arab Spring in North Africa', p. 522.

91. Peter Cole and Umar Khan (2015), 'The Fall of Tripoli: Part 1', in Peter Cole and Brian McQuinn (eds), *The Libyan Revolution and its Aftermath*, London: Hurst and Company, pp. 55–79, pp. 71–6; Lounnas, 'Confronting Al-Qa'ida in the Islamic Maghrib in the Sahel', p. 822.

92. Lounnas, 'Confronting Al-Qa'ida in the Islamic Maghrib in the Sahel', p. 822.

93. In addition to the fighters in Kabylia, there are around five hundred militants in the Sahel. Together, these two groupings form the main body of AQIM. Ibid. pp. 813–14 and 822.

94. Djallil Lounnas (2013), 'The Regional Fallouts of the French Intervention in Mali', *Mediterranean Politics*, 18: 2, 325–32, pp. 328–9; Yahia H. Zoubir (2012), 'The Sahara–Sahel Quagmire: Regional and International Ramifications', *Mediterranean Politics*, 17: 3, 452–8, p. 454.

95. Lounnas, 'The Regional Fallouts', p. 328.

96. Lounnas, 'Confronting Al-Qa'ida in the Islamic Maghrib in the Sahel', p. 820.

97. Francesco Cavatorta (2009), *The International Dimension of the Failed Algerian Transition: Democracy Betrayed?*, Manchester: Manchester University Press, pp. 110–12.

98. Martin Evans and John Phillips (2007), *Algeria: Anger of the Dispossessed*, New Haven, CT and London: Yale University Press, p. 240; Hugh Roberts (2003), *The Battlefield Algeria 1988–2000: Studies in a Broken Polity*, London: Verso, p. 309.

99. Evans and Phillips, *Algeria*, p. 223; Mohammed M. Hafez (2004), 'From Marginalization to Massacres: A Political Process Explanation of GIA Violence in Algeria', in Quintan Wiktorowicz (ed.), *Islamic Activism: A Social Movement Theory Approach*, Bloomington, IN: Indiana University Press, pp. 37–60, p. 46.

100. These accusations remain fiercely contested. See, for example, Hugh Roberts's careful consideration of some of the most notable claims. Roberts, *The Battlefield Algeria 1988–2000*, pp. 309–12.

101. Fawaz A. Gerges (1999), *Political Islam: Clash of Culture or Clash of Interests?*, Cambridge: Cambridge University Press, p. 144.

102. Cavatorta, *The International Dimension of the Failed Algerian Transition*, p. 110.

103. Evans and Phillips, *Algeria*, pp. 206–7.

104. In addition to night-vision equipment, France sold Algeria transport and attack helicopters. To circumvent the European Union's ban on the sale of

military materiel to the country, France's Interior Minister, Charles Pasqua, claimed that it was for civilian use only. Algiers concurred, stating that it was needed to survey the country's beaches. James D. Le Sueur (2010), *Between Terror and Democracy: Algeria since 1989*, London and New York: Zed Books, p. 107.

105. Ibid, p. 106.

106. James D. Le Sueur (2005), *Uncivil War: Intellectuals and Identity Politics during the Decolonization of Algeria*, 2nd edn, London and Lincoln, NE: University of Nebraska Press, p. 320.

107. Sonatrach is the state-operated hydrocarbon company. It owns around 80 per cent of all oil and gas produced in Algeria. Available at <http://www.eia.gov/countries/analysisbriefs/Algeria/algeria.pdf> (last accessed 19 July 2015), p. 3.

108. Yet, just as Algeria is a vital supplier to Europe, so the European Union is highly valued as a customer by Algiers. The EU is not alone, therefore, in being fearful. Algeria has its own concerns. Principally, the Commission's plans to restrict supplies from extra-European providers, increase nuclear power production, invest more in renewable sources, and achieve energy efficiencies of 20 per cent by 2020, and the growth in competition from Qatar (LNG) and fracking (the United States and several European countries). To counter these challenges, and thereby confirm its status as one of the EU's most important energy providers, Algeria would also like to sign a Strategic Energy Partnership. For different reasons, both Algiers and Brussels are keen to lock the other into an energy relationship. Darbouche, '"Energising" EU–Algerian Relations', pp. 79–80.

109. Available at <https://ec.europa.eu/research/iscp/pdf/policy/barcelona_declaration.pdf> (last accessed 5 July 2015).

110. World Trade Organization (2014), 'Algeria', February/March, <https://www.wto.org/english/thewto_e/acc_e/a1_algerie_e.htm> (last accessed 5 July 2015).

111. Börzel and van Hüllen, 'One Voice, One Message, but Conflicting Goals', p. 1034.

112. Ibid. p. 1034.

113. Ibid. p. 1034.

114. Ibid. p. 1034.

115. Ibid. p. 1034.

116. Ibid. p. 1033.

117. Ibid. p. 1034.

118. Ibid. p. 1034.

119. The precise composition of this troika is open to a little debate. Stone identifies its members as 'the army, the party and the state', while Entelis highlights 'the military and intelligence agency, Sonatrach, representing the economic engine of the country, and the ruling elite governing the party (*Front de Libération National* or FLN)'. Despite these slight discrepancies,

two conclusions can be drawn: that Algeria was ruled by a triad of institutions, one of which was the FLN. Martin Stone (1997), *The Agony of Algeria*, London: Hurst and Company, p. 249; Entelis, 'Algeria', p. 667.

120. Freedom House (2015), 'Algeria', available at <https://freedomhouse.org/report/freedom-world/2015/algeria#.VcxtNzZRGM8> (last accessed 13 August 2015), p. 1.

121. Volpi, 'Algeria versus the Arab Spring', p. 111.

122. More precisely, the government spent 3 per cent of GDP on the military in 1995, 3.1 per cent in 1996, 3.6 per cent in 1997, 4 per cent in 1998, 3.8 per cent in 1999, 3.4 per cent in 2000, 3.8 per cent in 2001, 3.7 per cent in 2002, and 3.3 per cent in both 2003 and 2004; World Bank (2015), 'Military Expenditure (% of GDP)', <http://data.worldbank.org/indicator/MS.MIL.XPND.GD.ZS?page=3> (last accessed 27 July 2015).

123. More precisely, the government spent 2.8 per cent of GDP on the military in 2005, 2.6 per cent in 2006, 2.9 per cent in 2007, 3 per cent in 2008 and 3.8 per cent in 2009; ibid.

124. More precisely, the government spent 3.5 per cent of GDP on the military in 2010, 4.3 per cent in 2011, 4.6 per cent in 2012, 5 per cent in 2013 and 5.5 per cent in 2014; ibid.

125. In 1995 defence spending was $1.23 billion, in 1996 $1.45 billion, in 1997 $1.75 billion, in 1998 $1.91 billion, in 1999 $1.82 billion, in 2000 $1.88 billion, in 2001 $2.09 billion, in 2002 $2.12 billion, in 2003 $2.20 billion, in 2004 $2.80 billion, in 2005 $2.92 billion, in 2006 $3.09 billion, in 2007 $3.94 billion, in 2008 $5.17 billion, in 2009 $5.28 billion, in 2010 $5.67 billion, in 2011 $8.65 billion, in 2012 $9.32 billion, in 2013 $10.4 billion and in 2014 $11.8 billion; Stockholm International Peace Research Institute (2015), 'SIPRI Military Expenditure Database', <http://www.sipri.org/research/armaments/milex/milex_database> (last accessed 27 July 2015).

126. Ibid.

127. Available at <https://freedomhouse.org/report/freedom-world/2015/algeria#.VcxtNzZRGM8> (last accessed 13 August 2015), p. 1.

128. Ibid. p. 1.

129. République Algérienne Démocratique et populaire, Ministère de l'Intérieur et de Collectivités Locale (2011), 'The Constitution of the People's Democratic Republic of Algeria', 25 November, <http://faolex.fao.org/docs/pdf/alg72556.pdf> (last accessed 30 July 2015).

130. Isabelle Werenfels (2007), *Managing Instability in Algeria: Elites and Political Change since 1995*, Abingdon: Routledge, p. 67.

131. Ibid. p. 67.

132. J. N. C. Hill (2012), 'Remembering the War of Liberation: Legitimacy and Conflict in Contemporary Algeria', *Small Wars and Insurgencies*, 23: 1, 4–31, p. 4.

133. Luis Martinez (2004), 'Why the Violence in Algeria?', *The Journal of North African Studies*, 9: 2, 14–27, p. 19.

134. These were: Hocine Ait Ahmed, Ahmed Ben Bella, Larbi Ben M'Hidi, Mustapha Ben Boulaid, Mohamed Boudiaf, Rabah Bitat, Mourad Didouche, Mohamed Khider and Belkacem Krim; David Ottaway and Marina Ottaway (1970), *Algeria: The Politics of a Socialist Revolution*, Berkeley and Los Angeles, CA: University of California Press, p. 14n.

135. Hill, *Identity in Algerian Politics*, p. 161.

136. Lise Storm (2014), *Party Politics and the Prospects for Democracy in North Africa*, Boulder, CO and London: Lynne Rienner Publishers, p. 153.

137. Ibid. p. 152.

138. Freedom House (2011), 'An Analysis of Democratic Governance: Countries at the Crossroad, 2011', available at <https://freedomhouse.org/report/countries-crossroads/2011/algeria#.VcxeoDZRGM8> (last accessed 13 August 2015), p. 1.

139. Lowi, *Oil Wealth and the Poverty of Politics*, p. 140; Bradford Dillman (1998), 'The Political Economy of Structural Adjustment in Tunisia and Algeria', *The Journal of North African Studies*, 3: 3, 1–24, pp. 13–14.

140. Salah Salhi (2004), 'Implications of Algeria's WTO Accession', in Ahmed Aghrout and Redha M. Bougherira (eds), *Algeria in Transition: Reforms and Development Prospects*, London: RoutledgeCurzon, pp. 58–72, p. 59.

141. The diminution of Algeria's debt-to-GDP ratio has not been constant under Bouteflika. After falling to 17.3 per cent by 2004, it then rose to 18.2 per cent by 2006 before dropping almost year on year until its present level. *The Economist* (2015), 'The Global Debt Clock', <http://www.economist.com/content/global_debt_clock> (last accessed 28 July 2015).

142. IMF Staff Country Report No. 98/97', *International Monetary Fund*, September, <http://www.imf.org/external/pubs/ft/scr/1998/cr9887.pdf> (last accessed 28 July 2015), p. 86.

143. Available at <http://www.eia.gov/beta/international/analysis_includes/countries_long/Algeria/algeria.pdf> (last accessed 28 July 2015).

144. Surprisingly, the act had been passed only the year before.

145. Available at <http://www.eia.gov/beta/international/analysis_includes/countries_long/Algeria/algeria.pdf> (last accessed 28 July 2015).

146. US Department of State (2013), '2013 Investment Climate Statement – Algeria', <http://www.state.gov/e/eb/rls/othr/ics/2013/204588.htm> (last accessed 24 October 2013), p. 1.

147. Algeria is ranked 154th out of 189 countries with the top-placed state being the easiest place to do business and the bottom the least. World Bank (2014), 'Doing Business 2015: Going beyond Efficiency', <http://www.doingbusiness.org/~/media/GIAWB/Doing%20Business/Documents/Annual-Reports/English/DB15-Full-Report.pdf> (last accessed 28 July 2015), p. 1.

148. Available at <http://www.eia.gov/beta/international/analysis_includes/countries_long/Algeria/algeria.pdf> (last accessed 29 July 2015).

149. Available at <https://freedomhouse.org/report/countries-crossroads/2011/algeria#.VcxeoDZRGM8> (last accessed 13 August 2015), p. 1.

150. Arguably this pressure peaked with the publication of the Sant'Egidio Platform on 13 January 1995. The platform was the outcome of a series of meetings held between the leaders of the main opposition parties – the National Liberation Front (Front de Libération Nationale, FLN), the Socialist Forces Front (Front des Forces Socialistes, FFS), the Movement for the Society of Peace (Mouvement de la Société pour la Paix, MSP), the Workers' Party (Parti des Travailleurs, PT) and the Movement for Democracy in Algeria (Mouvement pour la Démocratie en Algérie, MDA) – and the FIS at the Sant'Egidio religious community in Rome. In addition to calling for the separation of powers, the re-establishment of a multiparty system, Tamazight to be made the equal of Arabic and the government to stop using violence for political purposes, it demanded the relegalisation of the FIS. Even though he agreed with much of what it said, President Zéroual summarily rejected it on the grounds that he could not be seen to be capitulating to the FIS or other opposition parties. Le Sueur (2010), *Between Terror and Democracy*, pp.66–7.

151. RpCD is not the conventional abbreviation used for Sadi's party. It is used here to distinguish it from Ben Ali's RCD.

152. Storm, *Party Politics and the Prospects for Democracy*, p. 158.

153. Formally, parliament's powers are not as great as those invested in the presidency. And informally, it does not wield all of those which it is awarded. Though sanctioned under Article 160 of the constitution to oversee how the national budget is spent, it does not do so. Since 1982, in fact, 'financial laws have been enacted without parliamentary scrutiny'. Available at <https://freedomhouse.org/report/countries-crossroads/2011/algeria#. VcxeoDZRGM8> (last accessed 13 August 2015), p. 1.

154. Roberts, *The Battlefield Algeria 1988–2000*, p. 192.

155. Storm, *Party Politics and the Prospects for Democracy*, p. 204.

156. Yahia H. Zoubir (2004), 'The Dialectics of Algeria's Foreign Relations, 1992 to the Present', in Ahmed Aghrout and Redha M. Bougherira (eds), *Algeria in Transition: Reforms and Development Prospects*, London: RoutledgeCurzon, 151–82, p. 164.

157. Ibid. pp. 204–5; available at <http://www.reuters.com/article/2014/04/18/ us-algeria-election-idUSBREA3H0D620140418> (last accessed 29 April 2015), p. 1.

158. BBC (2004), 'Algerian Press Aghast at Election Result', 10 April, available at <http://news.bbc.co.uk/1/hi/world/africa/3616461.stm> (last accessed 13 August 2015), p. 1.

159. Carnegie Endowment for International Peace (2009), 'Lessons from Algeria's 2009 Presidential Election', 13 April, available at <http://carnegieendowment.org/2009/04/13/lessons-from-algeria-s-2009-presidential-election/i8t> (last accessed 13 August 2015), p. 1.

160. Available at <https://freedomhouse.org/report/countries-crossroads/2011/ algeria#.VcxeoDZRGM8> (last accessed 13 August 2015), p. 1.

161. Available at <https://freedomhouse.org/report/freedom-world/2015/algeria #.VcxtNzZRGM8> (last accessed 13 August 2015), p. 1.
162. Ibid. p. 1.
163. In 1997 they occupied 57.4 per cent of the National Assembly's seats (FLN 16.2/RND 41.1), in 2002 63.4 per cent (FLN 51.3/RND 12.1), in 2007 50.7 per cent (FLN 35/RND 15.7), and 2012 62.7 per cent (FLN 45/RND 14.7); Storm, *Party Politics and the Prospects for Democracy*, p. 203.
164. Freedom House (1998), 'Algeria', available at <https://freedomhouse.org/ report/freedom-world/1998/algeria#.Vc20lDZRGM8> (last accessed 14 August 2015).
165. Freedom House (2013), 'Algeria', available at <https://freedomhouse. org/report/freedom-world/2013/algeria#.Vc2zyjZRGM8> (last accessed 14 August 2015), p. 1.
166. Matthew Connelly (2002), *A Diplomatic Revolution*, Oxford: Oxford University Press, p. 357.
167. The next most successful second-placed candidate was Ali Benflis with 12.18 per cent in 2014. Available at <http://www.reuters.com/article/2014/ 04/18/us-algeria-election-idUSBREA3H0D620140418> (last accessed 29 April 2015), p. 1.
168. Hill, *Identity in Algerian Politics*, p. 195.
169. Storm, *Party Politics and the Prospects for Democracy*, p. 205.
170. Available at <https://freedomhouse.org/report/countries-crossroads/2011/ algeria#.VcxeoDZRGM8> (last accessed 13 August 2015), p. 1.
171. Available at <https://freedomhouse.org/report/countries-crossroads/2011/ algeria#.VcxeoDZRGM8> (last accessed 13 August 2015), p. 1.
172. Ibid. p. 1.
173. Storm, *Party Politics and the Prospects for Democracy*, p. 160.
174. Volpi, 'Algeria versus the Arab Spring', p. 112.
175. Ibid. p. 112.
176. Available at <https://freedomhouse.org/report/freedom-world/2015/algeria #.VcxtNzZRGM8> (last accessed 13 August 2015), p. 1.
177. Available at <https://freedomhouse.org/report/countries-crossroads/2011/ algeria#.VcxeoDZRGM8> (last accessed 13 August 2015), p. 1.
178. Reporters Without Borders (2015), 'New Cases of Media Censorship in Algeria', 27 April, available at <http://www.rsf.org/algerie-new-cases-of-media-censorship-in-27-04-2015,47819.html> (last accessed 17 August 2015), p. 1.
179. Available at <https://freedomhouse.org/report/freedom-world/2015/algeria #.VcxtNzZRGM8> (last accessed 13 August 2015), p. 1.
180. Available at <https://freedomhouse.org/report/countries-crossroads/2011/ algeria#.VcxeoDZRGM8> (last accessed 13 August 2015), p. 1.
181. Available at <https://freedomhouse.org/report/freedom-world/2015/algeria #.VcxtNzZRGM8> (last accessed 13 August 2015), p. 1.

182. Available at <https://freedomhouse.org/report/countries-crossroads/2011/algeria#.VcxeoDZRGM8> (last accessed 13 August 2015), p. 1.

183. Ibid. p. 1.

184. Available at <https://freedomhouse.org/report/freedom-world/2015/algeria#.VcxtNzZRGM8> (last accessed 13 August 2015), p. 1.

185. The state-controlled National Agency for Advertising and Publishing (Agence Nationale d'Edition et de la Publicité, ANEP) is the country's main distributor of advertising revenue. Available at <https://freedomhouse.org/report/countries-crossroads/2011/algeria#.VcxeoDZRGM8> (last accessed 13 August 2015), p. 1.

186. Ibid. p. 1.

187. Reporters Without Borders (2015), 'Algerian Authorities Step Up Harassment of Print Media', 25 March, available at <http://ww.rsf.org/algeria-algerian-authorities-step-up-25-03-2015,447725.html> (last accessed 17 August 2015), p. 1.

188. Robert Mortimer (2004), 'Bouteflika and the Challenge of Political Stability', in Ahmed Aghrout and Redha M. Bougherira (eds), *Algeria in Transition: Reforms and Development Prospects*, London: RoutledgeCurzon, pp. 183–98.

4

Morocco

Of all the cases examined here, Morocco presents some of the greatest challenges. For, despite appearances, Levitsky and Way's model cannot be easily applied to it. Indeed, they explicitly rule it out as a potential study on the grounds that 'the most important executive office is not elected'.[1] More specifically, they argue that 'the power of actors outside the electoral process' – in this case the monarchy – 'generates a distinct set of dynamics and challenges not found under competitive authoritarianism'.[2] That the king's powers are numerous and great is beyond question. That his political position is far more secure than those of elected heads of state is similarly irrefutable. Unlike the presidents of competitive authoritarian Algeria and Mauritania, he does not have to submit to the vote. And, even though Bouteflika and Abdel Aziz have successfully minimised the risk of defeat, they have been able to do so only through enormous and sustained effort and still cannot eliminate it entirely.

In fairness to Levitsky and Way, they did not argue that their model could *never* be applied to countries like Morocco. Rather, they were explaining their choice of case studies for their book. They also picked their words carefully. They ruled nothing in or out but, instead, spoke of uncommon dynamics and unusual challenges. Indeed, the only phrase they used which requires closer interrogation is 'outside the electoral process'. While this is, of course, literally true in the case of Morocco, it is also misleading. For the king is deeply affected by elections. Confirmation of just how important they are to him is provided by their very occurrence and by the palace's increasing efforts to ensure that they at least appear to be free and fair.[3] That a regime headed by an executive who supposedly occupies political space somewhere beyond the reach of ballots and voters should go to such lengths to hold elections and be so anxious about their conduct belies claims and suggestions that he is impervious to them.

The staging of these ballots has already led Immaculada Szmolka to describe Morocco as competitive authoritarian. She justifies doing so on the grounds that, even though elections are held regularly, opposition parties have been allowed to help reform the country's voting laws, and safeguards have recently been introduced to better ensure the integrity of the ballot, abuses still take place. In particular, 'the distribution of seats' in parliament continues to be fixed while parties and movements which 'might aim to modify the constitutional system' are routinely barred from the political process.[4] This final observation is especially important for, in identifying such a powerful motivation for the monarchy's high level of interest in the electoral system, Szmolka offers a compelling reason why Morocco can and should be labelled competitive authoritarian

Yet, frustratingly, having done so, she then drops this line of enquiry. Rather than explain why the monarchy is so wary of constitutional reform or how these fears engender competitive authoritarianism, she simply lapses into silence. This chapter, then, undertakes the analysis and offers the explanation that Szmolka alludes to but does not conduct or provide. Morocco is competitive authoritarian because the monarchy uses the limited amount of democracy it allows to take place to avoid and counter, diminish and contain those arguments and groups calling for significant reductions in its powers and greater political liberalisation. And, while it does not necessarily face the same level of existential threat as the regimes in Algeria and Mauritania – the king is as unlikely to be removed as head of state as the monarchy is to be abolished – its overriding objective is still largely the same as theirs. It does not want to surrender its great powers. It does not want to play the sort of decorative and symbolic role that most genuinely constitutional monarchies now have to perform. It does not want to be reduced to the status of mere figurehead. So, even though it could well survive democratisation, it would probably only do so much altered. And, at present, it would rather not undergo those changes.

The Moroccan regime, then, shares several notable similarities with its competitive authoritarian neighbours. Like its Algerian counterpart, it has emerged from the Arab Spring largely unchanged. Of course, the country experienced serious and sustained unrest. There were multiple demonstrations and riots in Rabat, Casablanca, Tangier and elsewhere throughout much of 2011 and the summer of 2012.[5] These protests were sufficiently frequent, large and angry to draw an official response. A Royal Commission was quickly established to consider and recommend changes to the constitution.[6] And the delayed Economic and Social Environment Council (Conseil Economique, Social et Environnemental, CESE), long portrayed as an at least partial solution to the country's endemic youth unemployment, was hastily launched.[7] Yet, despite these dangers and the reforms they elicited, the regime survived with its powers largely intact. Like its Algerian counterpart, the Moroccan regime entered the Arab Spring competitive authoritarian and emerged from the Arab Spring competitive authoritarian.

At least some of the reasons why it did are the same as those that enabled Ben Ali to remain in power for the better part of twenty-five years. For, like its Tunisian counterpart, the Moroccan regime continues to benefit from not having too much democratising pressure put on it by the West. For, despite having strong links to the country, their leverage over Rabat is only low. Furthermore, and just as they were with Ben Ali, they remain reluctant to bring to bear the full extent of the influence they do have. Their disinclination to do so stems from similar considerations to those that shaped their treatment of Tunisia. Morocco has long been one of the United States' and Europe Union's closest allies in North Africa. And the leniency this has led them to show the regime has only been strengthened by the Arab Spring's aftermath. As a stabilising influence in a less-stable region, the West is determined to avoid doing anything – including forcing the issue of democracy – that might undermine Morocco's current equilibrium. And, just as with Ben Ali's Tunisia and Bouteflika's Algeria, what tentative pressure they do apply is rendered less effective by its inconsistent application, by the discrepancies between individual Western governments' behaviour towards Rabat.

Nevertheless, the monarch's freedom from having to seek election has led the Moroccan regime to develop its organisational strength in a subtly different manner from that set out by Levitsky and Way. In so doing, it would appear to conform to their assessment about how the presence of a powerful non-elected official can alter the currents of power within a hybrid regime. Yet the palace's attitude towards, and treatment of, the country's political parties is not very far removed from President Bouteflika's handling of the RND, FLN and Algeria's other groups. Rather than create or elevate a party to a position of unrivalled supremacy, as Ben Ali did with the RCD, King Mohammed and, to a lesser extent, Bouteflika have both courted and divided power across a range of groups. As a result, none is in a position effectively to challenge or easily disobey either of them. By dissipating power and inculcating competition among their respective country's parties, they have enhanced their authority over their political systems. Not only, therefore, has the palace continued to act in a profoundly competitive authoritarian way but its behaviour is similar to that of another of the region's competitive authoritarian leaders.

To sustain this analysis and enable better Morocco's comparison with its near neighbours, the chapter is organised along the same lines as each of Levitsky and Way's original cases as well as this book's other country studies. The first section examines the strength of Morocco's links to both the United States and the European Union across their six categories of connection. The second section determines how much leverage

Washington and Brussels have over Rabat, and whether it has the backing of a Black Knight patron. The third section measures the regime's organisational power, whether it has the support of a ruling party, the scope and cohesion of its coercive forces and the amount of discretionary control the government exercises over the economy. And the final section charts the regime's origins and developments, paying particular attention to the period from 2005 onwards.

Linkage

Morocco has strong links to the United States and European Union across all six categories of connection. Both the number and quality of these ties have increased markedly under King Mohammed VI. Since his accession to the throne on 23 July 1999, the country has enthusiastically joined the same policy frameworks as Tunisia and Algeria, including the MEPI, the BMENA, the EMP, the UfM, the ENP and the PfDSP. In addition, it has secured other recognitions not extended to its near neighbours. It participates in the US-sponsored Millennium Challenge Corporation (MCC).[8] It has signed a Free Trade Agreement (FTA) with Washington. And its relations with the European Union have been granted Advanced Status by Brussels.

Morocco is one of Washington's oldest and closest allies in the region and a major recipient of US aid and development funding.[9] Between 2009 and 2015, it was awarded $232.11 million in financial assistance and $49.23 million in FMF credits. While this was less than that which was given to Tunisia over the same period ($424.6 million and $142.17 million respectively), it was substantially more than what was granted to either Algeria ($43.23 million and nothing) or Mauritania ($43.93 million and nothing).[10] Moreover, between August 2007 and September 2013, Rabat was awarded $649.37 million in MCC funding which no other Maghreb country received or was eligible to claim.[11] It is currently negotiating a second tranche of MCC investment.[12]

Another notable feature of Washington's aid and development assistance to Rabat is its focus. Since 2009, Morocco has been provided with significantly less security-related funding than Tunisia. While 41.5 per cent of the financial assistance it was granted over this period was set aside for Peace and Security projects, 57.93 per cent of that awarded to Tunisia was.[13] Moreover, Tunis was given nearly three times as much FMF credit as Rabat. Not only was the amount of security aid granted to Morocco less than that provided to its neighbour in absolute terms but this funding also comprised a much smaller portion of the total assistance it was given.

147

From an aid and development perspective, therefore, security concerns are less central to the United States' relations with Morocco than they are with Tunisia.

Morocco enjoys preferential trade relations with the United States compared to its neighbours. Rabat and Washington signed an FTA on 15 June 2004 and it came into force on 1 January 2006. Once it did, 95 per cent of bilateral trade became duty free,[14] with all remaining tariffs on US exports to Morocco to be phased out by 2024.[15] The agreement also regulates 'all forms of investment . . . including enterprises, debt, concessions, contracts and intellectual property'. And it allows investors from both countries to operate on largely equal footings with their local counterparts. No other North African country has signed an FTA. Its political and economic importance elevates Morocco's relationship with the United States 'to an altogether different level'.[16]

Like Tunisia, Morocco has consistently and energetically pursued closer relations with the European Union. It has continued to do so even after King Hassan II's ambition of acceding to the community was dashed by the European Council in 1987.[17] It has joined each policy framework at the earliest opportunity. It signed its association agreement just three months after the EMP was launched.[18] Similarly, it concluded its action plan scarcely seven months after the ENP was established.[19] In recognition of the strength of its commitment, Brussels upgraded Morocco's relationship with the EU to Advanced Status on 13 October 2008.[20] It is still the only North African partner state to receive this designation.

The European Union has also rewarded Morocco's enthusiasm with high levels of funding. The country has received more MEDA I (€660 million) and MEDA II (€980.1 million) investment than any of its neighbours, and Tunisia (€428 million and €517.6 million) and Algeria (€164 million and €338.8 million) combined (€592 million and €856.4 million).[21] Between 1996 and 2013, it was granted loans totalling €887 million by the EIB.[22] Between 2007 and 2010, it was given €654 million in development funding by the ENPI. Between 2011 and 2013, it was awarded a further €580.5 million by the ENPI.[23] And, between 2012 and 2013, it was granted €115 million in emergency assistance under the SPRING programme.[24] Since 2007, it has received more EU aid than any other North African country.[25]

Many of these intergovernmental accords and initiatives have important economic dimensions and implications. Since King Mohammed's accession to the throne, Brussels and Washington have been far keener to strengthen their economic relations with Morocco than they have to pressurise its ruling 'elite to implement meaningful political reform'.[26]

Little wonder that, by 2013, the European Union and the United States were the country's top two commercial partners. Like Tunisia and Algeria, Morocco does more trade with the European Union (53.6 per cent) than the rest of the world combined. And, while clearly not on the same scale (6.4 per cent),[27] its trade with the United States has steadily increased in value over the past twenty years.

Between 1995 and 1999, the annual average value of Morocco's exports to the United States was $188.29 million.[28] Between 2000 and 2004, that amount jumped to $280.8 million.[29] Then, between 2005 and 2009,[30] it rose again to $422.54 million before more than doubling to $861.1 million between 2010 and 2012.[31] The value of the country's imports from the United States has also increased significantly over this period. Between 1995 and 1999, their annual average value was $606.94 million.[32] Between 2000 and 2004,[33] that amount fell slightly to $575.19 million before tripling to $1.62 billion between 2005 and 2009.[34] And, most recently, between 2010 and 2012, it rose to $1.79 billion.[35] Tellingly, the most dramatic increases occurred shortly after the inauguration of the FTA in January 2006.

These rises have been mirrored by similar increases in the amount of FDI in the country. Between 1995 and 1999, Morocco attracted an average of $373.77 million of investment each year.[36] Between 2000 and 2004, that amount nearly doubled to $708.69 million.[37] Then, between 2005 and 2009, it more than tripled to $2.27 billion,[38] before rising again to $2.49 billion between 2010 and 2013.[39] And these figures do not include the millions of dollars in remittance payments made by the members of the country's extensive diaspora. There are currently 4.5 million Moroccan citizens living abroad.[40] Most are based in Europe (85 per cent),[41] with the largest communities in France (660,000), Spain (547,000), Italy (379,000), Belgium (285,000), the Netherlands (278,000) and Germany (130,000).[42] Between 1995 and 1999, their remittances were worth an average of $1.99 billion a year. Between 2000 and 2004, that amount climbed to $3.22 billion. Then, between 2005 and 2009, it nearly doubled to $5.98 billion, before rising again to $6.76 billion between 2010 and 2013.[43]

Like its Tunisian and Algerian equivalents, Morocco's diaspora also plays an important social role. And this cross-border flow of people is augmented by the tens of thousands of (mostly Western) tourists who travel to the country each year. Unlike Tunisia, Morocco did not experience any reductions in visitor numbers during the Arab Spring. On the contrary, there were small year-on-year increases throughout this period, from 9.28 million in 2010, to 9.34 million in 2011, to 9.37 million in 2012, to 10.04

million in 2013.[44] Clearly, these rises were not as great as those over the previous five years (from 5.84 million in 2005 to 8.34 million in 2009) but that there were any at all is telling. Firstly, because it offers additional insight into international – in this case public – attitudes towards what was happening in the Maghreb. While European travellers clearly had some concerns, they still viewed Morocco as more stable than Tunisia which experienced a big drop in visitor numbers over this period. And, secondly, this perception had a material consequence. When assessed in terms of tourist numbers, Morocco was less affected by the Arab Spring than its near neighbour.

A significant number of the millions of Moroccans living and working in the West are students. In the 2013/2014 academic year, there were 33,899 Moroccans enrolled at French universities alone. In addition, more Moroccan students have registered at French universities in each of the last ten academic years than any other foreign nationality.[45] Crucially, the vast majority of those who study in France, Spain and elsewhere in the West make their own arrangements to do so. Only a very small minority participate in one or other of the official exchange programmes run by Washington and Brussels, such as the US State Department's Kennedy–Lugar Youth Exchange and Study (YES) initiative,[46] and the European Union's Tempus and Erasmus Mundus schemes.[47] Since 2004 – the year the YES programme was extended to Morocco – less than 310 people have participated in them.[48]

Most of those who study in the West, therefore, are from well-to-do backgrounds. And, just as it is for their Tunisian and Algerian peers, spending a little time at a European or North American college or university is now an important rite of passage for many affluent young Moroccans. By virtue of the educations they receive and the qualifications they earn there, as well as having the sorts of socio-economic backgrounds that allow them to study abroad in the first instance, many of those who return home are well placed to secure gainful employment in either the public or private sectors. As a result, Morocco's strong technocratic links to North America and, in particular, to Europe are maintained.

The cross-border circulation of news these transnational populations both encourage and facilitate is enhanced by Morocco's much-improved and rapidly developing information links to the United States and Europe. Like its neighbours, the country has experienced an explosion in Internet and mobile phone use over the past decade. In 2000 just 0.7 per cent of the population had access to the World Wide Web. By 2005 this figure had leapt to 15.1 per cent. By 2010, it had more than tripled to 52 per cent. And, by 2013, it had risen again to 56 per cent.[49] And the increase in mobile phone subscriptions over this period has arguably been even more dramatic. In 2000 just 8 per cent of the populace had a contract. By 2005, this figure had soared to 41 per cent. By 2010, it had jumped again to 101 per cent. And, by 2013, it had risen still further to 129 per cent.[50]

These expansions mean that more ordinary Moroccans are better equipped than ever before to access additional information and alternative viewpoints on events and developments in their country. No longer must they rely exclusively on local and state-run news providers to learn about what has been happening. No longer must they content themselves with selected and officially sanctioned opinions and explanations. Through their improved links to friends, relations, contacts and media sources elsewhere they can find out better what is happening and decide for themselves what it means. And this includes questioning and challenging the regime's policies, actions and answers.

The existence of these large, mobile, cross-border populations has encouraged the proliferation of transnational civil society groups and networks. The European Union continues to make financial support available to a range of bodies and projects through the ENPI, CSF and other schemes. Especially strong ties have been forged between human rights groups. The Democratic Association of Moroccan Women (Association Démocratique des Femmes du Maroc, ADFM), Moroccan Human Rights Association (Association Marocaine de Driots Humains, AMDH), Moroccan Human Rights Organisation (Organisation Marocaine des Droits Humains, OMDH) and Espace Associatif all belong to the Euro-Mediterranean Human Rights Network (Réseau Euro-Méditerranéen des Driots de l'Homme, EMDH) which was established under the terms of the Barcelona Declaration,[51] and is funded by the European Commission and individual European Union member-state governments (Denmark and Sweden).[52]

Leverage

Despite these strong links, the West's leverage over Morocco is only low because the country meets at least one of Levitsky and Way's three criteria for determining a regime's ability to withstand outside influence. More specifically, it has a large economy of $107 billion.[53] So, even though it is not a major oil producer, does not possess or have access to nuclear weapons and is not supported by a Black Knight patron, it still has the economic wherewithal to cope with any democratising pressure put on it by the United States and European Union.

Crucially, though, this assessment, based on a fair and accurate application of Levitsky and Way's conditions, does not deny or preclude the

West's ability to put significant pressure on Morocco. Rabat's sustained determination to forge ever-closer relations with the United States and European Union has led it to join a range of policy frameworks that grant Washington and Brussels the authority to require it to modify its political behaviour. Through the MEPI, the BMENA, the FTA, the MCC, the EMP, the UfM, the ENP and the PfDSP, the West has the means to make some searching demands of the Moroccan regime. Yet, as great as its authority is, it still has only low leverage over the kingdom because Rabat's capacity both to refuse and to deal with any subsequent consequences is even greater. Furthermore, and just as importantly, the West has long shown a strong disinclination to bring as much pressure to bear on the country as it could. It has effectively abrogated, at least in part, its ability to hold Rabat to account.

Indeed, Western governments have consistently struggled to make more effective use of what leverage they do possess. The main cause of their failure is the same as that which colours and shapes their relations with Tunisia and Algeria – their profound fear that any serious instability in the region will soon spread to their own populations and territories. This anxiety makes them reluctant to do or say anything that might undermine those leaders and regimes which, they believe, are helping to maintain stability. Their policies towards Morocco, therefore, are marked by several inconsistencies. One of the most significant is the tension between their professed political expectations for the kingdom and the amount of undemocratic behaviour they are prepared to tolerate.

While this discrepancy predates King Mohammed's accession to the throne, it has been strengthened and entrenched throughout his reign, in large measure because of Western governments' eagerness to view him as a modernising and liberalising force. Their enthusiasm was born of a powerful collective desire to draw a line under the abusive and authoritarian rule of his father, Hassan II. They very much hoped that the youthful and westernised Mohammed would help strengthen democracy and human rights in Morocco and its neighbours. Their craving for stability was buttressed by a hunger to have the new king succeed. By extension, their reluctance to do anything which might destabilise this important ally or weaken its ability to act as a steadying influence in the region has been fortified by their determination to avoid undermining or alienating King Mohammed.

To a large extent, of course, these ambitions are complementary to the point of being indistinguishable. Symbolically, and in many substantive ways as well, Morocco and the monarchy are the same. To be an ally of one is to back the other. To put pressure on one is to compel the other.

To reform one is to change the other. Since Mohammed's accession to the throne, therefore, Western governments have adopted an '"applause policy"'.[54] This approach has at least three interconnected elements. The first is to shower the palace and regime with praise. Over the years, Western governments have been quick to commend Rabat for those reforms and initiatives of which they approve and appear to justify the high level of support they show it. King Mohammed's establishment of the Equity and Reconciliation Committee (Instance Equité et Réconciliation, IER) to investigate human rights abuses during the so-called Years of Lead, revision of the Family Code (the *Mudawana*) and reinforcement of women's rights, easing of some of the restrictions on political parties and the press, and willingness to allow international election monitors to oversee the 2007 parliamentary vote have all been lavishly extolled.[55]

The second part is to refrain from castigating Rabat too heavily for acting against democracy, backsliding on its promises, or not consolidating or extending those democratic reforms it has introduced already.[56] What criticisms of the regime Western governments have been prepared to make have either been muttered sotto voce, made with heavy caveat, or offset by encouragement. And the third part of their approach is to evaluate the regime's actions and progress in relative terms. Rather than judge its behaviour against fixed and predetermined criteria, they compare it backwards and sideways with that of earlier and neighbouring governments. When measured against that of King Hassan II, the current order appears far more enlightened. When compared with their Algerian and Mauritanian counterparts, the Moroccan elite seems more willing to work with international partners.

By adopting this policy, the West is predisposed to take a favourable view of Morocco's political development. In so doing, it has only increased the size of the challenge confronting the country's pro-democracy and human rights campaigners. For, to achieve change, they have to confront and try to reform a regime that enjoys the West's backing.[57] Moreover, by embracing this policy, Western governments have further compromised their ability to put pressure on Rabat. For, in perceiving and portraying the country in this way, they have not only effectively foresworn taking more punitive actions against the regime but rendered the application of any such measures both irrational and unfair. How can they punish that which they praise?

Paradoxically, and despite their solemn pledges to be more supportive of popular demands for greater democracy, the Arab Spring has only made Western governments more reluctant to do anything that might weaken or unsettle the Moroccan regime; and this includes pushing Rabat harder to reform and liberalise its political structures and processes. The primary triggers of this disinclination are the same today as they were before. In the years leading up to the Arab Spring, Western governments grew to value 'Morocco's stabilizing influence in the region' very highly, to the extent, that they did not want to jeopardise it 'for the sake of "optimizing" Moroccan democratic standards'. With political Islam seemingly on the rise across North Africa, Western governments looked to the country for 'positive regional spill-over', to be a calm and settling influence, to show its neighbours how to integrate peaceably and effectively manage Islamist parties, groups and societies.[58]

And the same is also true today. While religious organisations played only marginal roles in launching the Arab Spring protests, they have since reaped significant political benefits.[59] Ennahda and the Justice and Development Party (Parti de la Justice et du Développement, PJD) won the Tunisian and Moroccan parliamentary elections in 2011. And the Green Alliance of Algeria (Alliance de l'Algérie, AAV) came third in the Algerian National Assembly election in 2012.[60] Additionally, and more importantly for the West, violent Islamist factions continue to exploit and exacerbate the instability created by the Arab Spring. Libya is wracked by civil war and has become a safe haven for Islamic State fighters. Tunisia has suffered several devastating terror attacks and is struggling to cope with the twin threats of IS and the resurgent AQIM. And Algeria, which has long been plagued by Islamist terrorism, has been forced to strengthen security along its eastern and southern borders.

Like Algeria, Morocco emerged from the Arab Spring fundamentally unaltered. Despite the protests, riots and government reforms, power continues to be distributed along much the same lines as before. Decisive authority is still vested in the monarchy. The old order has survived largely intact. That it has is what now recommends the country to the West as a key regional partner. Or rather, it helps reaffirm the kingdom's importance as a vital source of stability in this unsettled region. Morocco is one of a diminished number of countries able to play this role just when it is needed most. Washington, Brussels and individual European governments still look to Rabat to project stability. They remain, therefore, as reluctant as ever to do anything – including '"optimizing" Moroccan democratic standards' – that might lessen its ability to play this part.

A second key constraint on the West's ability to put more democratising pressure on Morocco is the failure of its institutions and governments to co-ordinate better their policies towards the kingdom. Clearly, they agree on a great deal. Both the United States and the European Union are keen to strengthen their relations with the country, to the extent that each has concluded a special arrangement with Rabat: an FTA and Advanced Status respectively. And, of course, the European Union's position broadly reflects that of its member states. When taken together, most Western countries have the same goals in and for Morocco.

Yet divergences still persist. Some are almost entirely unavoidable. As Mouhib notes, the European Union's democracy-promotion efforts are less a coherent strategy and more a 'complex "political process"'.[61] This means that disagreements and deviations between the EU's organs and institutions are virtually inevitable. So it was in 2011 that the European Parliament 'questioned whether the financial and logistic assistance' the European Union provided Morocco and other southern Mediterranean partner states did enough to encourage the industrialisation that it deemed essential to promoting long-term growth in productivity and protecting their economies from the sorts of 'exogenous shocks' that commonly affect 'global agricultural and commodity markets'. And again in 2012, the European Parliament identified '"inconsistencies" in the EU's trade agreements' with the partner states that, it argued, prevented them from using 'trade barriers . . . to successfully promote infant industries'.[62]

Other divergences are perhaps less certain in that they are not structural, are not rooted in the EU's institutional make-up. Nevertheless, they are highly probable because they are geopolitical and exist between member states, and member states and the European Commission. These deviations result from national capitals taking different policy lines from each other and from Brussels. Both for them and for Rabat, bilateral relations take precedence over working either through or with the commission. France, Italy and Spain each looks to secure its own interests first before conforming to the position and approach adopted and set out by Brussels. Equally, 'the message from Paris, Rome and Madrid . . . remains far more significant because of their role as . . . security partners and exporters of defence equipment and training, than the EEAS's requests to talk about political reform'.[63]

This prioritisation sustains at least two significant paradoxes. The first is the extent to which the EU's policies towards its neighbours are decided by those member states most willing to deviate from them. It is now customary within the European Union for the members with the strongest, most immediate interests in a particular region to take the lead in formulating the bloc's relations with it. Northern European countries, therefore, 'looking more to the East than to the South', often let France and Spain shape 'Europe's relations with Morocco'.[64] This arrangement helps explain the EU's continuing reticence to press Rabat harder to democratise because its Mediterranean members remain reluctant to push 'for [greater] political change'.[65] And it also helps explain why the French and Spanish governments still prefer to work bilaterally with Morocco and the Maghreb's other countries than through the European Union.[66] For, even though the EU's policy towards the region reflects those countries' interests more closely than those of other member states, it still does not capture them precisely enough. As a result, both Paris and Madrid look to advance them by other means outside the European Union.

The second paradox is the extent to which, in so doing, the French and Spanish governments are encouraging their Moroccan counterpart to respond in kind, to prioritise dealing directly with them above working with and through Brussels. Clearly this is inevitable in those policy areas pertaining only or largely to themselves, to bilateral French–Moroccan and Spanish–Moroccan issues. Yet it is also encouraged by Northern Europe's deferment. For such is the French and Spanish governments' influence on European policy towards Morocco and the Maghreb that Rabat is well advised actively to engage with them. Brussels might declare what European Union policy is but its content, direction and tenor are mainly decided elsewhere, in Paris and Madrid.

Organisational Power

The Moroccan regime has high organisational power although its capacity varies across the three subdimensions and does not neatly conform to all aspects of Levitsky and Way's model. The mainstay of its strength is its large, well-funded and experienced armed and security forces. They have a meaningful and effective presence across much of the country, including the Western Sahara, and strong cohesion based, in part, on non-material ties. The regime does not incorporate or rely on a single ruling party but, instead, uses and controls several through its policy of political fragmentation. Its strength in this area, however, is still medium as these groups are all national forces, and its ability to influence the country's political processes remains considerable. Indeed, the only subdimension in which its organisational power is low is economic. Largely because of its conclusion of an FTA with the United States, it does not, unlike its Algerian counterpart, exercise decisive control over any key sectors so has less direct influence over the broader economy.

Over the past two decades, government investment in the military has remained steady. Between 1995 and 1999, the regime spent an average of 3.5 per cent annually of the country's GDP on the armed forces. Between 2000 and 2009, this allocation fell slightly to 3.3 per cent. Then, between 2010 and 2014, it rose a little to 3.6 percent.[67] This means that, in real terms, government spending on the military increased year on year almost without exception,[68] to the extent that, by 2014, the regime was spending nearly twice as much on defence ($4 billion) as it had been a decade earlier ($2.4 billion).[69]

The regime's sustained investment in the armed and security forces has enabled them to build up a wide and deep presence in the country. The military alone comprises 175,000 soldiers, 7,800 sailors, 13,000 air force personnel, 20,000 gendarmes, and 30,000 auxiliaries covering two zones, northern and southern.[70] This level of investment, number of troops and their disposition continue to be driven and justified by the existence and activities of the Popular Front for the Liberation of Saguia el-Hamra and Rio de Oro (Frente Popular para la Liberación de Saguia el-Hamra y Río de Oro, Polisario) and, increasingly since the start of the new millennium, the threat from Islamist terror groups, such as Salafia Jihadia (which carried out the 2003 Casablanca bombings) and AQIM.

The broad scope of Morocco's armed and security forces is confirmed by their ability to undertake low-intensity operations. While they do not carry out as many such actions as they once did or as their Algerian counterparts still do, they continue to harass, intimidate and persecute critics and opponents of the regime. Independent journalists, dissident intellectuals, and civil and human rights activists, in particular, are subjected to various forms of unpleasant and unsettling treatment as punishment for what they have done or are doing, and to try to make them desist.[71]

The security apparatus also has high cohesion based on non-material ties. Since achieving independence, Morocco's armed forces have fought and won two short wars against Algeria.[72] And, since 1973, they have waged a broadly successful counterinsurgency campaign against the Polisario. Its senior officers, therefore, have extensive experience of fighting and winning military campaigns. Moreover, they have proven their commitment to the regime and invested heavily in its survival. They not only know what to do to protect it, including how to carry out high-intensity operations, but, in defending it thus far, they have effectively committed themselves to doing so again in the future. For the sake of professional and personal consistency, these knowledgeable and experienced officers are bound to the status quo.

Just as the broad scope of the country's security apparatus is confirmed by its ability to conduct low-intensity operations, so its strong cohesion is demonstrated by its capacity to undertake high-intensity ones. Between January and September 2011 and again, albeit less frequently, during the summer of 2012, the country experienced numerous protests and the occasional riot.[73] Many of these demonstrations were inspired by what was taking place in Tunisia, Egypt, Libya and Algeria. Quite deliberately, especially following the establishment of the February 20th Movement (Mouvement du 20 Février, MVF), they were presented as the Moroccan phase of the Arab Spring,[74] to the extent that this was how they were quickly seen and understood domestically and internationally. That many of those who protested demanded economic, rather than political, reforms does not invalidate this perception. For the Arab Spring, in Morocco and elsewhere, was as much about unemployment, falling living standards and the absence of opportunity as it was about ousting authoritarian governments and winning greater political freedoms. Indeed, these goals were often viewed as complementary if not inextricably interlinked.

Yet, regardless of what was actually being demanded, the regime responded with force to a significant number of demonstrations.[75] Most of the occasions on which it did occurred in late February and early March, May and early June, and mid July and early August 2011.[76] Of course, this was never the sum of the regime's response. It took a range of additional political, economic and other measures concomitantly. Nevertheless, both the government and security apparatus were willing and able to use violence to break up rallies and marches. And, even though their actions prompted further, retaliatory demonstrations and 'made protestors more determined to press for' greater democracy, the regime and armed and security forces still had the resolve and ability to carry out these high-intensity coercive operations.[77]

One notable way in which the regime does not easily conform to Levitsky and Way's model is in party strength. To be consistent, this must be recorded as medium in as much that, even though the regime is not aided and abetted by a single ruling party, it has the loyal backing of the country's main groups, including those that won the most seats in the 2011 parliamentary election – the PJD (107), the Istiqlal (Hizb al-Istiqlal/Parti d'Independence) (sixty), the National Rally of Independents (Rassemblement National des Indépendants, RNI) (fifty-two), the Authenticity and Modernity Party (Parti Authenticité et Modernité, PAM) (forty-seven), the Socialist Union of Popular Forces (Union Socialiste de Forces Populaires, USFP) (thirty-nine), the Popular Movement (Mouvement Populaire, MP) (thirty-two), the Constitutional Union (Union Constitutionelle, UC) (twenty-three) and the Party of Progress and Socialism (Parti du Progès et du Socialisme, PPS) (eighteen).[78] As Morocco's largest and most electorally successful parties, they have each achieved the presence and penetration expected of national forces. The Istiqlal fielded candidates in all 395 constituencies, the PJD and USFP in 393, the PPS in 386, the RNI in 381, the MP in 377, the PAM in 365, and the UC in 340. And the government which was formed on the basis of this election result includes ministers belonging to the PJD, Istiqlal, MP and PPS.

Yet, even so, the regime does not depend on any of these parties as much as Ben Ali did on the RCD. That this is so is a consequence of the regime's 'policy of political fragmentation'.[79] Quite deliberately, King Mohammed, like his father before him, has foresworn relying too heavily on any one party. His objective is clear: to protect his own authority and influence by limiting that of any and all potential rivals. In this he demonstrates a zero-sum understanding of power. He hopes that, by containing and weakening that of his competitors – current and future – he can better defend and safeguard his position. The policy of fragmentation has several parts. One is the regime's tacit and explicit encouragement of party formation.

Since the mid 1990s, a succession of new parties has been established. No part of the political spectrum has been left unaffected. In 1982 the National Democratic Party (Parti National Démocrate, PND) broke away from the RNI. In 1991 the National Popular Movement (Mouvement National Populaire, MNP) broke away from the MP. In 1996 the Socialist Democratic Party (Parti Socialiste Démocratique, PSD) broke away from the Organisation of Democratic and Popular Action (Organisation de l'Action Démocratique et Populaire, OADP). In 1997 the Democratic Forces Front (Front de Forces Démocratiques, FFD) broke away from the PPS. In 2001 the Reform and Development Party (Parti de la Reforme et du Développement, PRD) broke away from the RNI. And, more recently in 2006, the Moroccan Union for Democracy (Union Marocaine pour la Démocratie, UMD) broke away from the UC.[80]

A few parties – including the RNI, the UC and the PAM – were founded by friends and allies of the king to help defend the palace's interests in parliament and the electoral sphere.[81] The PAM, for example, was established specifically to try to counter the growing popularity of the PJD whose ambitions and loyalty to the regime at that time were still not wholly trusted by the monarchy. In so doing, by allowing and encouraging the creation of new parties, the regime weakened those that existed already. Some, such as the RNI, the MP, the OADP, the PPS and the UC, have lost leaders, members, resources and voters directly to one or other of the parties that have been created. Yet, even those which have not had factions break away from them, must now compete on a more congested and competitive playing field.

Another facet of this policy is the high degree of consistency with which the monarchy treats many of the country's parties. The palace 'believes that it does not have permanent enemies, only political opponents'.[82] Nor does it seem to accept that it has any perpetual allies, just loyal subjects. While those groups which have shown it the most devotion over the years have undoubtedly accrued the greatest benefits, including being invited to contribute ministers to the largest number of governments, none has been allowed to assume the same position as the RCD. And, conversely, a few of the parties, not founded by palace stalwarts or which were initially a little more critical of the king, have been permitted to serve in governments provided they first accept the regime's rules and restrictions. The palace's actions were not wholly (or even mainly) motivated by a desire for fairness, a deep-seated belief that all groups should be treated the same. Rather, and as before, they were prompted by a careful political calculation. While, of course, the palace demands and rewards loyalty, it no more wants to be beholden to its friends than it does to its opponents. It opens its arms to many to avoid having to embrace a few. *Alternance* is both the doctrine and process by which this part of the policy is put into practice.

Indeed, and like their counterparts in Ben Ali's Tunisia and Bouteflika's Algeria, Morocco's political parties must accept and operate within certain parameters if they want to participate in the political process. The most important of these are the centrality of the monarchy and Islam to public life and the inviolability of the country's borders.[83] Crucially, these restrictions confirm both the purpose and existence of competitive authoritarianism in the country. Political parties can be established. Elections are held. Competing groups are permitted to take part in them. Yet, to do so, they must first accept, without question or caveat, the monarch's powers and prerogatives, Islam's role, and the country's claim to, and government of, the Western Sahara.

These conditions differ from the stipulations contained within Ben Ali's National Pact in at least two important ways: in what they emphasise and the level of dogmatism with which they are asserted. Nevertheless, their overall function is broadly similar. One of their shared goals is to fortify the powers and position of the head of state. And another is to do so forcibly by constraining the country's political imagination. Again, the National Pact is more subtle because it at least seems to invite, rather than compel, compliance. Yet, like the Moroccan conditions, it discouraged certain ideas and ways of thinking, ruled out particular possibilities and refused to countenance various reforms and changes.

One of the parties that has had to make the most compromises under Mohammed VI is the PJD. Over the past decade and a half, it has had to prove its loyalty to the crown to a greater extent than most of its rivals, and, arguably, the evidence as to its alleged perfidy and wrongdoing really warranted. Founded in 1997, it was initially willing to challenge the new king over issues of policy to the extent that it helped orchestrate and lead the successful campaign to dissuade him from relaxing the *Mudawana* when he first proposed reforming the code. Its readiness and ability to continue doing so, however, were severely curtailed as a result of the 2003 Casablanca suicide bombings. Even though it was in no way involved in these attacks and despite its fierce and repeated denunciations of those who carried them out, it was placed under enormous suspicion and pressure. Powerful and popular arguments were made for it to be outlawed.

Yet, regardless of the injustice of much of what it was subjected to, the PJD did not resist or even strongly object to the treatment it received. Rather, it set about trying to rehabilitate its reputation by adopting a policy of appeasement and conciliation. While it continued to protest its innocence, it tried to ingratiate itself with both the palace and the public by humbly acquiescing to whatever unique and arbitrary constraints the regime put upon it, and by supporting most of the government's major policy initiatives to the extent that, when, in the autumn of 2003, the king announced his intention to reconsider his earlier decision not to relax the *Mudawana*, it not only encouraged him to do so but supported the changes he eventually made to the code. And, to avoid fuelling popular concerns of a possible Islamist takeover, it agreed to field candidates in just 18 per cent of the country's constituencies in the 2003 local elections.[84] Nor did it seriously challenge either the gerrymandering or seat allocation of the 2007 parliamentary ballot even though these measures prevented it from becoming the largest party in the House of Representatives despite it winning the greatest share of the vote.

Under King Mohammed VI, the regime has successfully tamed much of the mainstream opposition. Indeed, to become part of it, to be granted official recognition, allowed to participate in elections, permitted to serve in government, an organisation must first accept the regime's rules. Yet, not all groups are prepared to. Some reject the current political order and refuse to comply. One of the largest and best-established groups to do so is the Justice and Benevolence Association (Justice et Bienfaisance/Al-Adl Wal-Ihsan, AWI). Founded by Sheikh Abdessalam Yassine in 1987 and led since his death in 2012 by Mohammed Abbadi, the AWI is a Sufi-influenced Islamist association. Its programme – which it both abides by and applies to everyone else – centres on three rejections: using 'violent methods', engaging in 'clandestine activity', and relying on foreign help 'including . . . funding'.[85]

On this basis, the AWI rejects parliamentary democracy as un-Islamic and the king's claim to be Commander of the Faithful.[86] It also calls for the 'weakening or abolition of . . . [the] monarchy' and for government 'dictated by Islamic law'.[87] These views and objectives not only led to Yassine being placed under house arrest for over a decade and the sustained harassment of some of his supporters but also resulted in the group being banned and its 'requests to form a political party systematically' turned down.[88] And, even though King Mohammed treats it a little more leniently than his father did, he still refuses to legalise it.[89] By these means, the regime has been able to manage and contain the opposition posed by the AWI and other non-mainstream groups. Perhaps more crucially, though, the AWI is precisely the sort of organisation that drives the regime to practise competitive authoritarianism.

Origins and Evolution of the Regime

Morocco's transition to competitive authoritarianism was protracted. It began late in the reign of King Hassan II but was not concluded (achieved rather than finished) until after Mohammed VI had ascended to the throne. Under Hassan, the regime was, for the main part, stridently authoritarian: reluctant to compromise, violent, a serial human rights abuser, to the extent that much of his reign overlaps with the so-called years of lead, an evocative depiction of a dark and difficult period in Morocco's recent past that falls entirely within his tenure.[90] In an effort to rehabilitate his regime's reputation and appease domestic sentiment, Hassan latterly embraced the concept and process of *alternance*. A distinctly Moroccan approach to democracy, it remains a programme of reforms intended and designed 'to allow the formation of governments based on any coalition of parties', centre left as well as 'loyalist right-wing'.[91]

The country's first *alternance* election was held in November 1997 for the House of Representatives. It was won by the left-of-centre USFP with fifty-seven seats.[92] The party's leader, Abderrahmane Youssoufi, was duly invited by King Hassan to serve as his prime minister. On 23 July 1999, King Hassan died and was succeeded by his son, Mohammed VI. The new king embraced and consolidated the *alternance* reforms introduced by his father. In September 2002, Morocco staged its second *alternance* election, also for the House of Representatives. Even though the USFP won the most seats again (fifty),[93] King Mohammed asked the Minister of the Interior, Driss Jettou, who had stood as an independent, to become prime minister. The next two parliamentary elections (2007 and 2011) were won by the Istiqlal and PJD with 52 and 107 seats respectively. The leader of each – Abbas El Fassi and Abdelilah Benkirane – was subsequently invited by the king to head the government.[94]

162

The quality of these votes has gradually improved with each one that has passed.[95] The 2007 vote was the first that international election observers were allowed to monitor. They duly described it as 'the most transparent in Moroccan history'. It also earned warm words from numerous Western governments and officials. The European Union's High Representative for the CFSP, Javier Solana, said that it confirmed 'Morocco's political maturity'. The Portuguese presidency of the European Council described the result as 'testament to Morocco's commitment to the reform process'. And Spain's Minister of Foreign Affairs, Miguel Angel Moratinos, even went so far as to proffer a positive interpretation of the low voter turnout, arguing that it provided 'proof that the elections were totally free'.[96]

International praise for the 2011 parliamentary election has been similarly fulsome. It was another important vote as it was the first held since the Arab Spring had begun. As such, it not only formed part of the regime's response to the protests but was conducted in accordance with the new constitution that had been approved by referendum just a few months earlier.[97] In response to the new constitution and election – the last held – France's president, Nicholas Sarkozy, commended the king for showing and taking 'the path towards a profound, peaceful and modern transformation of Moroccan institutions and society'.[98] The European Union's High Representative for Foreign Affairs and Security Policy (FASP), Catherine Ashton, and Commissioner, Stefan Fule, similarly pronounced that the constitutional reforms the palace had instigated and introduced represented 'a significant response to the legitimate aspirations of the Moroccan people' and were in keeping 'with Morocco's Advanced Status with the EU'.[99] And, speaking at the Opening Plenary of the US–Morocco Strategic Dialogue in September 2012, US Secretary of State, Hillary Rodham Clinton, declared that Washington looked 'to Morocco to be a leader and a model' before commending the palace and regime for their 'efforts to stay ahead' of the 'remarkable changes taking place across North Africa' by 'holding free and fair elections, empowering the elected parliament, [and] taking other steps to ensure that the government reflects the will of the people'.[100]

Yet, despite these improvements and this praise, the parliamentary elections held under King Mohammed VI have not been totally free and fair. The regime still practises gerrymandering to disadvantage and limit the gains made by parties it wishes to constrain. On 22 February 2007, the Council of Ministers (Conseil des Ministres, CM) 'passed a new seat distribution requirement', the purpose of which was 'to limit the representation of the party that was augured as victor . . . : the PJD'.[101] Despite winning the largest share of the vote in the 2007 House of Representatives election (10.9 per cent), the PJD received only the second highest number of seats (forty-six) in the chamber. The highest number (fifty-two) was secured by the second-placed Istiqlal (10.7 per cent) whose leader, Abbas El Fassi, was subsequently invited to become head of the new government.[102] The regime deliberately manipulated the country's constituency boundaries to prevent the PJD from taking power.[103]

Another enduring problem is the inability of journalists and news outlets to investigate and report openly and free from fear on events and individuals. Even though the 1996 constitution guarantees freedom of expression (Article 9b) and the 2011 version expression, creation, publication, presentation (Article 25) and the press (Article 28), the regime continues to harass, intimidate and persecute reporters, editors, bloggers and outlets.[104] Indeed, so numerous and serious have been the abuses perpetrated by the government that Morocco was ranked 130th (out of 180 countries) in the Reporters Without Borders' 2015 Press Freedom Index,[105] the lowest place of any of the book's four case studies.

Journalists, like opposition parties and politicians, are compelled to operate within fixed and inflexible parameters. Certain topics and issues are strictly off-limits upon pain of prosecution and/or extra-legal intimidation. Saying or writing anything critical of the monarch or causing him embarrassment, no matter how slight or justified, are completely forbidden. Querying either Islam's role within Moroccan society or the palace's interpretation of a particular religious matter is considered blasphemous and also outlawed. Questioning the country's territorial integrity, including the legitimacy of its claim to sovereignty over the Western Sahara or manner of its government of the region, is similarly prohibited. Journalists, editors and bloggers are routinely arrested for discussing, even briefly and seemingly benignly, these proscribed subjects.[106]

In October 2014, the Ministry of Communication belatedly responded to promises the regime had made during the 2011 constitutional referendum by announcing its intention to introduce three new media bills on the freedom of the press, the rights and responsibilities of journalists, and the remit and powers of the National Press Council (Conseil National de la Presse, CNP).[107] While these laws promised to help liberate the country's news outlets from official interference and better protect reporters from prosecution and persecution, they still fell a long way short of what domestic and international campaigners had hoped for.

The substantive constraints in which Morocco's news outlets have always had to work remain in place. The old prohibitions on criticising, or even discussing, the king, Western Sahara and Islam endure. Censorship continues to be practised. The government retains the right to appoint the heads of the country's television and radio stations. And, along with the prime minister and the presidents of the House of Representatives and the Senate, it selects all eight members of the High Authority for Audio-Visual Communication (Haute Autorité de la Communication Audiovisuelle, HACA), the body which both licenses and monitors the output of these stations.[108] Not only is the regime actively checking up on channels to make sure their programmes do not show or say anything of which it disapproves but it also has the capacity to revoke the official permissions they need to broadcast whenever it wants. And it can do the same to foreign-domiciled agencies operating in the country.

In 2010, it rescinded the accreditation of all journalists working for the Qatari-based news channel Al Jazeera, forcing the company's in-country office to remain closed until April 2013. And, in 2012, it twice banned the Spanish newspaper *El País* for publishing material it thought denigrated the monarchy.[109] Indeed, both the print and online media are subject to similar restrictions. The regime uses its control of advertising revenue and subsidies to put economic and financial pressure on independent news outlets. And, from time to time, it blocks access to online platforms – including websites, discussion forums, Instagram and parts of Skype – that are used to register and express criticism of the regime.[110]

As well as targeting media outlets, the regime actively and aggressively pursues individual journalists, editors and bloggers. It habitually brings defamation and other trumped-up charges – including for terrorism-related offences – against those who cross it.[111] Its purpose in doing so is always to punish, silence and discredit those who say anything it does not like, and to try to deter others from pursuing similar lines of enquiry. Its agents – police officers, soldiers and security services personnel – also occasionally attack and physically intimidate journalists. By these means, the regime has perpetuated the culture of self-censorship in which journalists and news outlets have long been forced to live, work and operate.[112] So, even though elections are held regularly and their conduct is often praised by foreign governments, Morocco's political playing field is far from level.

Moreover, and more importantly, these elections do not affect the established balance of power within the country's political order. The king still sits squarely at the heart of public life. He performs three essential roles, meaning that his position is thrice protected. The first is spiritual. He claims direct descent from the Prophet Muhammad and has the title Commander of the Faithful (*Amir al Mouminine*).[113] He is Morocco's most senior religious figure and leader of its Muslims. The second is political. He is head of the Moroccan state, its executive. And the third is legislative with a strong social element. Stemming from 'the long history of tribal arbitration that the Sultans used to perform', he is the country's mediator-in-chief, its foremost peacemaker, the bringer together of quarrelling parties, the settler of major disputes.[114]

In addition to affirming and protecting the king's position within public life, these roles are mutually reinforcing. As Commander of the Faithful, both his person and his word are touched by the divine, invested with sacred significance. At the very least, this sanctity informs and colours the cultural context in which he performs his other functions. He discharges his political and legislative responsibilities against this backdrop, making it even harder for his interlocutors and adversaries to disagree with or oppose him. All his pronouncements and judgements bear the unmistakable scent of infallibility. Thus, his political and legislative powers are enhanced.[115]

His role as the country's ultimate arbiter also offers significant subsidiary benefits. Most notably, it grants him great manoeuvrability, enables him to remain above the political fray, to evade censure and criticism, yet still dominate proceedings and actors. So it is that he can 'attack reformers and still present himself as their champion', and 'redirect any responsibility or accountability to the cabinet, its ministers, and the prime minister while maintaining his . . . power over' them.[116] Finally, as head of state, he can occupy, monitor and greatly influence the country's political space in order to prevent and stymie any challenges to, or debates about, his other roles: whether the state and religion should be disestablished; and what involvement, if any, the monarchy should have in discussions and disagreements in which it has clear interests and strong preferences.

In response to the Arab Spring, some of the king's rights and powers have been clipped a little. Whereas Article 24 of the 1996 constitution – which was in force when the protests broke out – allowed him to appoint whomever he pleased as prime minister and to the cabinet irrespective of the outcome of any election,[117] Article 47 of the new 2011 constitution requires him to fill these positions from the ranks of the party that won the most votes (*arrivé en tête des élections*).[118] And, unlike before when there were no 'significant constitutional restrictions' on the king's ability to dispense with individual members of the cabinet, the government (Article 24, 1996) or parliament (Article 27, 1996),[119] now he must at least talk to the prime minister (*après consultation du Chef du Gouvernement*) before acting (Article 47, 2011).[120]

Indeed, the extension and fortification of the premier's rights and responsibilities are arguably the most significant series of changes contained within the 2011 constitution. And it represents a very Moroccan response to the Arab Spring and the resultant clamour for political liberalisation. For, rather than rescind and reallocate any of the monarch's more notable powers, he is required – politely requested and encouraged in many instances – to share them with the prime minister. Changes are made, the king's prerogatives are curtailed and those of the people's elected representatives are enhanced but without inflicting any great loss of face on him or, more importantly, fundamentally weakening his position within the country's political order.

Indeed, these reforms are something of a *trompe l'œil* because they look more significant than they actually are. Save for one or two genuine limitations and alterations, the king's powers are largely the same as they were before. Moreover, the 2011 constitution preserves his three main roles – spiritual, political and legislative – and, in so doing, reaffirms his centrality to Moroccan public life.

He still presides over the Council of Ministers, Morocco's most important policy-formulating body with responsibility for – among other things – setting the legislative agenda, amending the constitution, overseeing the national budget, assessing all bills related to the armed forces, granting amnesties, declaring war, and appointing the head of the Bank Al-Maghrib, ambassadors, regional governors (*walis*) and the leaders of various other strategic establishments and enterprises (Article 48). He still presides over the Superior Council of the Judiciary (Conseil Supérieur du Pouvoir Judiciaire, CSPJ) and appoints – by royal decree – all the country's judges and magistrates (Articles 56 and 57). He is still the Supreme Head of the Royal Armed Forces (Chef Suprême des Forces Armées Royales, CSFAR) (Article 53). He still presides over the Superior Council of the Ulema (Conseil Supérieur des Oulémas, CSO), the only body empowered to comment on those religious matters he asks it to consider (Article 41). He is still Commander of the Faithful (Article 41), head of state, its supreme representative, guarantor of its permanence and continuity and supreme arbiter between its institutions, and the symbol of the nation's unity (Article 42). He appoints six of the Constitutional Court's (Cour Constitutionelle, CC) twelve members including its president (Article 130). And he now presides over the recently created Superior Council of Security (Conseil Supérieur de Sécurité, CSS) which oversees both the country's security and management of any crises that arise (Article 54).[121]

Despite King Mohammed's rejection of some of his father's more authoritarian ways and the constitutional reforms that were introduced to appease the Arab Spring protestors, the monarch's powers remain extensive and, in many instances, decisive. Yet, for all that, democratic institutions exist, procedures and processes are adhered to, and pretensions are maintained. The king may be unwilling to relinquish his prerogatives but he is still prepared to allow some democracy to take place and does not want to be thought of as authoritarian. Multiparty legislative elections and other votes, therefore, are regularly held.

Conclusions

Morocco presents a difficult and challenging case, not least because it appears to defy Levitsky and Way's model. They, in fact, reject it as a possible country study on the grounds that too much power is invested in its unelected executive. As a result, political life is subject to 'dynamics not found under competitive authoritarianism'.[122] Their charge is not without merit. The king's powers are great and he does not have to make many of the disparate, desperate calculations that so perplex and preoccupy his presidential peers. He never has to submit to the vote. His position is not up for regular renegotiation (even if the terms of the debate are heavily loaded and the outcome little in doubt). The institution of the monarchy is as secure as he is within it.

Yet he cannot escape the ballot entirely. While descriptions of him as 'constitutional' are certainly misplaced – since his powers fundamentally exceed those of most other,[123] similarly titled royal heads of state – the conduct and outcome of elections, especially national ones, still matter enormously to him,[124] for they not only affect the international standing of his regime but also determine the level of domestic influence attained by groups and parties seeking to curtail his power and authority. While the institution of the monarchy may well be free from any real danger, the king wants more. His ambition is not limited to simply defending the throne's existence. He wants to preserve its substantive powers, to avoid becoming a largely ceremonial figure, being reduced to the role of well-bred ribbon cutter.

This desire is the primary cause of Morocco's competitive authoritarianism. The regime holds regular elections because it feels that it must. It is sensitive to international opinion, to maintaining and strengthening its good relations with the West. Partly as a result, it is willing to address *some* domestic demands for democratic rights and civil liberties. Yet it remains determined to defend the monarchy's substantive powers. As a result, it organises elections that are neither free nor fair, and tilts the political playing field decisively in its own favour. The Moroccan regime is competitive authoritarian because it believes that its existence depends on preserving this deeply imperfect and weighted democratic process. The Moroccan regime is competitive authoritarian because it manipulates democracy to prevent groups and parties that want to constitutionalise the monarchy from extending their influence.

In this way, Morocco makes a valuable addition to the pantheon of competitive authoritarian case studies for it shows that, with a little care, Levitsky and Way's model can be applied to regimes in which unelected executives hold power. It also offers a clear exposition of leverage, particularly the interplay between pressure and resistance. The United States, European Union and various European countries have enormous influence over Morocco. Over the past twenty years, it has enthusiastically joined a succession of policy frameworks that have granted Washington, Brussels, Paris and Madrid both the right and the means to ask and compel Rabat to change its political and economic behaviour. Yet, despite these means, the West still has only low leverage over Morocco, in part because Western governments have shown themselves reluctant and unable to press the country too hard or to co-ordinate better their actions with one another. Primarily, though, it is because Morocco has a large economy. And, as a result, it has the economic means to withstand and mitigate whatever pressure the West is willing and able to bring to bear.

The Moroccan regime also makes an important addendum to the dimension of organisational power. Rather than nurture a single party to the point of overbearing dominance – as did Ben Ali with the RCD – it has cultivated numerous groups. In so doing, by dispersing limited amounts of power and prestige more widely across the political system, it has avoided becoming overly reliant on any one party. This means that no group can easily accrue sufficient influence and resources either to dominate its rivals or, more crucially, put real pressure on the palace. Moreover, because parties are compelled to compete for what opportunities and means there are, the regime is better able to play them off against each other, make them scrap among themselves rather than challenge its authority. This strategy was also employed – albeit less widely and explicitly – by President Bouteflika. That the Moroccan and Algerian regimes should do so – the two examined by this book in which unelected institutions (the monarchy and military) wield extensive political power – is telling, for, seemingly, the presence of these institutions at least partially liberates these countries' political leaders from having to establish, develop and rely upon ruling parties. They can afford to forgo such organisations and, as a result, manage and control their respective political systems in different ways from those outlined by Levitsky and Way.

Notes

1. Levitsky and Way, *Competitive Authoritarianism*, p. 32.
2. Ibid. p. 32.
3. Kristina Kausch (2009), 'The European Union and Political Reform in Morocco', *Mediterranean Politics*, 14: 2, 165–79, p. 170.
4. Immaculada Szmolka (2010), 'Party System Fragmentation in Morocco', *The Journal of North African Studies*, 15: 1, 13–37, p. 14.
5. Joffé, 'The Arab Spring in North Africa', p. 510.
6. Ibid. p. 511; Emanuela Dalmasso and Francesco Cavatorta (2013), 'Democracy, Civil Liberties and the Role of Religion after the Arab Awakening: Constitutional Reforms in Tunisia and Morocco', *Mediterranean Politics*, 18: 2, 225–41, p. 230.
7. Mounah Abdel-Samad (2014), 'Why Reform and No Revolution: A Political Opportunity Analysis of Morocco 2011 Protests Movements', *The Journal of North African Studies*, 19: 5, 792–809, pp. 802 and 804.
8. The MCC is an independent US foreign aid agency. It was established in January 2004 by Congress with strong bipartisan support. Millennium Challenge Corporation (2015), 'About MCC', available at <https://www.mcc.gov/about> last accessed 2 September 2015.
9. Famously, 'Morocco was the first country to recognize the independence of the United States'. As a result, it 'has the longest lasting uninterrupted friendship agreement' with Washington 'dating from 1787'; James N. Sater (2010), *Morocco: Challenges to Tradition and Modernity*, Abingdon: Routledge, pp. 134–5.
10. US Government (2015), 'Foreign Assistance', available at <http://beta.foreignassistance.gov/> (last accessed 28 August 2015), and US Department of State (2015), 'Foreign Military Financing Account Summary', available at <http://www.state.gov/t/pm/ppa/sat/c14560.htm> (last accessed 8 July 2015).
11. Millennium Challenge Corporation (2015), 'Morocco Compact', available at <https://www.mcc.gov/where-we-work/program/morocco-compact> (last accessed 1 September 2015).
12. Millennium Challenge Corporation (2015), 'Morocco Compact II', available at <https://www.mcc.gov/where-we-work/program/compact-morocco-compact-ii> (last accessed 1 September 2015).
13. In monetary terms, Morocco was awarded $96.52 million for these projects and Tunisia $245.98 million. Available at <http://beta.foreignassistance.gov/> (last accessed 28 August 2015).
14. Holden, 'Security, Power or Profit?', p. 18.
15. US Government (2011), 'The U.S.–Morocco Free Trade Agreement (FTS)', 12 October, available at <http://export.gov/FTA/morocco/index.asp> (last accessed 2 September 2015).
16. Holden, 'Security, Power or Profit?', p. 18.

170

17. This ambition was ruled out by the European Council in 1987; Iván Martín (2009), 'EU–Morocco Relations: How Advanced is the "Advanced Status"?', *Mediterranean Politics*, 14: 2, 239–45, p. 239.
18. The EMP was established in November 1995 and Morocco signed its AA on 26 February 1996; Holden, 'Security, Power or Profit?', p. 22.
19. The ENP was launched in May 2004 and Morocco concluded its AP on 9 December 2004; Holden, 'Security, Power or Profit?', p. 24.
20. Martín, 'EU–Morocco Relations', p. 239.
21. Available at <http://eeas.europa.eu/euromed/docs/meda_figures_en.pdf> (last accessed 20 March 2015).
22. European Neighbourhood and Partnership Instrument, 'Morocco: Strategy Paper 2007–2013', available <http://eeas.europa.eu/enp/pdf/pdf/country/enpi_csp_morocco_en.pdf> (last accessed 2 September 2015).
23. European Commission (2010), 'First EU–Morocco Summit in Granada on 7 March 2010', 5 March, available at <http://europa.eu/rapid/press-release_IP-10-242_en.htm> (last accessed 2 September 2015), and European Neighbourhood and Partnership Instrument, 'EU Supporting Morocco's Reforms with €580.5 Million in 2011–2013', available at <http://www.enpi-info.eu/files/publications/Morocco%20NIP%202010.pdf> (last accessed 2 September 2015).
24. Bicchi, 'The Politics of Foreign Aid and the European Neighbourhood Policy Post-Arab Spring', p. 329.
25. Kausch, 'The European Union and Political Reform in Morocco', p. 166.
26. Ibid. p. 165.
27. European Commission (2015), 'European Union, Trade in goods with Morocco', 10 April, available at <http://trade.ec.europa.eu/doclib/docs/2006/september/tradoc_113421.pdf> (last accessed 2 September 2015), p. 9.
28. More specifically, Morocco's exports to the United States were worth $159.66 million in 1995, $164.16 million in 1996, $164.71 million in 1997, $196.94 million in 1998 and $255.98 million in 1999; World Bank (2015), 'Morocco All Products Export Trade Value', 3 September, available at <http://wits.worldbank.org/CountryProfile/Country/MAR/StartYear/1994/EndYear/1998/TradeFlow/Export/Indicator/XPRT-TRD-VL/Partner/USA/Product/Total (last accessed 3 September 2015).
29. More specifically, Morocco's exports to the United States were worth $253.91 million in 2000, $276.81 million in 2001, $241.36 million in 2002, $245.93 million in 2003, and $385.98 million in 2004; ibid.
30. More specifically, Morocco's exports to the United States were worth $285.79 million in 2005, $243.91 million in 2006, $345.97 million in 2007, $793.7 million in 2008 and 443.32 million in 2009; ibid.
31. More specifically, Morocco's exports to the United States were worth $669.89 million in 2010, $983.63 million in 2011 and $929.77 million in 2012; ibid.

32. More specifically, Morocco's imports from the United States were worth $559.1 million in 1995, $611.97 million in in 1996, $513.4 million in 1997, $644.56 million in 1998 and $705.69 million in 1999; World Bank (2015), 'Morocco All Products Trade Import Value', 3 September, available at <http://wits.worldbank.org/CountryProfile/Country/MAR/StartYear/1994/EndYear/1998/TradeFlow/Import/Indicator/MPRT-TRD-VL/Partner/USA/Product/Total> (last accessed 3 September 2015).

33. More specifically, Morocco's imports from the United States were worth $643.52 million in 2000, $407.77 million in 2001, $511.38 million in 2002, $578.01 million in 2003 and $735.27 million in 2004; ibid.

34. More specifically, Morocco's imports from the United States were worth $690.32 million in 2005, $1.04 billion in 2006, $1.92 billion in 2007, $2.16 billion in 2008 and $2.28 billion in 2009; ibid.

35. More specifically, Morocco's imports from the United States were worth $2.49 billion in 2010, $3.59 billion in 2011 and $2.85 billion in 2012; ibid.

36. More specifically, the country attracted $923.86 million in FDI in 1995, $764.12 million in 1996, $35.68 million in 1997, $118.69 million in 1998 and $26.51 million in 1999. Available at <http://data.worldbank.org/indicator/BX.KLT.DINV.CD.WD/countries?page=3> (last accessed 7 July 2015).

37. More specifically, the country attracted $220.73 million in FDI in 2000, $143.83 million in 2001, $791.6 million in 2002, $2.31 billion in 2003 and $787.05 million in 2004; ibid.

38. More specifically, the country attracted $1.67 billion in FDI in 2005, $2.46 billion in 2006, $2.82 billion in 2007, $2.46 billion in 2008 and $1.97 billion in 2009; ibid

39. More specifically, the country attracted $1.24 billion in FDI in 2010, $2.52 billion in 2011, $2.84 billion in 2012 and $3.36 billion in 2013; ibid.

40. Ministère Chargé des Marocains Résident à l'Étranger et des Affaires de la Migration (2015), 'Dar Al Maghrib', available at <http://marocains-dumonde.gov.ma/fr/le-minist%C3%A8re/dar-al-maghrib> (last accessed 3 September 2015).

41. Mouna Cherkaoui (2012), 'Process and Implications of Morocco's Economic and Trade Liberalization', in Mahmoud A. T. Elkhafif, Sahar Taghdisi-Rad and Mutasim Elagraa (eds), *Economic and Trade Policies in the Arab World*, Abingdon: Routledge, pp. 115–55, p. 149.

42. Moha Ennaji (2014), *Muslim Moroccan Migrants in Europe: Transnational Migration in its Multiplicity*, New York: Palgrave Macmillan, p. 36.

43. Available at <http://data.worldbank.org/indicator/BX.TRF.PWKR.CD.DT/countries?page=3> (last accessed 8 July 2015).

44. World Bank (2015), 'International Tourism, Number of Arrivals', available at <http://data.worldbank.org/indicator/ST.INT.ARVL?page=1&order=wbapi_data_value_2010%20wbapi_data_value%20wbapi_data_value-first&sort=asc> (last accessed 4 September 2015).

45. Available at <http://www.iie.org/Services/Project-Atlas/France/Internatio nal-Students-In-France> (last accessed 4 September 2015).

46. US Department of State (2015), 'Kennedy–Lugar Youth Exchange and Study: Morocco', available at <http://www.yesprograms.org/country/ morocco> (last accessed 4 September 2015).

47. Available at <http://eacea.ec.europa.eu/erasmus_mundus/programme/about _erasmus_mundus_en.php> (last accessed 4 September 2015).

48. Since then, nearly three times as many students have completed the YES programme (230) as the Erasmus Mundus Master's (forty-seven) and Scholars (thirty) schemes. Available at <http://www.yesprograms. org/country/morocco> (last accessed 4 September 2015) and available at <http://eacea.ec.europa.eu/erasmus_mundus/programme/about_erasmus_ mundus_en.php> (last accessed 4 September 2015).

49. Available at <http://data.worldbank.org/indicator/IT.NET.USER.P2?page= 2> (last accessed 9 July 2015).

50. Available at <http://data.worldbank.org/indicator/IT.CEL.SETS.P2/coun tries?page=2> (last accessed 9 July 2015).

51. Euro-Mediterranean Human Rights Network (2015), 'Our Members', avail-able <http://euromedrights.org/members/> (last accessed 6 September 2015).

52. Euro-Mediterranean Human Rights Network (2015), 'Our Donors', avail-able at <http://euromedrights.org/about-us/our-donors/> (last accessed 6 September 2015).

53. World Bank (2015), 'Morocco', available at <http://data.worldbank.org/ country/morocco> (last accessed 5 September 2015).

54. Kausch, 'The European Union and Political Reform in Morocco', p. 172.

55. In response to Rabat's unprecedented decision to permit international observers to supervise the 2007 election, President Sarkozy wrote to King Mohammed stating his '"admiration for the democratic robustness your country has once again demonstrated"'; ibid. pp. 167 and 169.

56. Ibid. p. 169.

57. Ibid. p. 174.

58. Kausch, 'The European Union and Political Reform in Morocco', pp. 166 and 173.

59. Emmanuela Dalmasso and Francesco Cavatorta (2013), 'Democracy Civil Liberties and the Role of Religion after the Arab Awakening: Constitutional Reforms in Tunisia and Morocco', *Mediterranean Politics*, 18: 2, 225–41, p. 225.

60. Ennahda secured 34.8 per cent of the vote, the PJD 22.8 per cent and the AAV 10.6 per cent. The AAV comprises the MSP, Islamic Revival Movement (Mouvement de la Renaissance Islamique, MRI) and the National Reform Movement (Mouvement pour la Réforme Nationale, MRN); Storm, *Party Politics and the Prospects for Democracy*, pp. 162, 195, 199 and 203.

61. Mouhib, 'EU Democracy Promotion in Tunisia and Morocco', p. 352.
62. Fawaz Yusuf (2014), 'A Structural Change Analysis of EU–Moroccan Trade Liberalisation and Economic Development between 1995 and 2010', *The Journal of North African Studies*, 19: 3, 413–32, pp. 426–7.
63. Dennison, 'The EU and North Africa after the Revolutions', p. 123.
64. Kausch, 'The European Union and Political Reform in Morocco', p. 167.
65. Ibid. p. 167.
66. Ibid. p. 167.
67. World Bank (2015), 'Military Expenditure (% of GDP)', <http://data.worldbank.org/indicator/MS.MIL.XPND.GD.ZS?page=3> (last accessed 27 July 2015).
68. Indeed the one slight fall was between 2013 and 2014 when spending dropped from $4.094 billion a year to $4.032 billion; Stockholm International Peace Research Institute (2015), 'SIPRI Military Expenditure Database', available at <http://www.sipri.org/research/armaments/milex/milex_database> (last accessed 27 July 2015).
69. Ibid.
70. International Institute of Strategic Studies (2013), *The Military Balance 2013: The Annual Assessment of Global Military Capabilities and Defence Economics*, Abingdon: Routledge, pp. 394–6.
71. Emanuela Dalmasso (2012), 'Surfing the Democratic Tsunami in Morocco: Apolitical Society and the Reconfiguration of a Substantial Authoritarian Regime', *Mediterranean Politics*, 17: 2, 217–32, p. 226; and Erica Vásquez (2015), 'Morocco's Counterterrorism Strategy: Implications for Western Sahara', *Middle East Institute*, 13 August, available at <http://www.mei.edu/content/article/morocco%E2%80%99s-counterterrorism-strategy-implications-western-sahara> (last accessed 15 October 2015).
72. Hill, *Identity in Algerian Politics*, pp. 77–8 and 88–9.
73. The size of the protests decreased quite markedly from 1 July 2011 onwards; Mounah Abel-Samad (2014), 'Why Reform and No Revolution: A Political Opportunity Analysis of Morocco', *The Journal of North African Studies*, 19: 5, 792–809, p. 801.
74. The February 20th Movement was named for the date on which it was established in 2011. Like the CNCD in Algeria, it was an umbrella organisation that helped orchestrate protests and manage and co-ordinate the actions of its various participating groups and organisations; Joffé, 'The Arab Spring in North Africa', p. 510.
75. That said, the regime's use of repression decreased following the fall in the number of more explicitly democratic protests from 1 July 2011 onwards; Abel-Samad, 'Why Reform and No Revolution', p. 801.
76. Ibid. p. 799; Joffé, 'The Arab Spring in North Africa', p. 511; and Dalmasso (2012), 'Surfing the Democratic Tsunami in Morocco', p. 228.
77. Ibid. p. 802.
78. *The Economist* (2011), 'Yet Another Islamist Victory', 3 December,

available at <http://www.economist.com/node/21541058> (last accessed 14 October 2015).

79. Abel-Samad, 'Why Reform and No Revolution', p. 796.
80. Szmolka, 'Party System Fragmentation in Morocco', p. 16.
81. The RNI was established in 1978 by King Hassan's brother-in-law, Prime Minister Ahmed Osman, the UC in 1983 by Prime Minister Maati Bouabid, and the PAM in 2008 by former Minister of the Interior and adviser to King Mohammed VI Fouad Ali El Himma.
82. Abel-Samad, 'Why Reform and No Revolution', p. 797.
83. Ibid. p. 796.
84. Howe, *Morocco*, p. 345.
85. Vish Sakthivel (2014), 'al-Adl wal-Ihsan: Inside Morocco's Islamist Challenge', The Washington Institute for Near East Policy, August, available at <http://www.washingtoninstitute.org/uploads/Documents/pubs/ PolicyFocus135_Sakthivel_v2.pdf> (last accessed 18 October 2015), p. 4.
86. Lise Storm (2007), *Democratization in Morocco: The Political Elite and Struggles for Power in the Post-Independence State*, Abingdon: Routledge, pp. 188–9.
87. Available at <http://www.washingtoninstitute.org/uploads/Documents/pubs /PolicyFocus135_Sakthivel_v2.pdf> (last accessed 18 October 2015), p. viii.
88. Howe, *Morocco*, pp. 129–30.
89. Available at <http://www.washingtoninstitute.org/uploads/Documents/pubs /PolicyFocus135_Sakthivel_v2.pdf> (last accessed 18 October 2015), p. vii.
90. Fadoua Loudiy argues that the years of lead ran from the early 1960s until the late 1990s; Fadoua Loudiy (2014), *Transitional Justice and Human Rights in Morocco: Negotiating the Years of Lead*, Abingdon: Routledge, p. 5.
91. Storm, *Democratization in Morocco*, p. 118.
92. Ibid. p. 83.
93. Eva Wegner (2011), *Islamist Opposition in Authoritarian Regimes: The Party of Justice and Development in Morocco*, Syracuse, NY: Syracuse University Press, p. 106.
94. Ibid. p. 117 and European Forum for Democracy and Solidarity (2014), 'Morocco', 4 June, available at <http://www.europeanforum.net/country/ morocco> (last accessed 19 October 2015).
95. Ibid. p. 90.
96. Kausch, 'The European Union and Political Reform in Morocco', p. 172.
97. The referendum was held on 1 July 2011. The changes to the constitution proposed by the regime were approved by 98.5 per cent of voters; Abdelilah Bouasria (2013), 'The Second Coming of Morocco's "Command of the Faithful": Mohammed VI and Morocco's Religious Policy', in Bruce Maddy-Weitzman and Daniel Zisenwine (eds), *Contemporary Morocco:*

State, Politics and Society under Mohammed VI, Abingdon: Routledge, pp. 37–56, p. 49. The election took place on 25 November 2011.

98. *Le Monde* (2011), 'La France salue les réformes annoncées par le roi du Maroc', 18 June, available at <http://www.lemonde.fr/afrique/article/2011/06/18/la-france-salue-les-reformes-annoncees-par-le-roidu-maroc_1538011_3212.html> (last accessed 9 October 2015).

99. European Commission (2011), 'Joint statement by High Representative Catherine Ashton and Commissioner Stefan Fule on the Referendum on the New Constitution in Morocco', 2 July, available at <http://europa.eu/rapid/press-release_MEMO-11-478_en.htm?locale=en> (last accessed 9 October 2015).

100. Hillary Rodham Clinton (2012), 'Remarks at the Opening Plenary of the US–Morocco Strategic Dialogue', US Department of State, 13 September, available at <http://www.state.gov/secretary/20092013clinton/rm/2012/09/197711.htm> (last accessed 9 October 2015).

101. Szmolka, 'Party System Fragmentation in Morocco', pp. 19–20.

102. Wegner, *Islamist Opposition in Authoritarian Regimes*, p. 117.

103. Eva Wegner and Miquel Pellicer (2010), 'Islamist Moderation without Democratization: The Coming of Age of the Moroccan Party of Justice and Development', in Michelle Pace and Peter Seeberg (eds), *The European Union's Democratization Agenda in the Mediterranean*, Abingdon: Routledge, 157–75, p. 168.

104. Available at <http://unpan1.un.org/intradoc/groups/public/documents/undpadm/unpan041912.pdf> (last accessed 7 October 2015), Article 9b. Available at <http://www.maroc.ma/en/system/files/documents_page/bo_5964bis_fr_3.pdf> (last accessed 7 October 2015), article 25 and 28.

105. Reporters Without Borders (2015), 'Press Freedom Index', available at <http://index.rsf.org/#!/> (last accessed 8 October 2015).

106. Freedom House (2015), 'Morocco', available at <https://freedomhouse.org/report/freedom-press/2015/morocco> (last accessed 12 October 2015).

107. Reporters Without Borders (2015), 'Details About Morocco', available at <http://index.rsf.org/#!/index-details/MAR> (last accessed 12 October 2015).

108. More specifically, the government appoints four members, the prime minister two and the presidents of the House of Representatives and Senate one each. Available at <https://freedomhouse.org/report/freedom-press/2015/morocco> (last accessed 12 October 2015).

109. Ibid.

110. Ibid.

111. Ibid.

112. Ibid.

113. Marvine Howe (2005), *Morocco: The Islamist Awakening and Other Challenges*, Oxford: Oxford University Press, p. 3.

114. Abel-Samad, 'Why Reform and No Revolution', p. 796.

115. Ibid. p. 796.
116. Ibid. p. 796.
117. Kingdom of Morocco (1996), 'Constitution', 13 September, available at <http://unpan1.un.org/intradoc/groups/public/documents/un-dpadm/unpan 041912.pdf> (last accessed 7 October 2015), Article 24.
118. Kingdom of Morocco (2011), 'Constitution', 29 July, available at <http://www.maroc.ma/en/system/files/documents_page/bo_5964bis_fr_3.pdf> (last accessed 7 October 2015), Article 47.
119. James N. Sater (2009), 'Reforming the Rule of Law in Morocco: Multiple Meanings and Problematic Realities', *Mediterranean Politics*, 14: 2, 181–93, pp. 181–2, and available at <http://unpan1.un.org/intradoc/groups/public/documents/un-dpadm/unpan041912.pdf> (last accessed 7 October 2015), Articles 24 and 27.
120. Available at <http://www.maroc.ma/en/system/files/documents_page/bo_5964bis_fr_3.pdf> (last accessed 7 October 2015), Article 47.
121. Ibid; Articles 41, 42, 48, 53, 54, 56, 57 and 130.
122. Levitsky and Way, *Competitive Authoritarianism*, p. 32.
123. Available at <http://www.maroc.ma/en/system/files/documents_page/bo_5964bis_fr_3.pdf> (last accessed 7 October 2015), Article 1.
124. Indeed, and as Kausch records, the king's own characterisation of the monarchy as executive is closer to the mark; Kausch, 'The European Union and Political Reform in Morocco', p. 168.

5

Mauritania

Mauritania presents a quite different explanatory challenge from Morocco. For, unlike its near neighbour, Nouakchott seems to offer a near textbook exposition of Levitsky and Way's ideas and arguments, starting with their foundational observation that not all political transitions 'lead to democracy'.[1] The country's 2005 turn towards more liberal and open government proved to be short-lived and, over the course of the next couple of years, it steadily regressed into authoritarianism, albeit of a more competitive form. That the self-installed Military Council for Justice and Democracy (Le Conseil Militaire pour la Justice et la Démocratie, CMJD) felt obliged to launch this experiment at all was mainly due to the political and economic pressure Western governments were beginning to put on them for having ousted their long-time ally, President Maayouya Ould Sidi Ahmed Taya. Anxious to avoid the imposition of any further sanctions, the CMJD quickly sought to mollify the West. On this occasion, therefore, the threat of further Western pressure succeeded in altering the regime's behaviour, in making it democratise, in creating the political opening.

Yet the speed with which this opportunity passed continues to raise difficult questions about the true extent of the West's support for this democratic turn and leverage over the regime. Western governments may have been pleasantly surprised by the course of events but their optimism has proved insufficient to sustain the country's experiment with democracy. This, by extension, generates doubts about how much influence they actually have over Nouakchott because they have failed to discipline subsequent governments into respecting and consolidating these earlier reforms. Why, if they have been able to make the regime democratise once, have they not done so again? Is this failure due to disinterest, incompetence or inability?

Then there were the causes of the West's ire, of the irritation and anger which prompted the regime to make these changes. While Western governments welcomed Nouakchott's democratic turn, their pleasure stemmed, at least in part, from their surprise. They did not expect it to respond in this way. Nor, crucially, did they *demand* that it do so. On the contrary, the regime took the initiative by introducing reforms calculated to appeal to Western sensibilities and prevent the imposition of any further sanctions. It felt compelled to do so because of the West's reaction to the removal of President Taya. So, while Western governments might have successfully disciplined Nouakchott into becoming more democratic, they did not instigate the reform process and initially demanded the reinstatement of a fairly authoritarian leader who had held power continuously for more than two decades.[2] The West's leverage over the regime might have been medium but its democratic intent – to begin with at least – was decidedly low.

For Desha Girod and Meir Walters, the West's initial disinterest in Mauritania's democratic turn exposes an important explanatory blind spot within the transition literature and Levitsky and Way's model. They contend that the country's experiences defy at least two of the literature's key conventions. The first, which Levitsky and Way express and, therefore, reinforce, holds 'that Western strategic interests in states with crucial natural resources . . . or vital security ties . . . trump democracy promotion efforts'.[3] Mauritania is just such a country. Its generous deposits of iron ore and oil and established role as a bulwark against illegal migration to Europe and Islamist terrorism within North Africa make it an important regional partner for the West.[4]

And the second is that low levels and slow rates of modernisation often mean that there is little domestic pressure for greater democratisation.[5] Girod and Walters point to the high incidence of poverty in the country as one important indicator of its underdevelopment. In addition, they observe that successive regimes have repeatedly demonstrated their willingness to ignore popular demands, such as breaking 'diplomatic ties with Israel'.[6] So, even if domestic pressure for democratisation was stronger, there are still no guarantees that those in power would respond in kind. On this basis, Girod and Walters conclude, Mauritania's democratic turn seems to defy conventional wisdom and, in so doing, pose a serious problem for Levitsky and Way's model.

But what of the turn's brevity? Within just a few years, many of the democratising reforms which had been introduced had either fallen into abeyance or been undone. Certainly, the promise the country seemed to show in 2007 has not been maintained or replicated. And, more fundamentally, what of Levitsky and Way's emphasis that 'Western powers have *exerted* little democratizing pressure on major energy producers . . . or states that are deemed strategically important' (emphasis added)?[7] The active element in this observation is crucial for, while Western governments might not always press for greater political liberalisation if they deem the potential risks and losses too high, that does not mean they will try to stop such transitions from happening without them or oppose those that succeed. On the contrary, Mauritania's turn shows that the West is only too willing to accept serendipitous democratic turns.

Girod and Walters, therefore, are only partly right. While the West's strategic interests in Mauritania remain a critical influence on its political development, they do not invalidate Levitsky and Way's model, render it unable to explain what is happening there. On the contrary, and as this chapter shows, the country closely conforms to their thesis. Crucially, the United States and European Union have only medium linkage to Mauritania. This means that, despite their medium leverage over Nouakchott and occasional application of significant liberalising pressure, they do not consistently press the regime to democratise and are often satisfied if it holds 'minimally acceptable elections'.[8] As a result, the regime's medium organisational power is sufficient to maintain the country's competitive authoritarian order and prevent the onset of unstable authoritarianism, a sometime consequence for states with less capable governments.[9]

Like Morocco and Algeria, Mauritania both entered and emerged from the Arab Spring competitive authoritarian. Unlike its near neighbours, however, it did so for different reasons. Whereas Rabat and Algiers had sufficient organisational power to resist whatever democratising pressure local protestors and the West could put on them, Nouakchott benefited from Western inattention born of its weaker links. Moreover, Mauritania's transition to competitive authoritarianism started from a different point on the political compass. Unlike its neighbours, the Mauritanian regime became less, not more, democratic, discarding or compromising the liberalising reforms that had recently been introduced rather than offering new (albeit severely constrained) electoral opportunities.

To sustain this analysis and facilitate Mauritania's comparison with its near neighbours, this chapter is structured along the same lines as each of Levitsky and Way's original cases and this book's other country studies. The first examines the strength of Mauritania's economic, intergovernmental, technocratic, social, information and civil society links to the United States and the European Union. The second section begins by assessing the extent of the West's leverage over Nouakchott before considering the lasting effects of the Black Knight patronage the regime once received. The third section then measures the regime's organisational strength, the scope and cohesion of both its security apparatus and ruling party, and how much control it exercises over the country's economy. And, finally, the fourth section traces the regime's development, especially since 2005.

Linkage

Overall, Mauritania has medium links to the United States and the European Union. It has stronger connections in some categories (intergovernmental and economic) than in others (technocratic, social, information and civil society). Moreover, its ties to the US and EU have grown both in number and quality over the past twenty years. Since the rapid and irretrievable decline of its Black Knight patron (Iraq) in the early 1990s, successive regimes have consistently sought closer relations with the West. Nevertheless, its connections to the United States and European Union are not as numerous and robust as those of its northern neighbours, including Algeria, the other case study with medium-strength links.

Like Tunisia and Morocco, Mauritania is a member of the MEPI, the BMENA and the UfM. And, unlike any of its neighbours, it is a core participant – along with Mali and Niger – in the European Union's Strategy for Security and Development in the Sahel (SSDS). Launched in March 2011, the SSDS's longer-term goals include 'enhancing political stability, security, good governance, social cohesion . . . economic and education opportunities' in the region's countries so that they might 'prosper and no longer be . . . potential safe haven[s] for AQIM and criminal networks'.[10] And, like Morocco, it was admitted to the Millennium Corporation Challenge in 2007.[11]

Since the United States and European Union relaunched their respective aid programmes to the country – after suspending them in retaliation for the military's overthrow of President Sidi Ould Cheikh Abdallahi in August 2008 – Mauritania has been granted significant amounts of development and other support. Between 2009 and 2015, it was awarded $43.93 million in financial assistance by the United States, more than Algeria (which received $43.23 million over the same period) and more per capita than Morocco.[12] And, between 2010 and 2013,[13] it was given €209.3 million by the EU under the tenth European Development Fund (EDF).[14] Some of this money (€22 million) was disbursed as part of the SSDS to which was added a further €1.2 million by the Instrument for Stability (IfS).[15]

Nevertheless, Mauritania has still not entered into as many agreements with the West as Tunisia, Morocco or even Algeria. It was expelled from the MCC as a consequence of the 2008 *coup d'état*.[16] It has not signed any sort of free trade agreement with the United States. It does not receive any Foreign Military Financing credits from Washington. It has not joined the EMP, the ENP or the PfDSP. It has not concluded an association agreement or an action plan with the European Union. And it has not been given any MEDA I or II or SPRING funding. Its relations with the United States and the European Union, therefore, are conducted outside most of the policy frameworks to which its neighbours belong.

Perhaps unsurprisingly, this difference is reflected in Mauritania's economic relations with the West. Like its neighbours, its commercial links to the United States and European Union are important and improving. Between 2004 and 2014, the total value of its trade with the EU more than doubled from €734 million to €1.6 billion.[17] And, while starting from a much lower level, its trade with the US has grown at an even faster rate. Between 2000 and 2004, the annual average value of the country's exports to the United States was just $122,010.[18] Between 2005 and 2009, that amount fell even lower to $82,521.[19] Then, between 2010 and 2014, it leapt to $5.52 million.[20] And the value of the country's imports from the United States has also grown exponentially over this period. Between 2000 and 2004, their annual average value was $30.79 million.[21] Between 2005 and 2009, that amount more than doubled to $75.89 million.[22] And, between 2010 and 2014, it nearly quadrupled again to $275.2 million.[23]

This growth has been mirrored by similar increases in the amount of FDI in the country. Between 1995 and 1999, Mauritania attracted an average of $36.95 million of investment a year.[24] Between 2000 and 2004, that amount soared to $135.53 million.[25] Then, between 2005 and 2009,[26] it more than doubled again to $289.55 million before leaping to $807.84 million between 2010 and 2013.[27] Just as they are to Tunisia, Algeria and Morocco, therefore, the European Union and United States are two of Mauritania's most important economic collaborators. Yet neither of them dominates commercial activity with the country to quite the same extent that the European Union does with Tunisia, Algeria and Morocco. While Mauritania might import more goods from Europe than anywhere else (37.6 per cent), its biggest export market, by some margin, is China (45.3 per cent). So, even though the EU is Nouakchott's top trading partner, China is its close second (30.7 per cent).[28] Mauritania's economic links to the West may be strong but they are not as strong as those of each of its northern neighbours.

This comparative difference is mirrored in the global distribution of the country's diaspora. As of 2012, there were 198,307 Mauritanians living and working abroad out of a total population of 3.77 million.[29] And like the hundreds of thousands of Tunisians, Algerians and Moroccans who do the same, they continue to make vital economic, political and social contributions back home. In 2006, they remitted $103 million which amounted to 3.9 percent of the country's total GDP.[30] And, in accordance with Article 47 of the constitution, they elect three of the Senate's 56 members.[31]

A significant number of these migrants are based in the West, mainly in France (13,699) and Spain (10,821). Nevertheless, the vast majority (145,000) live elsewhere in Africa. So, while Mauritania may have a large diaspora like its neighbours, most of its expatriates do not reside in Europe and North America. This difference both reflects and reinforces the country's weaker links to the United States and the European Union compared to those of Tunisia, Algeria and Morocco. Fewer Mauritanians live in the United States and Europe because the country has not joined several key Western policy frameworks. As a result, the country's human connection to the West is not as strong. And this bond has been undermined still further of late by the fall in tourist numbers caused by the 'general threat from terrorism, including kidnapping'.[32] Indeed, the famous Paris–Dakar car rally has not been staged in the country (or even Africa) since 2007.[33]

With fewer of its nationals living and working in the United States and European Union, Mauritania's technocratic links to the West are also weaker than those of its northern neighbours. Both in total and proportionally, not as many Mauritanians are learning and acquiring the attitudes and skills that will encourage them to remain emotionally and intellectually connected to where they studied, and diffuse democracy when they return home. And, of those who are based in Europe and North America, very few are students. Indeed, most are 'men . . . with a low level of education . . . employed in low skilled occupations, including elementary jobs . . . [such] as service workers . . . shop and market sales workers . . . craft and related trades workers . . . and . . . plant and machine operators and assemblers'.[34]

Mauritanians also have weaker information links to the West than other Maghreb populations. While the country has experienced some growth in Internet and mobile phone use over the past fifteen years, this increase has not been as rapid or widespread as that of its neighbours. In 2000, just 0.2 per cent of its inhabitants had access to the World Wide Web, a smaller proportion than that of Tunisia (2.8 percent), Algeria (0.5 per cent) and Morocco (0.7 per cent). By 2005, this figure had crept up to 0.7 per cent before rising more quickly to 4 per cent by 2010, and 6.2 per cent by 2013. By then, however, the gap in access between Mauritania and its neighbours had grown into a chasm, with 43.8 per cent of Tunisians, 16.5 per cent of Algerians and 56 per cent of Moroccans able to go online.[35]

And, while the spread in mobile phone use across the Maghreb has been more consistent, Mauritania still lags a little behind most of its neighbours. In 2000, the number of people subscribing to a cell phone service was roughly the same throughout the region; 1 per cent of Mauritanians and Tunisians, 8 per cent of Moroccans and virtually no Algerians. By

2005, 24 per cent of Mauritania's populace had a contract, and then 77 per cent by 2010 and 103 per cent by 2013. This dramatic growth, though, was more than matched in most other countries, with subscription rates of 116 per cent in Tunisia, 101 per cent in Algeria and 129 per cent in Morocco in 2013.[36]

Perhaps inevitably, with fewer of its nationals living in the West, Mauritania's civil society links to the United States and European Union are not as numerous and strong as those of its neighbours. Moreover, because it does not belong to the EMP, the ENP or the PfDSP, and does not receive any MEDA or SPRING funding, its groups and organisations are not eligible to access certain sources of EU money, most notably the CSF. Of course, there are organisations in Europe and North America that cater to parts of this smaller, cross-border population, and West-based networks that collaborate with local, Mauritanian partners but not nearly as many as work with Tunisian, Algerian and Moroccan émigrés, groups and bodies. Indeed, and tellingly, Mauritania is the only Maghreb country that is not part of the Euro-Mediterranean Human Rights Network.[37]

Leverage

Perhaps unsurprisingly, in the light of these weaker links, the West's leverage over Mauritania is middling rather than high. With a GDP of just $5.061 billion, the country has neither a large nor medium-sized economy.[38] Pumping only 6,000 barrels of crude oil a day during the course of an average year, it is not a major or intermediate oil producer.[39] It does not possess, or have easy access to, nuclear weapons. And, without the backing of a Black Knight patron, it is not well placed to resist whatever democratising pressure the West might put on it. Indeed, the only one of Levitsky and Way's criteria the country satisfies, is the persistence of 'a major security-related foreign-policy issue for the United States' and European Union within its territory.[40] This alone reduces the West's leverage from high to medium.

In actual fact, Mauritania is vital to at least two such issues. The first is the same as that which continues to mark the West's relations with the region's other countries: the existence and activities of Islamist terror groups within and across its borders. Between October 2004 and January 2010, at least thirteen serious attacks were carried out there, mainly by AQIM.[41] The high number of incidents – which included shootings, bombings and abductions – and the inability of Mauritania's armed and security forces adequately to protect the country's territory and resources,[42] have prompted the United States, the European Union and individual European governments to provide Nouakchott with significant security-related assistance. It is a member of the US-sponsored Trans-Sahara Counterterrorism Partnership (TSCTP), the UN-recognised Middle East and North Africa Financial Action Task Force (MENAFATF), and the EU–Arab Maghreb Union's 5 + 5 Initiative.[43] Through these programmes, its armed and security forces have been provided with money, equipment and training.

And the second security-related foreign-policy issue is migration, and Mauritania's dual role as 'receiver of "returned" migrants from Europe and . . . as "returner" of sub-Saharan migrants who may attempt to proceed' there.[44] Again, the importance of these functions has increased markedly as a result of the Arab Spring. As one of the region's less-affected countries, Mauritania is still in a position to play these parts in a way in which Libya no longer easily can. Moreover, the instability which was generated by the Arab Spring, along with that caused by the civil war in Mali and the ongoing unrest in northern Nigeria and elsewhere, have led to an increase in the number of people trying to enter Europe by irregular means. Partly as a result, and because of the vast and still unfolding human tragedy in Syria and northern Iraq, European Union governments and citizenries are now acutely sensitive to the issue of migration.

The centrality of these issues to the West's relationship with Mauritania does not mean that the dangers posed by the country are significantly greater than those presented by its neighbours. Rather, the United States' and European Union's dealings with it are not as deep and diverse as their interactions with Tunisia, Algeria and Morocco. These issues, therefore, only appear more important in Mauritania's case because its links to the United States and European Union are fewer and weaker.

Moreover, the United States and European Union have been far more willing to use their leverage over Mauritania than they have over Tunisia, Algeria and Morocco. Of course, their influence over Algiers and Rabat is only low. Yet, even so, they have consistently refrained from pressing either of these regimes as hard as they could. And they certainly did not maximise their high leverage over Ben Ali. Nouakchott, in contrast, has been repeatedly disciplined, with Washington and Brussels (and other Western governments) suspending their aid programmes to the country after both the 2005 and 2008 *coups d'état*. And, in response to the HCE's overthrow of President Abdallahi, it was expelled from the MCC and barred from receiving any Foreign Military Financing credits.[45]

Mauritania's ability and willingness to withstand and resist Western pressure are further complicated by the Black Knight patronage it used to receive from Libya, Syria and, in particular, Iraq.[46] Or, perhaps more accurately, given the United States' and European Union's sustained disinclination to try to make Nouakchott democratise, its *relationship* with the West is still affected by the now long-ended support it received from Damascus, Tripoli and Baghdad. This patronage did not last for very long – a few years in the early 1990s – and was not especially expansive in form, mainly military equipment and some financial assistance and diplomatic support. And, at least some of what was provided was 'driven by status rivalries' as Libya and Syria sought to match Iraq's beneficence and reinforce their own claims to be leading Arab powers.[47]

Nevertheless, this patronage has profoundly affected both Mauritania's relations with the West and political development over the past two decades. First, it helped establish Nouakchott's dependence on outside help. Since then, the regime has remained reliant on (mainly Western) donor assistance, and on international financial and technical support to launch and sustain many of the country's most ambitious development programmes.[48] Second, it antagonised the West. While Taya was mindful not to accede to all Saddam Hussein's requests and offers – which included allowing the Iraqi army to test fire surface-to-air missiles in the Mauritanian Sahara and provide the members of his personal bodyguard – he was still sufficiently friendly towards Baghdad to anger and alienate Western governments;[49] hardly surprising given that they went to war with Iraq in January 1991. And third, it has, as a result of these other effects, led Nouakchott to adopt a policy of appeasement towards the West. Taya and his successors have anxiously sought to repair and strengthen their relations with the United States and Europe, not least because they have needed to find new sources of development assistance to make up for that which Iraq stopped providing. To the extent that Taya was even prepared to establish diplomatic relations with Israel, an act that was deeply unpopular at home and led most of the country's Arab donors promptly to withdraw their support to Nouakchott.

Indeed, perhaps the most significant long-term consequence of the Black Knight patronage Mauritania received from Libya, Syria and Iraq, certainly the most paradoxical, has been the inexorable growth in Nouakchott's dependence on the West. To the extent that the regime is now acutely sensitive to Western opinions and attitudes, and eager and committed, through the weight of past compromises, current obligations and near-future ambitions, to satisfy them. As a result of once accepting help from Saddam Hussein, the country has felt obliged to try to win and retain the West's support by means of sustained supplication. As a result of this strategy, Mauritania no longer has or wants the backing of (another) Black Knight patron.

Yet the United States' and European Union's disciplining of Mauritania

– the exercise of their leverage – is also marked by several inconsistencies. These tensions lie less between the US and EU, whose 'relationship . . . has been described as . . . one of "cooperation and division of labour"', and more in the countermeasures they have taken against the regime and continue to enforce.[50] In response to the 2008 coup, Washington refused to grant Nouakchott any FMF credits. This prohibition was aimed directly at the military – at least part of which was responsible for the overthrow of President Abdallahi – and is still in force today. Yet, at the same time, Mauritania was allowed to remain in the TSCTP and became one of the 'core Sahelian states and . . . focus of' the EU's SSDS which was launched soon thereafter.[51] The tension, therefore, derives from Western governments' willingness to punish the regime and desire to make sure it can still effectively combat their common enemies: the Islamist terrorists. Furthermore, these inconsistencies do not seem to have greatly impaired their ability to discipline Nouakchott.

Organisational Power

Unlike any of the other regimes examined here, Nouakchott has only medium-low organisational power. Even though it continues to exercise a fair degree of control over the country's economy, its coercive apparatus and ruling party both have middling scope and low cohesion. Paradoxically, some of the greatest constraints on the armed and security forces are of their own making, the result of their prolonged involvement in Mauritanian politics. Six of the country's nine heads of state since independence have been either serving or recently retired army officers. And, to date, military-led *coups d'état* have brought more administrations to an end than any other process. Not one of the country's leaders has been voted out of office by the electorate.

Perhaps unsurprisingly, given the backgrounds of so many heads of state and the ways in which they acquired power, which gave them a keen appreciation of the military's political import and the need to keep its officers and personnel onside, government investment in the armed forces over the past two decades has increased steadily. Between 1995 and 1999, the regime spent each year an average of 2.4 per cent of the country's GDP on the armed forces. Between 2000 and 2004, this allocation rose markedly to 3.4 per cent before falling slightly to 3.3 per cent between 2005 and 2009. And, between 2010 and 2014, it climbed again to 3.9 per cent. This means that, in real terms, government spending on defence over this period has quadrupled from \$37.3 million in 1995 to \$150.3 million in 2014.[52] This funding supports a military of 15,850 soldiers, sailors and airmen,[53] and five thousand gendarmes and National Guards, one of the largest per capita forces in the region.[54]

This investment, and the financial and other assistance provided by the United States and Europe, ensure that Mauritania's armed and security forces are able to conduct low-intensity operations in most of the country's urban centres. In the months immediately following both the 2008 *coup d'état* and the start of the Arab Spring, they successfully contained and dispersed many of the protests and rallies staged in Nouakchott, Maghama, Zouerate and elsewhere. They also occasionally arrest and harass journalists and opposition figures.[55] Nevertheless, they still struggle to maintain an effective presence outside the main towns and cities. Much of their equipment is outdated while a lack of air transport means they cannot easily monitor and police large swathes of the country's vast territory.[56] The seriousness of these limitations is confirmed by both the number of terror attacks carried out over the past decade and the level of support being provided by the West.

This investment is also insufficient to counteract the huge damage the military's repeated interventions in the political process has caused its cohesion. These coups have not only established and reinforced a precedent that normalises and legitimises the seizure of power but has also helped factionalise the armed forces. Four of the six *coups d'état* which have been carried out since independence were launched by army officers against other army officers who had themselves seized power. And even though Colonel Vall came to support Abdel Aziz's intervention, the HCE's removal of Abdallahi was an at least partial repudiation of the CMJD's efforts and legacy.

The debilitating effect of political power on the armed forces' unity is exacerbated by the absence of any significant non-material ties. Unlike its Algerian and Moroccan counterparts, the Mauritanian military does not have any recent glorious campaigns upon which to build an *esprit de corps*: quite the reverse, in fact, since it was defeated by Polisario,[57] and its recent successes against AQIM are largely the result of the extensive and sustained help it has been given by the West.[58]

The party set-up in Mauritania is also different from those in Algeria, Morocco and Ben Ali's Tunisia. Unlike Algiers and Rabat, Nouakchott is supported by a more conventional ruling party: the Union for the Republic (Union pour la République, UR). The UR commands a small majority in the National Assembly which is augmented by the other members of the ruling coalition. Together they control 75 per cent of the seats giving the regime considerable influence over what parliament ponders, proposes and promulgates. Yet, unlike Ben Ali's RCD, the UR has far less influence over the rest of the political system. It does not have a mass membership so cannot easily mobilise large portions of the population. It is not particularly popular in some parts of the country, most notably the south. And it must compete – for candidates, members and voters – with other, older, better-established groups. Its lack of deeper and wider roots reflects its origins, for it was established only in 2009 to help Abdel Aziz compete in the presidential election. It remains, therefore, a top-down creation, an electoral vessel, a means by which the regime can influence the National Assembly more effectively.

Despite the regime's reduced coercive capacity and lesser party strength, the ruling elite continues to exercise significant control over the country's economy. Since President Taya launched his strategy to reposition Mauritania as an ally of the West, successive governments have, with fluctuating enthusiasm, introduced a range of liberalising reforms.[59] While these changes have helped to attract more foreign investment,[60] large parts of the economy remain unreconstructed. 'Less formal state intervention' has not led to 'better state intervention or less informal state intervention',[61] to the extent that the country was ranked 176th (out of 189 countries) in the World Bank's 2015 Doing Business Index.[62]

This lack of fundamental reform is both a cause and an effect of the local elite's continuing economic influence. It emerged from the 2008 *coup d'état* mostly unchanged and with its interests largely intact. Indeed, its durability provides perhaps the clearest confirmation of the strength of its links to the new regime. Its members 'control most of the sectors of the market economy, including transport, banking, telecommunications, food imports, and construction'. The '"four-firm concentration ratio for the imports of wheat and sugar tops 90 percent"' while the '"two firms [that] dominate . . . rice imports . . . [have] a combined market share of 80 percent"'.[63] The regime also dominates, by means of the state-owned National Industrial and Mining Company (Société Nationale Industrielle et Minière, SNIM), the extractive industries sector which currently generates just over half (50.12 per cent) of the country's total export earnings.[64]

The regime's ability to control and influence the country's politics is enhanced by the continuing disunity of its domestic rivals. Serious efforts have been made by opposition leaders in the wake of the 2008 *coup d'état* to co-ordinate better the activities of those groups hostile to Abdel Aziz's takeover. A National Front for the Defence of Democracy (Front National Pour la Defénse de la Démocratie, FNDD) was quickly formed by four of the main opposition parties to defend both President Abdallahi's claim to power and his person, and, subsequently, help set the conditions in which the 2009 presidential election was conducted. Eleven parties then established the Coordination of Democratic Opposition (Coordination de l'Opposition Démocratique, COD) coalition which organised fairly successful boycotts of the 2013 parliamentary and 2014 presidential elections. And, just as they were in Tunisia, Algeria and Morocco, the Arab Spring protests in Mauritania soon came to be orchestrated by an umbrella body called the February 25th Movement (Mouvement du 25 Février, MVCF).

To date, these bodies have met with some success. The FNDD was able to wring a number of notable concessions out of the HCE over the conduct of the 2008 election and help ensure that no serious harm befell Abdallahi. The COD has not only held together but was able to undermine the legitimacy of the 2014 ballot by persuading thousands of Mauritanian voters not to participate. And the MVCF has sustained itself and, in so doing, become an important voice on youth issues. Yet, despite their individual and combined efforts, these coalitions have not stopped Abdel Aziz from strengthening his grip on power. Moreover, they have never commanded the support of all of the country's opposition groups and parties.

For, in truth, the 2008 coup was not met with universal or consistent condemnation. Even though they initially refused to serve in the regime-sponsored government, three of the largest opposition parties – the Rally of Democratic Forces (Regroupement des Forces Démocratiques, RFD) led by defeated 2007 presidential candidate, Ahmed Ould Daddah, the Republican Party for Democracy and Renewal (Parti Républicain Démocratique et Renouvellement, PRDR) headed by ex-CMJD chair, Ely Ould Mohamed Vall, and the Union for Democracy and Progress (Union pour la Démocratie et le Progrès, UDP) founded and fronted by former Minister of Foreign Affairs, Hamdi Ould Mouknass – united to form the broadly pro-coup coalition called Mithaq El Wihda. Despite initially opposing the 2009 election, the FNDD duly participated and was represented by the leader of the Popular Alliance for Progress (Alliance Populaire Progressiste, APP), Messaoud Ould Boulkheir. One of the COD's member organisations, the National Rally for Reform and Development (Tawassoul/Rassemblement National pour la Réforme et le Développement, RNRD), broke the coalition's boycott of the 2013 election. And, even though it has a majority, Abdel Aziz's UR is part of the Coalition of the Majority (Coalition des Partis de la Majorité, CPM) which together controls 110 (out of 147) seats.[65] While genuine opposition to the regime still exists, Abdel Aziz has successfully drawn a range of groups and parties to his banner.

Origins and Evolution of the Regime

Competitive authoritarianism has been restored to Mauritania by President Abdel Aziz. The main system and style of government for much of the past twenty-five years, it had, immediately prior to his taking office, given way to more democratic processes and institutions. The first significant step in its introduction was taken by Colonel (as he was then) Taya on 12 July 1991 when he held a referendum to secure popular approval for his new constitution. This generally liberal and encouraging document committed the state and government to respect and defend human rights, hold regular elections and allow the establishment of an unrestricted number of political parties.[66] In accordance with its strictures, Colonel Taya held a succession of parliamentary (1992, 1996 and 2001) and presidential (1992, 1997 and 2003) elections, each one competed for by several parties.

Yet, contrary to the letter of the new constitution – if perhaps not the intention of its drafter – none was ever free and fair. In the 1992 legislative ballot, Taya's Democratic and Social Republican Party (Parti Républicaine Démocratique et Social, PRDS) secured 85 per cent of the seats with 67 per cent of the vote. The next best-placed party – the Rally for Democracy and Unity (Rassemblement pour la Démocratie et l'Unité, RDU) – returned just a single member of parliament. And the 1992 presidential election, which resulted in a landslide victory for Taya, was marred by serious allegations of fraud as supporters of the Union of Democratic Forces (Union des Forces Démocratiques, UFD) were prevented from registering to vote, sometimes forcibly, by military personnel.[67] Such outcomes and patterns of behaviour were repeated throughout Taya's time in office. While not quite as remarkable as the victories secured by the RCD and Ben Ali, the PRDS and Taya never took less than 67.6 (1996) or 62.7 (1992) per cent of the vote respectively.[68]

On 3 August 2005, President Taya was ousted in a *coup d'état*. He was initially replaced by the CMJD led by Colonel Ely Ould Mohamed Vall. In an effort to appease the West, which was much aggrieved by Taya's removal, the CMJD did what few expected it to do: strengthen the country's democratic processes and institutions. For, by the time it struck, Mauritania had long grown used to such military interventions. The independence years were studded with a succession of depositions, four in total with Taya's the fifth. Each ousting was accompanied by similar justifications: decisive action was needed to save the country which would, as a result, undergo a political renaissance. Yet, not once had an intercession led to democracy. The closest the country had come had been under Taya whose new constitution outlined a competitive multiparty system that was never fully implemented. There were, in short, few precedents for what the CMJD did.

One of the council's earliest reforms was to establish the Independent National Electoral Commission (Commission Electorale Nationale Indépendante, CENI) to organise and oversee all future ballots. Despite lacking sufficient trained personnel and much essential equipment, the commission's creation marked a vital first step, a declaration of liberalising intent by the new regime and, more practically, a bulwark against the undemocratic influence of the Ministry of the Interior. Other reforms soon followed. Presidential term limits – two periods of no more than five years each – were introduced. The practice of transporting military personnel to vote in opposition constituencies was ended.[69] Members of the CMJD and other military officers were barred from standing for election either in or out of uniform. And United Nations help organising fresh elections was formally requested.[70]

In accordance with these changes, local, parliamentary and presidential elections were staged in November and December 2006, and March 2007 respectively. And, while not perfect – 'the military's chosen candidates . . . took over both the National Assembly and the presidency' – they were still freer and fairer than any held before or since.[71] The 2007 election was a landmark occasion for both country and region. It was the first time Mauritania elected a civilian – Sidi Ould Cheikh Abdallahi – in an open and competitive vote. And it was the first time an Arab League member staged a free and fair executive election.[72] So impressed were the United States and European Union by the CMJD's reforms that they lifted the aid embargo they had imposed shortly after Taya's removal.

On 6 August 2008, however, Mauritania's democratic experiment came to a juddering halt when former CMJD member, Colonel Mohamed Ould Abdel Aziz, ousted President Abdallahi in yet another military-led *coup d'état*. The country's retreat into competitive authoritarianism since then has been inexorable but erratic, mainly because Abdel Aziz cannot afford completely to ignore or totally undo all the liberalising reforms his predecessors introduced. Like every competitive authoritarian leader, he needs to maintain a degree of democracy to satisfy Western sensibilities, and he must also calm the significant domestic discontent that his actions provoked. Preserving some of what he inherited, therefore, has been one of the ways in which he has tried to persuade sceptical and agitated Mauritanians to come to terms with what he has done.

Power was initially invested in the High Council of State (Haut Conseil d'État, HCE) led by Abdel Aziz.[73] Over the next ten months, the council engaged in protracted negotiations with the opposition, led by the FNDD and the RFD, over the fate of Abdallahi and the staging of a new presidential election. These talks were finally concluded on 4 June 2009 with the signature of the Dakar Accords. Under the terms of this agreement, the HCE relinquished power to a Transitional Government of National Unity (Gouvernement d'Union Nationale de Transition, GUNT) on 27 June 2009 which was initially headed by Abdallahi who promptly resigned in order to allow the country's political order to return to a more regular constitutional footing.[74] The Transitional Government then remained in power to organise the presidential election before being dissolved on election day (18 July 2009).[75]

By these means, Abdel Aziz hoped to appease his domestic opponents and Western governments, and reconcile them to what he had done. His willingness to negotiate with the FNDD and RFD was a key part of this strategy and, even though the HCE used some force against the protestors who took to the streets in the days and weeks immediately following the coup, it did not rely on coercion alone.[76] And, by delegating responsibility for organising and conducting the 2009 presidential election to the Transitional Government, it was better able to present the vote as free and fair.

Indeed, the ballot was held under much the same terms as the 2008 election. The CENI was again put in charge of making the arrangements and overseeing the conduct of the vote. Each candidate was allowed to send two observers to every polling station to monitor what was taking place. Media coverage of the competing campaigns was mostly fair and equal.[77] And, while Abdel Aziz's eventual victory was both predictable and handsome, the size of his winning margin was not an affront to credibility.[78] The country's Constitutional Council (Conseil Constitutionnel, CCo) duly declared him the winner and the result was 'recognized by the international community'.[79]

The FNDD and other opposition groups rejected the outcome, however, on the grounds that the election was flawed. The Transitional Government and CENI had been given just twenty-one days in which to prepare, not nearly enough time to do everything that was needed to ensure a free and fair vote. Most credible international election monitors had declined to participate, arguing that conditions prevented them from carrying out a 'complete and effective observation mission'.[80] The Constitutional Council had acted with suspicious haste, declaring the winner just forty-eight hours after the polls had closed, far earlier than it had to and before the Electoral Commission's final report into the conduct of the ballot had been published. The chairman of the CENI, Sidi Ahmed Ould Deye, had sufficient doubts about the 'reliability' of the result to resign from his post.[81] And the constitutional ordinance barring members of the armed forces and CMJD from standing for election had simply been ignored.[82]

But the opposition's biggest grievance was about the broader context in which the vote had been held, for it had not been staged in accordance with established and accepted constitutional practice as part of a long-standing and culturally embedded political routine. On the contrary, it had taken place because a cabal of usurpers had demanded that it did. After overthrowing the legally elected president, they wanted the chance to acquire retrospective public approval, clearly not because they valued and respected the democratic will of the people but because they needed to normalise and legitimise what they had done. The election, then, was never intended to be an open competition. No amount of promises and concessions was going to alter the almost certain outcome. Its function, instead, was as an electoral coronation, to give Abel Aziz a mandate after the fact. Not only was the staging of the 2009 election an affront to the very principles it was supposed to embody and implement but its inevitable conclusion marked the final triumph of the 2008 *coup d'état*. In conception, design and conduct, therefore, it was a profoundly competitive authoritarian exercise.

So, too, were the 2013 parliamentary and 2014 presidential elections, in part because many of the issues and antagonisms which had defined both the content and conduct of the previous ballot also dominated these later votes. Indeed, ten of the largest and most popular parties – belonging to the anti-regime Coordination of Democratic Opposition coalition – boycotted the 2013 election in protest at the government's preparations for it.[83] The only COD member to participate was the Tawassoul which was beaten into a distant second by Abdel Aziz's Union for the Republic. Conveniently, the UR secured exactly enough seats (seventy-four out of 147) to form a majority while the Tawassoul gained only sixteen, prompting its leader,[84] Jemil Ould Mansour, to complain to the CENI about 'ballot stuffing in some places and the resumption of the vote after the count in others'.[85]

The 2014 presidential election was also boycotted by the COD – including the Tawassoul this time – leading to a turnout rate of just 56 per cent.[86] Further serious doubts about the credibility of the process were stirred by the eventual result, as Abdel Aziz secured victory with 82 per cent of the vote, a triumph on a comparable scale to those of Ben Ali. Furthermore, his nearest challenger, Biram Ould Dah Ould Abeid, standing for the Resurgence of the Abolitionist Movement (Initiative pour la Resurgence du Mouvement Abolitioniste, IRMA), was able to muster only 9 per cent. Despite his complaining to the CENI, Western governments quickly recognised the outcome and congratulated 'the people of Mauritania on the successful completion of peaceful and orderly presidential election'. Tellingly, they did not praise the regime for the freeness and fairness of the ballot.[87]

The recurrence of many of the same allegations and arguments across these elections highlights just how much less affected by the Arab Spring Mauritania has been than its northern neighbours. While protests were staged in many of the country's larger urban centres throughout 2011 and early 2012, they were not as numerous or as large as those organised elsewhere in the region. And, even though a higher proportion of these rallies was more overtly political (rather than economic) than those held in Algeria and Morocco, the *casus belli* was often an older, more enduring grievance linked to the 2008 *coup d'état*. Perhaps unsurprisingly, given that the 2009 election – arguably the final act in the coup – took place just eighteen months earlier, the country's Arab Spring protests were profoundly shaped and coloured by what had gone on before. Certainly, locally, they were both seen and presented as a continuation of this earlier unrest.

Partly as a result, the regime has remained alive to its origins, to how it initially acquired power. In addition to respecting *some* of the political reforms introduced by the CMJD and Abdallahi, therefore, it has preserved the country's generally permissive media environment. In this, Mauritania is far more liberal than its northern neighbours. In the Reporters Without Borders' 2015 Press Freedom Index, it was ranked 55th (out of 180 countries), well ahead of Algeria (119th), Tunisia (126th), Morocco (130th), Libya (154th) and Egypt (158th).[88] And, since taking power, the regime has broadly strengthened the media reforms made by its predecessors. It does not interfere in the workings of the High Authority for the Press and Broadcasting (Haute Autorité de la Presse et de l'Audiovisuel, HAPA), the independent body established by Abdallahi in October 2006 to oversee the media. Nor does it seek to control or curb the activities of the Mauritanian Journalists' Union (Syndicat des Journalistes Mauritaniens, SJM). In 2011, it 'abolished prison sentences for slander and defamation, including for speech about heads of state'. And, in late 2011, it approved the launch of several new, independent television and radio stations, thereby bringing its fifty-one-year monopoly over the country's broadcast media to an end.[89]

Nevertheless the regime still actively restricts both freedom of speech and the media. And, perhaps more worryingly, over the past couple of years it has contemplated passing new legislation which, if introduced, would greatly undermine existing liberties. Many of the abuses which are perpetrated presently are (over-) reactions to something said or written about one of Mauritania's sensitive topics – Islam, the military, high-level corruption and slavery. While these issues are not quite as taboo as the monarchy, Islam and the Western Sahara are in Morocco – not least because they are not proscribed to the same extent either in law or by culture – the authorities still tend to treat harshly those deemed to have said something offensive.

Indeed, in March 2014, six journalists were detained by the security services for covering a press conference held by the banned Islamist group, Friends of the Prophet (Ahbab Errassoul). Then, in December 2014, a journalist at the *Al-Layl* newspaper, Abeh Ould Mohammed Lafdal, was arrested by police and detained without charge for several days following an argument he had with President Abdel Aziz. And, also in December 2014, Mohamed Cheikh Ould Mohamed Ould Mkhaitir was sentenced to death for apostasy for arguing in a blog post that local interpretations of Islam helped legitimise and entrench the country's rigid caste system. Such cases only encourage journalists to keep practising self-censorship.[90]

And what protections the law currently provides may soon be legally pared back if the government passes the cybercrime bill it has been preparing with intermittent urgency since early 2013. If promulgated, it 'would establish jail time and heavy fines for disseminating certain types of politically sensitive content over the internet', 'bring encryption technology under heavy state regulation' and, most notably, 'nullify previous laws extending protections to journalists using digital technologies'.[91]

Conclusions

Mauritania's political development over the past decade tests all aspects of Levitsky and Way's model. Its earlier turn towards democracy (2005–8) seems to provide a textbook demonstration of how Western pressure can affect political change. So great was the country's dependence on international aid and such was the West's displeasure at President Taya's defenestration, that the HCE felt compelled, in a last-ditch attempt to regain the trust of the donors whose support was so essential, to introduce a raft of political reforms. This programme culminated in the 2008 presidential election, still the freest and fairest vote ever held in the country, and the first of its kind staged by an Arab League member. Western pressure, carefully targeted and judiciously applied, drove an illegitimate and usurping regime to democratise.

Yet the new order was short-lived and its demise posed difficult questions for Levitsky and Way even though, in the first instance, its fate confirmed their most basic premise: that not all political transitions result in democracy. The HCE's armed intercession brought an abrupt halt to the country's liberalising march. President Abdallahi was overthrown and barred from standing in the 2009 election which, while conducted in accordance with many of the reforms he and the CMJD had introduced, was not as free and fair as before. And, inevitably, Abdel Aziz's victory cast huge doubt on the West's intent. Its complaints about the HCE's intervention did not prevent it from recognising and collaborating with the new regime. It appeared to have lost both the will and the way to sustain the democracy it had helped bring about.

Yet, in one crucial respect, the West's behaviour was entirely consistent. Mauritania's democratic turn did not occur because of Western intentions, but despite them. Democratisation was a happy, yet unexpected and unsolicited, outcome for Washington and Brussels. Abdel Aziz's ascension simply pulled back the curtain, therefore, on the West's true motivations and objectives. And, even now, despite the Arab Spring and their promises better to support what liberalising ambitions the region's inhabitants harbour, Western governments do not crave democracy for Mauritania above all else. Their most fervent desire remains, as always, security and stability, to the extent that they are prepared to support Abdel Aziz because he is the incumbent and sensitive to their fears for and in the region.

Both the West's seeming erraticism and privileging of strategic considerations are well explained by Levitsky and Way's model. The United States and European Union have only medium links to Mauritania. This means that their investment in democracy there is entirely inconsistent. So, even though their leverage over Nouakchott is medium and the regime's ability to withstand their influence reduced, they have exerted uneven democratising pressure. The regime has medium organisational power. While the security apparatus is well funded, it is factionalised and, therefore, lacks cohesion. And, despite the ruling UR's dominance of the National Assembly, it was established only recently as a vehicle for Abdel Aziz and, as such, lacks deep roots in large parts of the country.

The regime's susceptibility to the West's authority, even if irregularly wielded, provides an intriguing corollary to Levitsky and Way's model because its vulnerability is largely and deliberately self-induced as a result of the Black Knight patronage it once accepted from Libya, Syria and, above all, Iraq. By aligning with Baghdad, President Taya not only made an opponent of the West but developed a dependence on a country whose ability to provide patronage was irreparably curtailed. When this happened, Taya's response was completely to reposition Mauritania and actively seek Western approval and support. He therefore acquiesced to many of the West's core demands. He liberalised the country's politics but this amounted to little more than holding regular, but uncompetitive, elections and, far more significantly, established diplomatic relations with Israel, a decision that is still widely resented at home. Yet, despite such bitter opposition, this compromise, arguably more than any other, helped shift Mauritania to where Taya wanted it to be: firmly in the West's political orbit.

And, in making this journey, the country has conformed to another of Levitsky and Way's foundational observations: that, in the immediate aftermath of the Cold War, 'the primary sources of external assistance were . . . located almost exclusively in the West', driving 'many autocrats [to] adopt formal democratic institutions in an effort to "position their countries favorably in the international contest for scarce development resources"'.[92] Mauritania's initial shift to competitive authoritarianism, therefore, formed part of the main wave of transitions identified by Levitsky and Way and examined in their book. And, though its shift was triggered by Iraq's demise rather than that of the Soviet Union,[93] the principal causes of its transformation are otherwise largely the same as those captured in their model. In more ways than one Mauritania is a near textbook case study.

Notes

1. Levitsky and Way, *Competitive Authoritarianism*, p. 3.
2. Taya came to power in December 1984 after overthrowing his predecessor, Colonel Mohamed Khouna Oul Haidalla; Desha M. Girod and Meir R. Walters (2012), 'Elite-Led Democratisation in Aid-Dependent States: The Case of Mauritania', 17: 2, 181–93, p. 184.
3. Ibid. p. 182.
4. Hannah M. Cross (2011), 'Rents, Rights, Rejections and Resistance: West African Migrants, the EU's Migration Regime and Militarisation in Mauritania', *The International Journal of Human Rights* 15: 6, 827–46, pp. 832 and 836.
5. Girod and Walters, 'Elite-Led Democratisation in Aid-Dependent States', p. 182.
6. Ibid. p. 182.
7. Levitsky and Way, *Competitive Authoritarianism*, p. 41.
8. Ibid. p. 53.
9. Ibid. p. 53.
10. European External Action Service (2015), 'Strategy for Security and Development in the Sahel', available at <http://eeas.europa.eu/africa/docs/sahel_strategy_en.pdf> (last accessed 31 October 2015), p. 4.

11. Curt Tarnoff (2015), 'Millennium Challenge Corporation', *Congressional Research Service*, 11 March, available at <https://www.fas.org/sgp/crs/row/RL32427.pdf> (last accessed 31 October 2015), pp. 15–16.

12. Like those used in earlier chapters, this figure is based on planned disbursements since they more accurately reflect the United States' intent. The Maghreb country that received the largest amount of per capita financial assistance was Tunisia. US Government (2015), 'Foreign Assistance', available at <http://beta.foreignassistance.gov/> (last accessed 31 October 2015).

13. The funding period was supposed to start in 2007 but was delayed because of the suspension.

14. European External Action Service (2015), 'EU Relations with Mauritania', available at <http://eeas.europa.eu/mauritania/index_en.htm> (last accessed 31 October 2015).

15. Available at <http://eeas.europa.eu/africa/docs/sahel_strategy_en.pdf> (last accessed 31 October 2015), p. 9.

16. Available at <https://www.fas.org/sgp/crs/row/RL32427.pdf> (last accessed 31 October 2015), pp. 15–16.

17. European Commission (2015), 'European Union, Trade in Goods with Mauritania', 20 October, available at <http://trade.ec.europa.eu/doclib/docs/2011/january/tradoc_147323.pdf> (last accessed 1 November 2015), p. 8.

18. More specifically, Mauritania's exports to the United States were worth $83,730 in 2000, $231,390 in 2001, $76,950 in 2002, $29,880 in 2003 and $188,100 in 2004. World Bank (2015), 'Mauritania All Products Export Trade Value', 31 October, available at <http://wits.worldbank.org/CountryProfile/Country/MRT/StartYear/2010/EndYear/2014/TradeFlow/Export/Indicator/XPRT-TRD-VL/Partner/USA/Product/Total> (last accessed 31 October 2015).

19. More specifically, Mauritania's exports to the United States were worth $29,820 in 2005, $7,700 in 2007, $68,290 in 2008 and $43,070 in 2009; ibid.

20. More specifically, Mauritania's exports to the United States were worth $5,140 in 2010, $303,180 in 2011, $23,870 in 2012 and $26.06 million in 2013; ibid.

21. More specifically, Mauritania's imports from the United States were worth $29.14 million in 2000, $42.46 million in 2001, $23.7 million in 2002, $17.5 million in 2003 and $41.16 million in 2004. World Bank (2015), 'Mauritania All Products Import Trade Value', 31 October, available at <http://wits.worldbank.org/CountryProfile/Country/MRT/StartYear/2010/EndYear/2014/TradeFlow/Import/Indicator/MPRT-TRD-VL/Partner/USA/Product/Total> (last accessed 31 October 2015).

22. More specifically, Mauritania's imports from the United States were worth $107.99 million in 2005, $59.36 million in 2006, $64.12 million in 2007, $52.72 million in 2008 and $54.11 million in 2009; ibid

23. More specifically, Mauritania's imports from the United States were worth $63.99 million in 2010, $74.25 million in 2011, $145.44 million in 2012, $225.42 million in 2013 and $866.92 million in 2014; ibid.

24. More specifically, the country attracted $6.98 million in FDI in 1995, -$0.43 million in 1996, -$3.32 million in 1997, $0.13 million in 1998 and $15.11 million in 1999. Available at <http://data.worldbank.org/indicator/BX.KLT. DINV.CD.WD/countries?page=3> (last accessed 7 July 2015).

25. More specifically, the country attracted $40.09 million in FDI in 2000, $76.7 million in 2001, $67.4 million in 2002, $101.89 million in 2003 and $391.6 million in 2004; ibid.

26. More specifically, the country attracted $814.1 million in FDI in 2005, $154.6 million in 2006, $139.37 million in 2007, $342.77 million in 2008 and -$3.07 million in 2009; ibid

27. More specifically, the country attracted $130.52 million in FDI in 2010, $588.74 million in 2011, $1.38 billion in 2012 and $1.12 billion in 2013; ibid.

28. Available at <http://trade.ec.europa.eu/doclib/docs/2011/january/tradoc_ 147323.pdf> (last accessed 1 November 2015), p. 8.

29. Migration Policy Centre (2013), 'Mauritania', June, available at <http:// www.migrationpolicycentre.eu/docs/migration_profiles/Mauritania.pdf> (last accessed 1 November 2015), p. 1; and World Bank (2015), 'Population, total', available at <http://data.worldbank.org/indicator/SP.POP.TOTL> (last accessed 1 November 2015).

30. International Fund for Agricultural Development (2007), 'Sending Money Home: Worldwide Remittance Flows to developing and Transition Countries', December, available at <http://www.ifad.org/remittances/maps/ brochure.pdf> (last accessed 1 November 2015), p. 8.

31. République Islamique de Mauritanie (2015), 'Ordonnance no. 91.022 du 20 Juillet 1991 portant Constitution de la République Islamique de Mauritanie', available at <http://www.mauritania.mr/fr/index.php?niveau=5&coderub= 4&codsoussous=74&codesousrub=11> (last accessed 1 November 2015), Article 47.

32. Foreign and Commonwealth Office (2015), 'Foreign Travel Advice: Mauritania', 1 November, available at <https://www.gov.uk/foreign-travel-advice/mauritania> (last accessed 1 November 2015).

33. Cross, 'Rents, Rights, Rejections and Resistance', p. 835.

34. Available at <http://www.migrationpolicycentre.eu/docs/migration_pro files/Mauritania.pdf> (last accessed 1 November 2015), pp. 1–2.

35. Available at <http://data.worldbank.org/indicator/IT.NET.USER.P2?page= 2> (last accessed 9 July 2015).

36. Available at <http://data.worldbank.org/indicator/IT.CEL.SETS.P2/coun-tries?page=2> (last accessed 9 July 2015).

37. Available at <http://euromedrights.org/members/> (last accessed 6 September 2015).

38. World Bank (2015), 'Mauritania, <http://data.worldbank.org/country/mauritania> (last accessed 2 November 2015).
39. US Department of Energy (2015), 'International Energy Statistics: Total Petroleum and Other Liquids Production 2014', <http://www.eia.gov/beta/international/rankings/#?prodact=53-1&cy=2014> (last accessed 2 November 2015).
40. Levitsky and Way, *Competitive Authoritarianism*, p. 372.
41. Girod and Walters, 'Elite-Led Democratisation in Aid-Dependent States', p. 188.
42. International Institute of Strategic Studies, *The Military Balance 2013*, p. 393.
43. US Department of State (2013), 'Chapter 2. Country Reports: Africa Overview', 30 May, available at <http://www.state.gov/j/ct/rls/crt/2012/209979.htm> (last accessed 2 November 2015).
44. Cross, 'Rents, Rights, Rejections and Resistance', p. 827.
45. Ibid. p. 835.
46. A Black Knight is a 'high-income country (per capita GDP of $10,000 or higher) or a major military power (annual . . . [defence] spending in excess of $10 billion)' that is neither the United States nor (usually) a member of the European Union. Levitsky and Way, *Competitive Authoritarian*, pp. 372–3. Iraq qualified as such on the grounds that, in 1990, the year before the Gulf War started, which brought its patronage of Mauritania to an end, its defence budget is estimated to have been $14.11 billion. It was, according to Levitsky and Way's criteria, therefore, a major military power. Anthony H. Cordesman (1999), *Iraq and the War of Sanctions: Conventional Threats and Weapons of Mass Destruction*, Westport, CT and London: Praeger, p. 38.
47. Girod and Walters, 'Elite-Led Democratisation in Aid-Dependent States', p. 184.
48. In July 2014, the European Union Africa Infrastructure Trust Fund awarded the Mauritanian Electricity Company (Société Mauritanienne d'Électricité, SOMELEC), a €5.5 million Technical Assistance grant to help it develop its gas-powered electricity generation capability. European Union Africa Infrastructure Trust Fund (2014), 'Technical Assistance for the Mauritania Senegal Power Interconnection Project', July, available at <http://www.eu-africa-infrastructure-tf.net/activities/grants/mauritania-senegal-power-ic.htm> (last accessed 25 October 2015).
49. Girod and Walters, 'Elite-Led Democratisation in Aid-Dependent States', p. 184.
50. Cross, 'Rents, Rights, Rejections and Resistance', p. 836.
51. Available at <http://eeas.europa.eu/africa/docs/sahel_strategy_en.pdf> (last accessed 31 October 2015), p. 1.
52. Available at <http://www.sipri.org/research/armaments/milex/milex_database> (last accessed 3 November 2015).

53. International Institute of Strategic Studies, *The Military Balance 2013*, pp. 393–394.

54. Girod and Walters, 'Elite-Led Democratisation in Aid-Dependent States', p. 189.

55. Available at <https://freedomhouse.org/report/freedom-press/2015/mauritania> (last accessed 29 October 2015).

56. International Institute of Strategic Studies, *The Military Balance 2013*, p. 393.

57. To secure peace, Nouakchott was forced to renounce its claim to the southernmost third of the Spanish Sahara on 5 August 1979. The territory was occupied by Moroccan troops nine days later. Hill, *Identity in Algerian Politics*, pp. 89 and 109.

58. Lounnas, 'Confronting Al-Qa'ida in the Islamic Maghrib in the Sahel', p. 820.

59. Jan-Erik Lane and Hamadi Redissi (2009), *Religion and Politics: Islam and Muslim Civilisation*, 2nd ed., Farnham: Ashgate, pp. 217–18.

60. US Department of State (2015), 'Mauritania: Investment Climate 2015', June, available at <http://www.state.gov/documents/organization/241868.pdf> (last accessed 4 November 2015), p. 4.

61. Cédric Jourde (2011), 'Countries at the Crossroads 2011: Mauritania', available at <https://freedomhouse.org/report/countries-crossroads/2011/mauritania> (last accessed 26 October 2015).

62. World Bank (2014), 'Doing Business 2015: Going beyond Efficiency', <http://www.doingbusiness.org/~/media/GIAWB/Doing%20Business/Documents/Annual-Reports/English/DB15-Full-Report.pdf> (last accessed 28 July 2015), p. 4.

63. Available at <https://freedomhouse.org/report/countries-crossroads/2011/mauritania> (last accessed 26 October 2015).

64. World Bank (2015), 'Mauritania Trade Summary 2014 Data', 4 November, available at <http://wits.worldbank.org/CountryProfile/Country/MRT/Year/2014/Summary> (last accessed 4 November 2015).

65. Jeune Afrique (2014), 'Mauritanie: L'Opposition Radicale Boycottera la Présidentielle', 4 May, available at <http://www.jeuneafrique.com/148002/politique/mauritanie-l-opposition-radicale-boycottera-la-pr-sidentielle/> (last accessed 4 November 2015).

66. This he did with 97.94 per cent of the vote; Janet Fleischman (1994), *Mauritania's Campaign of Terror: State-Sponsored Repressions of Black Africans*, Human Rights Watch/Africa, p. 126.

67. Ibid. p. 130.

68. Dieter Nohlen, Michael Krennerich and Bernard Thibault (eds) (1999), *Elections in Africa: A Data Handbook*, Oxford: Oxford University Press, p. 595.

69. Available at <https://freedomhouse.org/report/countries-crossroads/2011/mauritania> (last accessed 26 October 2015).

70. Girod and Walters, 'Elite-Led Democratisation in Aid-Dependent States', pp. 186–7.

71. Available at <https://freedomhouse.org/report/countries-crossroads/2011/mauritania> (last accessed 26 October 2015).

72. Girod and Walters, 'Elite-Led Democratisation in Aid-Dependent States', p. 181.

73. He remained in this role until he resigned from the military on 22 April. He was subsequently replaced as the country's de facto head of state by the president of the Senate, Ba Mamadou Mbaré; Embassy of the United States Nouakchott, Mauritania (2010), 'Human Rights Report 2010', available at <http://mauritania.usembassy.gov/hrr2010.html> (last accessed 27 October 2015).

74. US Department of State (2010), 'Mauritania (04/04/10)', 4 April, available at <http://www.state.gov/outofdate/bgn/mauritania/167886.htm> (last accessed 27 October 2015).

75. Available at <http://mauritania.usembassy.gov/hrr2010.html> (last accessed 27 October 2015).

76. BBC (2008), 'Mauritania Coup Protest Broken Up', 6 October, available <http://news.bbc.co.uk/1/hi/world/africa/7654148.stm> (lasted accessed 27 October 2015).

77. Available at <https://freedomhouse.org/report/countries-crossroads/2011/mauritania> (last accessed 26 October 2015).

78. Abdel Aziz won with 52 per cent of the vote from Messaoud Ould Boulkheir (16 per cent) and Ahmed Ould Daddah (13 percent). *The New York Times* (2009), 'Coup Leader Wins Election Amid Outcry in Mauritania', 19 July, available at <http://www.nytimes.com/2009/07/20/world/africa/20mauritania.html?_r=0> (last accessed 27 October 2015).

79. US Department of State (2009), 'Mauritania (09/09)', available at <http://www.state.gov/outofdate/bgn/mauritania/129314.htm> (last accessed 28 October 2015).

80. Available at <https://freedomhouse.org/report/countries-crossroads/2011/mauritania> (last accessed 26 October 2015).

81. BBC (2009), 'Mauritania Election Chief Quits', 23 July, available at <http://news.bbc.co.uk/1/hi/world/africa/8165979.stm> (last accessed 27 October 2015).

82. Available at <https://freedomhouse.org/report/countries-crossroads/2011/mauritania> (last accessed 26 October 2015).

83. Reuters (2013), 'Mauritanian Opposition Parties to Boycott Legislative Election', 4 October, available at <http://www.reuters.com/article/2013/10/04/mauritania-politics-idUSL6N0HU2E920131004> (last accessed 28 October 2015).

84. US Department of State (2013), 'Mauritania 2013 Human Rights Report', available at <http://www.state.gov/documents/organization/220348.pdf> (last accessed 28 October 2015), p. 14.

85. Agence France-Presse (2013), 'Mauritania Election "Marred by Ballot-Stuffing"', 25 November, available at <http://www.globalpost.com/dispatch/news/afp/131125/mauritania-election-marred-ballot-stuffing> (last accessed 28 October 2015).

86. Reuters (2014), 'Mauritanian President Abdel Aziz Easily Re-Elected in Boycotted Vote', 22 June, available at <http://uk.reuters.com/article/2014/06/22/uk-mauritania-election-idUKKBN0EX14F20140622> (last accessed 28 October 2015).

87. US Department of State (2014), 'Mauritania's Presidential Election', 30 June, available at <http://www.state.gov/r/pa/prs/ps/2014/06/228630.htm> (last accessed 29 October 2015).

88. Reporters Without Borders (2015), 'Press Freedom Index', available at <http://index.rsf.org/#!/> (last accessed 8 October 2015).

89. Freedom House (2015), 'Mauritania', available at <https://freedomhouse.org/report/freedom-press/2015/mauritania> (last accessed 29 October 2015).

90. Ibid.

91. Ibid.

92. Levitsky and Way, *Competitive Authoritarianism*, p. 17.

93. Ibid. p. 17.

Conclusions

The past few years have been a period of unprecedented political upheaval for the Maghreb. While each country had, of course, experienced dramatic moments before – Ben Ali's ousting of Bourguiba, Algeria's Black October riots, the Casablanca bombings and Mauritania's 2005 and 2008 *coups d'état* to name but some – nothing of the breadth, depth or duration of the Arab Spring, a protest that began in a provincial city in one of North Africa's quieter corners and quickly engulfed the entire region. Presidents of decades' standing – latter-day imperators – were swept from office on waves of public discontent while their counterparts elsewhere nervously and hurriedly tried to calm the mob.

In several places, these protests are still being played out: in the law courts of Egypt; on the bloody battlefields of Libya; and in the leaking tubs carrying migrants to Europe. And, even where the winds of change seem to have died down, the political and social landscape is different from before, sometimes markedly so. Algeria has dispensed with its nineteen-year-long state of emergency. King Mohammed VI is now obliged – constitutionally, at least – to consult his prime minister more frequently and widely. Mauritania has a new youth movement. Tunisia has become a democracy.

And herein lies one of the defining paradoxes of the Arab Spring; its ubiquity and singularity. Nearly all of the region's countries have been directly affected, have experienced some domestic manifestation of this transnational phenomenon. Anti-government rallies were staged everywhere throughout early 2011. Umbrella bodies mushroomed better to co-ordinate, direct and motivate protestors. Public squares were occupied, government buildings targeted, symbols of the regime attacked, yet, despite making similar demands in largely the same ways over much the same period, the outcomes of these protests varied hugely. These transnational forces were given local faces. Domestic factors and concerns helped generate unique results.

Regional specialists were repeatedly confounded – initially at least – by this interplay of generalities and specificities. They compounded their collective failure to anticipate the start of the Arab Spring first by being too conservative and then too ambitious. They misdiagnosed what would become of Ben Ali's regime and the speed of its collapse. They then overcompensated and predicted sweeping changes everywhere all at once: Algeria was to be next, Bouteflika's days were definitely numbered. And, while the tide of change certainly swept through the streets of Algiers, the regime survived along with those in Rabat and Nouakchott.

An important aim of this book, therefore, has been to chart and explain these discrepancies: why Tunisia, Algeria, Morocco and Mauritania have reached different political outcomes. It has done so by contextualising each country's experiences both temporally and regionally. Their individual political development has been examined over the past decade and set alongside those of their three near neighbours. The examination and comparison have been guided and structured according to Levitsky and Way's model. Nevertheless, the book is not primarily about the Arab Spring protests: why they began; how they developed as they did; and with what consequences. It is not a taxonomy of who did what and when. Rather, the unrest represents a vital moment in the recent political lives of these countries, a crucial turn in the development of the book's true focus on modern Tunisia, Algeria, Morocco and Mauritania.

Formulated in response to events from a different period, Levitsky and Way's model both anticipates these variations and offers a framework for explaining them. One of their foundational assumptions – that political, even liberalising, transitions do not always lead to democracy – has certainly been borne out. Of the four case studies examined here, only Tunisia has achieved this transformation. The other three have all remained largely as they were: 'civilian regimes in which formal democratic institutions exist and are widely viewed as the means of gaining power, but in which incumbents' abuse of the state places them at a significant advantage vis-à-vis their opponents';[1] that is to say, they are still competitive authoritarian.

Levitsky and Way's model places more emphasis than most on the United States and European Union as democratising forces. In particular, it assesses both their links to, and leverage over, regimes. Linkage is measured across six categories of connection – economic, intergovernmental, technocratic, social, information and civil society. Leverage is determined by the amount of democratising pressure the United States and the European Union can bring to bear balanced against the regime's ability to resist their influence. If these links are numerous and good, and Western leverage high, then democratisation is more likely, no matter how much organisational power the regime has. But, if linkage and leverage are weaker, then the regime's coercive, political and economic capabilities play a more decisive role.

Conclusions

The United States and European Union had high linkage to, and high leverage over, Ben Ali's regime. Nevertheless, they did not put as much democratising pressure on Tunis as they could have done. Their failure to do so was born of reluctance and the inability and unwillingness of Western governments and different parts of the European Union to co-ordinate their leverage better. Ben Ali's regime fell, and the country made the transition to democracy, because of the weakness of its organisational power caused by an insuperable division between the armed and security forces, and the RCD's brittle cohesion owing to a lack of non-material ties.

The United States and European Union have medium linkage to, and low leverage over, Bouteflika's regime. Some connections (technocratic, social, information and civil society) are stronger than others (economic and intergovernmental). For reasons rooted in history, Algiers remains far more wary about joining Western policy frameworks and agreeing treaties with Washington and Brussels than Tunis and Rabat do for fear of diminishing its hard-won sovereignty and freedom of manoeuvre. And, as a major oil producer with a large economy, it is well equipped to resist whatever democratising pressure the US and EU might want to put on it. In fact, they are disinclined to press Algiers to democratise for fear of undermining its ability to counter Islamist terror groups in the region or impair its oil and gas provision. Algiers also has strong organisational power based on its large, well-funded and battle-hardened security apparatus which is led by men who have extensive experience of winning and retaining power by force of arms.

The United States and European Union have high linkage to, and low leverage over, the Moroccan regime. Rabat is the West's closest ally in the region and has eagerly joined all the policy frameworks that it can at the earliest opportunity. Its large economy, though, means that it is well placed to withstand whatever democratising pressure the US and EU might wish to put on it. It also has high organisational power based on an effective and cohesive security apparatus. But, as with Tunis and Algiers, Washington and Brussels are disinclined to try to compel Rabat to democratise for fear of undermining the regime and eroding its ability to act as a bulwark against Islamist extremism and terrorism in the region. Furthermore, and again as before, this pressure is further compromised by the failure of Western governments and different parts of the European Union to co-ordinate their efforts better.

The United States and European Union have medium links to, and medium leverage over, Abdel Aziz's regime. Of the four case studies examined here, Mauritania has the fewest ties to the United States and Europe. It belongs to only one EU policy framework (the UfM) and has no trade agreements with the United States. And, uniquely, most members of its diaspora do not live in Europe but in other African countries. It is neither a major nor an intermediate oil producer, does not possess nuclear weapons, has a small economy and no longer has the backing of a Black Knight patron. It also has only medium organisational power as both its security apparatus and ruling party lack scope and cohesion. Nevertheless, its medium links to the West mean that Washington and Brussels, Paris and Madrid do not put consistent democratising pressure on it. Furthermore, and as with Tunis, Algiers and Rabat, they remain reluctant to press it harder through fear that they will weaken its ability to combat Islamist terrorism and deal with illegal migration.

Levitsky and Way's model, therefore, has been used to structure the analysis of each case study and facilitate their comparison. This is the first time the model has been applied to these countries. Its application has provided fresh insight into why they each developed in the ways that they did – including their respective experiences of the Arab Spring – and how they are similar to, and differ from, their neighbours. The case studies have, in turn, tested and extended some of Levitsky and Way's ideas, most notably about history and geography, unelected executives, ruling parties, the relationship between high- and low-intensity coercion and the cohesion and scope of armed and security forces, and Western intent.

Algeria shows us that history and geography are not neutral enablers of stronger links between a country and the West. Sometimes, in fact, shared experiences, facilitated in Algeria's case by geographic proximity, can have the reverse effect and deter the forging of certain types of connection. Algeria's wariness about joining some of the European Union's policy frameworks, most notably the UfM, is directly informed by its extended colonisation by France and the high price it had to pay to secure its independence. Algiers continues to guard very jealously its hard-won sovereignty and freedom of manoeuvre. This lesson also reinforces the value of comparative analysis because Algeria's weaker intergovernmental links become more apparent when contrasted with those of Tunisia and Morocco.

Morocco and Algeria also demonstrate that Levitsky and Way's model can be applied to regimes in which unelected executives and tutelary authorities wield significant political power. While neither King Mohammed nor the Algerian armed forces have to submit to the vote to renew their mandates, their authority and positions in their respective political systems are still profoundly affected by elections and their outcomes. Who wins and on what platform have huge implications for their roles and the extent of their influence. They, like all competitive authoritarian regimes, need a degree of democracy – achieved mainly through the staging of regular multiparty elections – to satisfy Western opinion and assuage domestic opposition. Yet these ballots are rarely free and fair, and the political playing field remains heavily tilted in favour of pro-regime parties and candidates.

The Moroccan and Algerian regimes have also forged different working relationships with their respective ruling parties. Unlike either Abdel Aziz or, in particular, Ben Ali, who more closely conform to Levitsky and Way's ideal arrangement, King Mohammed and Bouteflika do not rely on one group that they have privileged and elevated above all others. Instead, they court and favour several, both alternately and simultaneously. The Istiqlal and the PJD, the RND and the FLN must compete with one another and others for posts, power and prestige. That these two regimes, of the four examined, should take this approach suggests an interesting correlation between the presence of an unelected executive or tutelary authority and the ability of those in power to dispense with a more conventional ruling party. Seemingly, because they are less directly dependent on elections – in that neither the king nor the armed forces must submit to the vote themselves – they can afford not to create or build up organisations that can subsequently limit their actions. They are able to avoid Ben Ali's symbiosis with the RCD whereby the party relied on him but he, in turn, depended on it.

This observation is buttressed by the lesser gradations between these four case studies. King Mohammed is arguably the most able to dominate his country's political parties because he is the least dependent on elections. Bouteflika, with the backing of the military, can afford to play off the RND and FLN against each other to a greater extent than Abdel Aziz who, in turn, does not need to elevate the UR to the same position as the RCD because he has the support of parts of the Mauritanian armed forces. Again, comparative analysis is crucial to highlighting these differences, to exposing the subtle contrasts between the various case studies and suggesting what they might mean for Levitsky and Way's model.

The book also deliberately inverts another of Levitsky and Way's observations better to appraise and demonstrate organisational power. They argue that 'scope is particularly important for low-intensity coercion' and that 'cohesion is critical to the success of high-intensity coercion',[2] that is, that a regime's armed and security forces can conduct certain types of operation only if they have good reach and are unified. The book reasons that, on this basis, the reverse can also be demonstrated, that a security apparatus's capacity to undertake low- and high-intensity actions can be used to determine its scope and cohesion. This logical innovation offers another means of evaluating a regime's coercive capability and organisational power, and forms part of the book's assessment of each of its case studies.

Finally, the book confirms the great importance of one of Levitsky and Way's caveats: that 'where Western powers have countervailing economic or strategic interests at stake, autocratic governments often possess the bargaining power to ward off external demands for democracy by casting themselves – and regime stability – as the best means of protecting those interests'.[3] The same can also be said of competitive authoritarian regimes. A common feature of all the case studies examined here is the extent to which the West has avoided putting as much democratising pressure on them as it could for fear of impairing their ability to pursue some strategic line deemed essential by the United States, European Union and European governments. This vital qualification not only helps preserve the analytical rigour of Levitsky and Way's model but also explain why Ben Ali's Tunisia was, and Algeria, Morocco and Mauritania have remained, competitive authoritarian.

Notes

1. Levitsky and Way, *Competitive Authoritarianism*, p. 5.
2. Ibid. pp. 59–60.
3. Ibid. p. 41.

Index

Abbadi, Mohammed, 161
Abdallahi, Sidi Ould Cheikh, President, 181, 185,
    187, 188, 189, 190, 192, 193, 195, 197
Abdel Aziz, Mohamed Ould, President, 1, 144,
    188, 189, 190, 191, 192, 193, 194, 196, 197,
    203n78, 204n86, 207, 209
Abeid, Biram Ould Dah Ould, 194–5
advocacy networks, 15, 42n30
Ahbab Errassoul *see* Friends of the Prophet
aid, 63–4, 65, 185
al-Ghannushi, Rashid, 73, 95n212
Al Jazeera news channel, 165
Al-Layl (newspaper), 196
al-Qaeda in the Islamic Maghreb (AQIM), 99,
    101, 109, 110, 111, 131n14, 137n93, 154,
    157, 181, 184, 188
Algeria, 98–130
    al-Qaeda in the Islamic Maghreb (AQIM), 99,
        101, 109, 110, 184; *see also* terrorism
    Arab Spring, 1, 4, 10, 98–9, 100, 110, 128,
        205
    Armed Islamic Group (Groupe Islamique
        Armé, GIA), 109
    Armed Islamic Movement (Mouvement
        Islamique Armé, MIA), 109
    Black October riots (1988), 100, 118
    Charter for Peace and National Reconciliation
        (Charte pour la Paix et la Réconciliation
        Nationale, CPRN) (2005), 127
    civil society groups, 102, 108–9, 136n77
    coercion, 118–19, 121–2
    competitive authoritarianism, 4, 115, 128–9,
        210
    constitution, 119–20
    Department of Intelligence and Security
        (Département du Renseignement et de la
        Sécurité, DRS), 116, 118, 128
    diaspora, 107–8
    divisions, 116
    economy, 109, 115, 120–1, 129–30
    education (Western), 107–8
    elections, 98, 107, 117, 119, 123–5, 126,
        128–9, 208–9
    elites, 101, 116, 119, 139n119
    energy, 101, 104–5, 109, 113, 129; *see also*
        gas; hydrocarbons
    Euro-Mediterranean Partnership (EMP),
        103–4, 112

European Neighbourhood and Partnership
    Instrument (ENPI), 105
European Neighbourhood Policy (ENP), 85n46
European Union Strategic Energy Partnership
    (SEP) Memorandum of Understanding
    (MOU), 105
expatriots, 107
Foreign Direct Investment (FDI), 107
gas, 105–6, 109, 113, 115, 121, 129
High State Council (Haut Comité d'État,
    HCE), 120, 122, 124, 130n1, 188
hydrocarbons, 105–6, 121
Internet, 108, 183
Islamic Salvation Army (Armée Islamique du
    Salut, AIS), 41n11, 98, 103, 112, 118, 122,
    141n150
Islamic Salvation Front (Front Islamique du
    Salut, FIS), 98, 112, 118, 119, 141n150
leverage, 109–14, 185, 207
linkage, 129; Europe, 100, 101, 102, 103–9;
    United States, 100, 101, 103
media, 126, 127–8
military, 99, 100, 116–17, 129
military aid to, 111
mobile phones, 108, 183–4
Movement for the Islamic State (Mouvement
    pour l'État Islamique, MEI), 109
National Assembly, 119–20, 124, 125, 126
National Coordination for Change and
    Democracy (Coordination Nationale pour le
    Changement et la Démocratie, CNCD), 123
National Organisation of the Children of
    Mujahidin (Organisation Nationale des
    Enfants de Moudjahidine, ONEM), 117–18
opposition groups 98, 115, 116, 117, 127, 129
organisational power, 100, 115–23, 129
parties: accreditation, 126; Justice and
    Development Party (Parti de la Justice et
    du Développement, PJD), 122–3, 154;
    Movement for Democracy in Algeria
    (Mouvement pour la Démocratie en Algérie,
    MDA), 141n150; Movement for the Society
    of Peace (Mouvement de la Société pour la
    Paix, MSP), 141n150; National Liberation
    Front (Front de Libération Nationale, FLN),
    115, 119, 120, 125–6, 141n150; National
    Rally for Democracy (Rassemblement
    National Démocratique, RND), 115, 119,

211

Index

Index